# MisLeadership

*This book is dedicated to those people who fear:*

*– They are living in a world full of **MisLeadership**;*
*– Such **MisLeadership** threatens the survival of humanity*
*– And achievement of our potential*

*And they want to do something about it.*

# MisLeadership

## Prevalence, Causes and Consequences

JOHN RAYMENT and JONATHAN SMITH

GOWER

**Gower Applied Business Research**
Our programme provides leaders, practitioners, scholars and researchers with thought provoking, cutting edge books that combine conceptual insights, interdisciplinary rigour and practical relevance in key areas of business and management.

Published by
Gower Publishing Limited
Wey Court East
Union Road
Farnham
Surrey, GU9 7PT
England

Ashgate Publishing Company
Suite 420
101 Cherry Street
Burlington,
VT 05401-4405
USA

www.gowerpublishing.com

**British Library Cataloguing in Publication Data**
Rayment, John.
  Misleadership : prevalence, causes and consequences.
  1. Leadership. 2. Decision making. 3. Business planning.
  I. Title II. Smith, Jonathan.
  658.4'092-dc22

  ISBN: 978-0-566-09226-8 (hbk)
       978-0-566-09227-5 (ebk)

**Library of Congress Cataloging-in-Publication Data**
Rayment, John.
  Misleadership : prevalence, causes and consequences / John Rayment and Jonathan Smith.
      p. cm.
  Includes bibliographical references and index.
  ISBN 978-0-566-09226-8 (hbk.) -- ISBN 978-0-566-09227-5 (ebook)
  1. Leadership. 2. Leadership--Moral and ethical aspects. 3. Decision making. 4.
Management.
  I. Smith, Jonathan Ashley. II. Title.
  HD57.7.R39 2010
  658.4'092--dc22

                                                                          2010025554

MIX
Paper from
responsible sources
FSC    FSC® C018575
www.fsc.org

Printed and bound in Great Britain by the
MPG Books Group, UK

AFB

# Contents

# List of Figures

# List of Tables

# Abbreviations

| | |
|---|---|
| ACCA | Association of Chartered Certified Accountants |
| BCCI | Bank of Credit and Commerce International |
| CBC | Canadian Broadcasting Corporation |
| CEO | Chief Executive Officer |
| CIA | Central Intelligence Agency |
| CIMA | Chartered Institute of Management Accountants |
| CIPD | Chartered Institute of Personnel and Development |
| DNA | Deoxyribonucleic acid |
| EPO | Erythropoietin |
| G8 | A forum for governments of the eight richest countries |
| G20 | A bloc of developing nations |
| GDP | Gross Domestic Product |
| GFL | Globally Fit Leadership |
| GFF | Global Fitness Framework |
| GRLI | Globally Responsible Leadership Initiative |
| HR | Human Resources |
| HSE | Health and Safety Executive |

| IMF | International Monetary Fund |
| IPCS | International Programme on Chemical Safety |
| MAC | Mines and Communities |
| MP | Member of Parliament |
| NHS | National Health Service |
| NINJA | No Income, No Job or Assets |
| PRME | Principles for Responsible Management Education |
| r-EPO | Recombinant EPO |
| TUC | Trades Union Congress |
| UCI | Union Cycliste Internationale (UCI) |
| UGI | Urgent Global Issue |
| UK | United Kingdom |
| UN | United Nations |
| UNICEF | The United Nations Children's Fund |
| US | United States (of America) |
| USGS | United States Geological Survey |
| VAT | Value Added Tax |
| WHO | World Health Organization |

# About the Authors

**John Rayment** is a Principal Lecturer in Leadership and Management at the Ashcroft International Business School, Anglia Ruskin University, where he is Programme Leader for the Chelmsford-based MBA programme.

Coming from an accounting background, John moved increasingly toward problem-solving, including writing the text 'Mind Morphing – Decision Making Using Logic and Magic'. This led him to consider whether mental fitness could be thought of in similar fashion to physical fitness, that is, in terms of strength, stamina and suppleness, and the role such mental fitness should play in successful leadership, particularly in the solution of urgent global issues (UGIs).

These thoughts drew the conclusion that while mental processes are vital for good decision-making, they are not sufficient to provide and ensure such factors as strong motivation and valid mission and values. This caused John to consider whether another element was necessary, which he ultimately identified as spirituality, loosely defined as 'a sustainable, just and fulfilling human presence on the planet'.

John's search for ways in which these ideas can be taken to the key decision-makers of our time was the original drive for this book.

John acts as a consultant to a range of international private and public sector bodies, leads international postgraduate programmes in leadership and management and facilitates adoption of his ideas by organisations. In April 2008 he and Jon Smith co-organised and led an international conference on Global Leadership.

John is a member of CIPFA, ACCA and ACMA and has an MBA. He is most easily contacted by e-mail on john.rayment@anglia.ac.uk

**Dr Jonathan Smith, MA, Chartered FCIPD** is a Senior Lecturer in the Ashcroft International Business School, Anglia Ruskin University, where he leads international postgraduate programmes in leadership, management and human resource management (HRM). He designs and facilitates innovative Masters level courses in leadership, strategy, organisational change, HRM and research methods. Jon coaches and supports a large number of HR professionals in the research, design and implementation of best practice HR initiatives in organisations. As a member of the university senate Jon has been involved in establishing the strategic direction of the university. His current research, consulting and development interests are focused on organisational, team, and individual transformation through spiritual leadership; development and training within the police; and sustainable development for businesses. In April 2008 he and John Rayment co-organised and led an international conference on Global Leadership.

He is a member of the Academic Advisory Board at Saint Mary's University in Nova Scotia, member of the Board of the Chinese American Scholars Association and has been a judging panellist for the International Spirit at Work Awards. He has been a visiting speaker at Sydvast University in Finland, and Concordia University in Montreal.

Jon has experience in a variety of managerial and training roles in a number of public and private-sector organisations. Prior to working at the university Jon was a director of studies at the UK National Police Training and Development Authority, working with the 43 Home Office Forces of England and Wales to shape and drive the training agenda to achieve world-class performance within police training. This was both a strategic and hands-on role and included his designing and facilitating six-week residential programmes of trainer development involving use of experiential learning and andragogical approaches to attitudinal development.

Jon is a Chartered Fellow of the CIPD, and Fellow of the HE Academy. He has a PhD in Education, MA in HRM, and a first-class honours degree in Mechanical Engineering. He is a trained mechanical engineer and has undertaken a wide range of production, research and project management roles. Jon's e-mail is jonathan.smith@anglia.ac.uk

# *Reviews for* MisLeadership

'We are in the midst of a leadership crisis that extends to all spheres of society. The lack of trustworthiness amongst leaders has contributed to the erosion of trust amongst the general public. With its fresh thinking and practical wisdom, this book will help arrest the crisis and inspire us to become the leaders we have it within us to be.'

Peter S. Heslam, Transforming Business, University of Cambridge.

'MisLeadership analyses a widespread phenomenon of today's leadership: leaders solve wrong problems precisely. The authors call for a holistic and globally fitting approach to leadership where ethical and stakeholder considerations play a vital role. The book is a welcome contribution to the transformation of leadership toward a truly human profession.'

Laszlo Zsolnai, Professor and Director, Business Ethics Center, Corvinus University of Budapest

'The authors' trademark is a re-definition of fair-play concerning managerial, corporate, entrepreneurial and integration decisions, both in interior and exterior relations. Their concept of GFF provides a check-list that could serve as a compass for stakeholders and shareholders of any sector likewise to invest into more sustainable than volatile goals. This goes beyond thinking in iterative structures of well-accepted standards.'

Uwe TORSTEN, MD, PhD, MBA, Director of the Dept of GYN at the Vivantes Hospital Neukoelln, Germany

'Effective leadership is one of the most critical and important factors for our long term survival and wellbeing on this planet. Given the current problems in the world isn't it time for a new 'kind' of leadership - one in which progress is actually experienced? One way to look at the current position must surely be that we suffer from MisLeadership and that this MisLeadership is embedded in our system. We need to identify its scope and scale and break out of the embedded cycle. This book is a ground-breaking leader in that journey.'

Martin Rutte, Founder & Chair of the Board, The Centre for Spirituality and the Workplace, Saint Mary's University, Canada; Founder of Project Heaven on Earth

# 1

# Introduction

## When Were You Last Misled?

- By someone at work, promising help but failing to deliver; saying that if you worked hard you would get promoted and have job security; they were too busy to help you; promising to achieve a sales figure which they subsequently failed to make? They would all fit our definition.

- Accidentally by a stranger you asked for directions? That too would fit – MisLeadership doesn't have to be on purpose.

- Deliberately by a tennis opponent disguising a drop shot, or card player fooling you into thinking they did not have the King of Spades? That would be misleading but is all part of the false situation of a game. Should it come under the MisLeadership umbrella?

- Exploitatively, by someone selling you a house knowing it regularly floods? Now that would fit anyone's definition – or would it? Perhaps it is a case of 'caveat emptor' – let the buyer beware. If you were fool enough to buy without checking important facts …

- Negligently by someone who forgot to warn you the petrol tank was almost empty? That is a tricky one. They presumably didn't do it on purpose and perhaps it was your responsibility to check before setting off but it would have been helpful if they had said something.

- Thirty seconds ago, intrigued by the title of this book? 'MisLeadership – I'm not sure exactly what it means, but I'm sure I've experienced it!' Or did you read it as 'MisLeadership by John Rayment and Jonathan Smith'? That isn't what we meant!

## When Were You First Misled?

Can you remember a specific instance, or was it even before you can remember? Perhaps you were told about the tooth fairy? Or given medicine disguised in a sugar cube? If so, were your parents wrong to do either or both of them?

## When Did You Last Mislead Someone?

Most of us think we are misled more often than we mislead but by definition the two are opposites of the same coin, so we are probably misleading ourselves. We can tend to treat our own acts of MisLeadership as justified in some way while decrying that displayed by others. In the business world, most people believe they keep their staff well informed but that their supervisors keep them in the dark.

We hope you find the above questions challenging and thought-provoking, but if you do, this may end up being the hardest book you have ever read. Not because it is written in a foreign or difficult language, uses advanced mathematics or contains complicated theories or hypotheses – it does none of those. You may find it tough going because it will cast doubt on much of what you have been taught to believe in, much of what you, your friends and your family hold dear.

We hope to raise your awareness of and provide insights into the prevalence and causes of MisLeadership, why it is creating such problems for humanity and help you identify and overcome the MisLeadership that surrounds you. It introduces MisLeadership as having many guises and being found in all walks of life including public and private sectors, family, work and society, education and religion. It is only one book, however, and cannot cover all these areas in detail so we hope you will consider the points made and how they apply to your circumstances. We use a range of short illustrations and simplified case studies but are aware that these are complex issues and have many more factors and sides to the argument than we are able to include so again we encourage you to think about them, challenge our view and read around them further.

We want you to be active when reading this book, reflecting, questioning what it says, coming up with your own ideas and models, thinking of how the points made might apply to situations more personal and relevant to you, and recording your thoughts while they are fresh. At the end of each chapter we offer specific 'Points to Ponder' and considered also providing occasional blank spaces throughout the text for your thoughts but decided it would be preferable for you to keep them on a separate notepad. We have, however, inserted occasional mini-spaces to encourage you to record your thoughts in whatever way you feel appropriate.

This book is of particular relevance to managers, leaders, educators and coaches but is also aimed at anyone who is frustrated with current leadership at any level and wants to help initiate change. We look to encourage and empower every individual to think on a vastly different scale and in new ways, to challenge assumptions and take an effective leadership role.

We challenge the fundamentals of current thinking on history, leadership, economic and social theory, and show how we have all been misled, both as individuals and humanity, in many of these areas right from birth. Worse – having broken up the jigsaw, we make scant attempt to put the pieces back together. To do that will take a great deal of work, which we are starting but need your involvement. We believe the situation is so dire that everyone who is able to help bring about change must take part.

If you agree with the fundamental concepts presented but feel daunted by the prospect of striving to achieve the required changes, do not despair; you are not alone. We too felt the weight as we explored the issues. Remember what Hellen Keller said:

> I am only one; but still I am one.
> I cannot do everything, but still I can do something;
> I will not refuse to do something I can do.

And Frances Hodgson Burnett:

> At first people refuse to believe that a strange new thing can be done,
> then they begin to hope it can be done,
> then they see it can be done
> – then it is done
> and all the world wonders why it was not done centuries ago.

We believe passionately in what we say and want to challenge and empower you to think anew and join us in our search for humanity's well-being in both the short and long-term. If it fits with your own thoughts, so much the better – let's get together to find a way forward. If, however, what is written here goes against your fundamental beliefs and you remain convinced that they are right and we are wrong, so be it. At least you will have read what we have to say. All we ask is that you do so with as open a mind as possible because that is the only way any new approach has a chance of getting past the comfort zone we all tend to slip into.

Imagine for a moment …

*Two babies enter our world*
*Each weighing 7 pounds*
*Unable to focus, naked and with no teeth*
*Unable to feed themselves*
*Or keep themselves safe and warm*
*Unable to walk or talk*
*Communicating only through crying …*
*Squirming and messing themselves*
*BUT with fantastic minds*
*Beating hearts*
*Able to control most of the functions*
*Of their incredible bodies*
*Each with amazing spirit*
*And zest for life*
*Lacking all forms of prejudice*
*Equal to all other babies*
*Perhaps one might be your child, grandchild or great grandchild.*

Now imagine that these two babies arrive in two very different locations: one in a well-off family in a rich and powerful country, the other in a poor family in a weak and unsettled land. Take a moment to reflect on the difference this arrival location will make to the rest of their lives when there are:

- More than one billion people in the world living on less than US$1 a day

- 2.7 billion struggling to survive on less than US$2 per day

- More than 800 million people going to bed hungry every day, including 300 million children

- A person dying of starvation every 3.6 seconds, most of them being children under the age of 5

- 6,000 people every day who die from HIV/AIDS and another 8,200 who are infected with the deadly virus. (Source: Rural Poverty Portal.)

Is that how our world should be? Remember that one of those babies might be yours – which one should be irrelevant since we are all part of the same family and need to change the current situation.

There are plenty of reasons and explanations for the inequalities those two little babies may experience throughout their lives, but our starting point for this book is that these are fundamentally just excuses. There is something innately wrong with a world where such inequalities occur routinely on such a frequent and widespread basis. It does not have to be like that and we want to do something about it. Do you?

## Messages in Childhood

Depending on our background and the beliefs of our parents, we all have particular childhood memories, some that we cherish and others we are loath to recall. For those from a Christian background many of these may revolve around Christmas but we are sure that if you have different roots you will have equivalent tales to tell. Warm and cosy, away from the cold and dark, we snuggle into cushions on the settee while our parents tell us stories like:

> *Twas the night before Christmas*
> *When all through the house*
> *Not a creature was stirring, not even a mouse*
> *When what to my wondering eyes should appear*
> *But a miniature sleigh, and eight tiny reindeer*
> *With a little old driver, so lively and quick*
> *I knew in a moment it must be St Nick*

*(Moore, 1822)*

We are told that Father Christmas will bring us lots of wonderful things as long as we are good, so on Christmas Eve we put out some carrots for the reindeer and a biscuit for Father Christmas, then go to bed early not daring to get up because if we see Father Christmas, he won't leave anything.

Other stories are told to us forming a vast jumble of myths, legends and hard facts, some vital for our survival, others not: ... 'Mummy and Daddy love you' ... 'don't play in the road' ... 'always tell the truth' ... 'blue is for boys, pink is for girls' ... 'don't talk to strangers' ... 'listen to teacher' ... 'two twos are four' ...

Slowly we begin to sort out fact, fiction, and what might be fact or fiction but it probably doesn't matter. If from a Christian background we will have been told by our parents, grandparents, other relations and friends how little baby Jesus was born of the Holy Spirit to the Virgin Mary long ago in a town called Bethlehem so He could die for our sins and we can be saved and not go to hell but instead go to heaven and live for ever in glory with God.

Unquestioning we trust our parents to be honest, truthful, look after us, protect and love us and each other. They are all-powerful and know the answers to everything. We trust our family and their friends, police officers and teachers but not strangers – they are outsiders and not to be trusted.

We start to play games ... 'Kiss Chase' and 'Cowboys and Indians' ... and really enjoy them but they turn into sport and we are encouraged to try to win and beat the opposition, be competitive, that cuddles and crying are only for sissies.

One can really only begin to surmise the impact all this information in our formative years has on our thinking, our views of the world and our values, our views about leadership and *MisLeadership*. What is the long-term effect when we discover the truth about all the 'little white lies' we have been fed? It may dent our faith and trust in what adults tell us, which may be a necessary part of growing up, but may also make us think that lying is OK and natural.

Indoctrination goes on and on as we are continually exposed to such commonly propounded views as 'education is good for you', 'the church will look after you', 'people can be managed', 'members of parliament are trustworthy', 'bankers have you best interests at heart', 'leaders of organisations know where the organisation is going and how to get there', and so on. Having discovered the truth behind some lies we are loath to fall for them again, so are left in a state of wanting to believe what we are told but becoming increasingly cynical and sceptical, reinforced every time we discover another lie.

**ALMOST ALL MPS STILL FACING QUESTIONS OVER EXPENSES**

Nine out of ten MPs are still facing questions over their expenses following an audit by the parliamentary authorities.

*Source*: Hope, 2009.

The above points begin to show how embedded and engrained MisLeadership can be. It starts as soon as babies are born through the things parents and grandparents say and do, then broadens to include family and friends, school teachers, leaders of clubs, university lecturers, people they are led by, work with or see on television.

From the above indoctrination, patterns of action, thoughts, opinions and beliefs are quickly developed, slip into our mind and gradually move further and further out of our consciousness until they simply become 'the way things are'. They form the context of our life, shaping everything we say and do, unseen but all-pervasive. Like an iceberg where the bulk of the ice is unseen below the waterline, our innermost values, beliefs and attitudes are the things with the largest effect on our actions but are kept hidden in our subconscious. We depict this in the Embedded Values Cycle shown in Figure 1.1

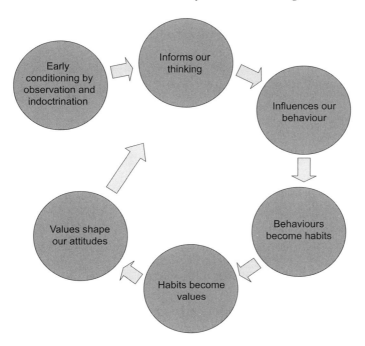

**Figure 1.1** **The Embedded Values Cycle**

The cycle in Figure 1.1 illustrates how early conditioning leads to early behaviours which shape our thinking and future behaviours and start to become habits and values. We show this process to encourage you to reflect on how your current values and habits have developed and, where necessary, to begin to undo the process by challenging your values and thereby freeing up your habits, behaviour and thinking to ultimately rid yourself of the undesirable influences of the accumulated MisLeadership you have been saturated with since birth.

One of the authors describes a 'eureka' moment – when he realised a truth previously hidden by MisLeadership from Hollywood:

> *It was not until I was in my twenties watching an old 'Cowboy' film that I realized some of my values were completely wrong. I had believed Red Indian savages attacked wagon trains to kill the men, capture the women and steal the horses and supplies. Heroes like John Wayne led the US Cavalry to the rescue, killed the evil Indians and sent the wagon train safely on its way. Suddenly it occurred to me that a bow and arrow would have been fairly useless against rifles and the famous Colt 44.*

> *I then watched, with open eyes and mind, the Indians trying to fire arrows while riding horses round a circle of wagons, while the Cowboys, stationary and protected by the wagons, took careful aim and shot them dead. The odds were heavily stacked against the Indians – which thinking about it was obvious since even in cowboy films there are always many more Indians killed than cowboys.*

> *This made me start to rethink the whole situation: why would the Indians have behaved in such a suicidal manner? Who were the heroes and who the villains?*

## A Crisis of Leadership

We argue that effective leadership is one of the most critical and important factors for our long-term survival and well-being on this planet. More often, however, we see leadership that does not come up to the mark. This is so frequent that professional bodies such as the CIPD (2008:5) are suggesting that we are now in the throes of a crisis: a crisis in leadership as people begin to recognise that what they are doing isn't working, that they do not know what to do, that they cannot cope, and that people are losing confidence and trust in their leaders.

The leadership crisis is evident globally in the financial sector, parliamentary system, environment and the lack of meaning many are experiencing. The loss of trust and confidence is illustrated by Talbott (2009:1) who argues that the cause of the current economic crisis, resulting in the most serious global recession the world has seen in its history (2009:227) is that our entire financial system over the years has been corrupted, and how 'endemic it is to our largest corporations, our biggest financial institutions and, yes, our government.'

More significant and crucial still, the leadership crisis is evident in the many urgent global issues (UGIs) now facing everyone and everything on our planet. A sample of these is shown in Table 1.1 and we explore many of these issues in this book.

**Table 1.1     Illustrative urgent global issues**

| |
|---|
| Climate change |
| Resource depletion/sharing, e.g., water, oil, deforestation |
| Domination by corporations |
| Wealth/power distribution |
| Extreme poverty and hunger endured by more than a billion people in the world |
| Economic system failure |
| Soil degradation |
| Toxic childhood/protection |
| HIV/AIDS |
| Religious and other armed conflicts/extremism/radicalisation |
| Mass epidemics, resistance of bugs to antibiotics |
| Species being wiped out, including all large animals |
| Lack of education/lack of basic numeracy and literacy |
| Roles of nation states |

According to Smircich and Morgan (1982:258), leadership is an obligation or perceived right on the part of certain individuals to define the reality of others. We argue that this obligation for all aspects of humanity has not always been recognised or honoured and as a result has led to MisLeadership in one form or another.

Most definitions of leadership reflect the assumption that it involves a process whereby intentional influence is exerted by one person over other people to guide, structure and facilitate activities and relationships in a group or organisation (Yukl 2006:8). This intentional influence of a leader is used to enable followers to achieve a particular entity's objectives, be that entity a team, business, public or private sector body, religious group, government or a global group like the United Nations.

Leaders over the centuries have often been viewed as highly successful in this role but we wonder whether this apparent success may have been due to the way in which it was assessed and measured. From a global perspective, what appeared to be successful in earlier times may now be seen as short-sighted, parochial or just plain wrong.

What we are doing now is beginning to question the traditional measures of success. Leadership actions that stem from a way of thinking that might have been appropriate some time ago may no longer be so. Some (such as Senge et al. 2008) are recognising that our global organisations, our nations and our planet are not machines but living systems, and we need to work in these living systems in different ways than we have been doing:

> As long as our thinking is governed by habit – notably by industrial, 'machine age' concepts such as control, predictability, standardisation, and 'faster is better' – we will continue to re-create institutions as they have been, despite their disharmony with the larger world, and the need of all living systems to evolve.

A lot of our thinking is informed by education, and this returns us to the cycle shown earlier in Figure 1.1. One of the major points in this book is that one of the reasons why leaders may not have been as genuinely successful as they believed is that the practice of MisLeadership has been such an embedded, prolific and often unconscious part of people's upbringing, socialisation and education over many hundreds of years. As a result leaders face an almost impossible task to break free from this constraining system. It has become the habit, embedded in all our systems of development and cultures as the informed, expected and accepted way to lead. The start of this chapter provided initial illustrations of how embedded in our psyche, thinking and systems this MisLeadership is and we will see many more examples as the book progresses. This is Institutional MisLeadership on a global scale.

One of the biggest difficulties with tackling MisLeadership is that it has been apparently tremendously successful, particularly when seen from its own viewpoint. If someone wins a game of football by deliberately getting another player sent off, from their narrow viewpoint they may believe they have been successful. Similarly, a person who gains promotion at work by undermining the credibility of their rival or a king who leads an army to conquer a neighbouring kingdom may feel justified and successful.

This way of thinking and leading has led from its viewpoint to enormous success and development in a huge range of areas. As we will see when we study resource consumption in Chapter 2, however, it has led humanity to the brink of catastrophe and possible extinction. Let us emphasise it again, as a consequence of past MisLeadership we are at the brink of catastrophe and possible extinction and have to enact massive change on a global scale urgently.

## MisLeadership

Underpinning the kind of thinking that continues to develop unsustainable working practices is that a lot of what we learn, claim to know about, and practise as good leadership is actually nothing of the sort, but MisLeadership.

One way of looking at the leadership crisis is through the lens of the Leadership Fitness Continuum shown in Figure 1.2. In this figure Globally Fit Leadership is our term for the best possible leadership that humans are capable of while Diabolical Leadership would be the worst possible. Actual Leadership Fitness represents the quality or fitness level of leadership currently taking place. By fitness here we do not just mean physical fitness but a holistic physical, mental and spiritual fitness. We discuss this more in Chapter 3. The gap between actual and globally fit leadership is the room for improvement and that between actual and diabolical leadership the extent to which we should be pleased with the leadership we have.

The reason behind the current crisis in leadership is that the fitness level of current leadership is not sufficiently high to cope with the challenges of the modern environment. The issues discussed earlier in this chapter may justify the argument that leadership fitness has probably declined in recent times but it should be borne in mind that the challenges faced may be much greater so the Globally Fit Leadership goal is much harder to achieve. There is a leadership crisis, though, because the gap between actual and globally fit leadership is large and growing. This gap represents MisLeadership and is the focus of this book.

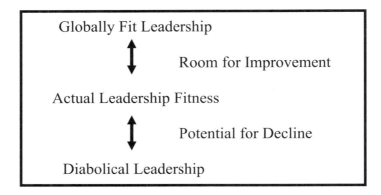

**Figure 1.2    Leadership Fitness Continuum**

The Leadership Fitness Continuum is useful for identifying a number of points for reflection. What would globally fit leadership look and feel like? What would be the outcomes if globally fit leadership were present? How fit is your own leadership?

To close the gap between actual and globally fit leadership we need to identify and reduce the MisLeadership that is taking place. It is a continuum so every improvement we make to actual fitness will move toward globally fit leadership. It is difficult to stand still so unless we work on our fitness it is likely to decline – perhaps the current crisis is partly due to historic complacency that current leadership was resulting in great success.

Globally fit leadership is that which results in optimum achievement of an entity's overall objectives. MisLeadership is then any leadership action or inaction which results in less than optimum achievement of objectives. When we think big and include the global situation in our considerations we realise that an entity's overall objectives should include consideration of the objectives of humanity. This definition of MisLeadership includes, but greatly extends, many other definitions with a similar principle, such as the one given by the US Federal Trade Commission Act (FTC 1984). This Act prohibits unfair or deceptive business practices defined as 'a representation, omission, or practice that is likely to mislead the consumer acting reasonably in the circumstances, to the consumer's detriment'. We include consumers under the 'objectives of humanity' although humanity incorporates many more things such as communities and society. We also believe the objectives of humanity should include caring for the planet and all its inhabitants, not just humans.

We argue that MisLeadership per se is wrong even though there are many acts that are intended to mislead that we would not categorise as MisLeadership. Examples of such activities can be found in art, entertainment, comedy, drama, storytelling, magic, theme parks and visual effects, where misleading the participants may be part of the 'show'. This is why our definition emphasises that actions must result in less than optimum achievement of objectives for them to be classed as MisLeadership. The line between what is and what is not MisLeadership is fuzzy but that is exactly why the issues are challenging and complex, difficult, interesting and exciting. The complexities of ethical decisions and the basis on which judgements are made are brought to bear on these ambiguous, socio-culturally constructed notions.

## Categories of MisLeadership

To us, there are two main categories of MisLeadership, the first being unwitting MisLeadership which results from leadership that is missing, misguided, or misinformed. The second category is what most people think of when they hear the term 'MisLeadership': a deliberate attempt by a leader to achieve hidden personal objectives. We call this Machiavellian, after the author of *The Prince*, a book written in the early sixteenth century as a guide to the deceptive ways in which those in power can keep and use it:

MISSING LEADERSHIP

Is where appropriate and necessary leadership simply does not take place.

MISGUIDED LEADERSHIP

Is where the leadership could be seen to be effective, but is targeted at the wrong objectives, or the approaches and processes used could not lead to achievement of the objectives.

MISINFORMED LEADERSHIP

Is where the leader is unaware of important information, skills, techniques or consequences, or misunderstands their importance or how to use them.

## MACHIAVELLIAN LEADERSHIP

As stated above, this is the only form of MisLeadership that we say is deliberate. It is where the leader attempts to achieve hidden personal objectives and does this by deliberately misleading their followers.

The extent of and reaction to MisLeadership varies across cultures and generations and may be more embedded in the national psyche of some countries than others. It is evident, though, in all cultures (Boush et al. 2009:3). MisLeadership has exacerbated a large number of issues for us as a human race:

- We often do not know, or work with, the correct information

- We have lost touch with reality

- We do not recognise or acknowledge the complexity or seriousness of the problems we face

- Crucial issues are not resolved effectively

- Many have experienced a loss of meaning, both in work, community and society

- It is difficult to develop close, meaningful working relationships and trust others. This applies in our homes, workplaces, communities, countries and globally

- We are emotionally immature and unable to deal with reality

- We are currently experiencing the biggest economic crisis the world has ever known

- We are facing a huge range of urgent global issues of the type shown in Table 1.1, and

- We are on the brink of catastrophe and possible extinction.

## Structure of the Book

This first chapter of the book has introduced MisLeadership and our four categories.

Each of the next four chapters details one of these four categories of MisLeadership, its scope, causes and potential remedies including the related element of Globally Fit Leadership.

Chapter 6 pulls together the concepts and approaches covered in earlier chapters, including further discussion of the Global Fitness Continuum and the complexities involved in solving many live issues.

A wide range of situations and applications are used throughout the book to illustrate examples of MisLeadership. Chapter 7, however, is devoted to three more substantive case studies which illustrate the findings from Chapter 6, then reveals actions that have already been taken by practitioners at all levels to implement these findings.

Chapter 8 summarises the book, concepts and models developed and approaches to their use. It concludes with a framework for action including practical suggestions for implementation.

Table 1.2 indicates the chapter containing each category of MisLeadership and the related element of Globally Fit Leadership. It also summarises the case studies examined and suggested action points.

Our approach throughout is to emphasise that we, the authors, do not have all the answers and accept that the issues involved in the rapidly changing global environment are of such complexity that we as humanity often do not even know the right questions to ask let alone know how to find the right answers. With this complexity, though, there is a danger of analysis paralysis, where action becomes frozen through long circular debates that attempt to bring in and understand all relevant factors and their interaction. We do not have the luxury of time to do this given the many urgent global issues facing humanity and it is extremely unlikely that we would be able to predict and quantify all the relevant factors, however long we spent on the attempt.

We therefore suggest an approach which Quinn (1980) terms 'logical incrementalism'. This is a process of iterative small steps by which new ideas and

**Table 1.2     Summary of book content**

| Chapter | Type of MisLeadership | Globally Fit Leadership Element | Main Case Studies |
|---|---|---|---|
| 2 | Missing | Effective decision-making | Sinking of the *Titanic* <br> Climate change and resource depletion <br> Toxic childhood |
| 3 | Misguided | Global perspective | Business environment <br> A level grades in the United Kingdom <br> King Henry V at the Battle of Agincourt <br> Christopher Columbus' exploits in the Caribbean at the end of the 15th century |
| 4 | Misinformed | New paradigm | Global financial markets <br> Bank of Credit and Commerce International <br> Nick Leeson and Barings Bank |
| 5 | Machiavellian | Contemporary mission | The baby milk industry <br> Ecuador vs. Chevron |
| 6 | Complexities | Consolidation | Forced marriage <br> Swine flu and Tamiflu <br> The police |
| 7 | Cases | Actions taken | Religion <br> The Tour de France <br> The asbestos and tobacco industry <br> Globally Responsible Leadership Initiative <br> Avaaz <br> State of the World Forum <br> Al Gore <br> Jeremy Gilley <br> Center For Spirituality and the Workplace <br> CIMA's Business Trust: A Critical Time Initiative <br> Aspen Institute's Corporate Values Strategy Group <br> The Gates Foundation |
| 8 | Summary | Framework for action | |

changes are tested to avoid risk and damage while striving to meet overarching strategic aims and keeping site of the long-term goal. We urge people to get started on the journey to resolution, evaluate as we progress and keep looking for emerging factors. Thus we view our ideas as initial steps on the journey: they are only the start of the path and we need your help in creating the route forward.

## Summary

This first chapter has been focused on introductions. We have defined leadership and emphasised how important this is in the current rapidly changing, complex and global environment. We have said that we believe Globally Fit Leadership is often lacking and that we are experiencing a crisis of leadership as people begin to feel there is little point to what they are doing recognise that what they are doing isn't working, that they do not know what to do, that they cannot cope, and lose confidence and trust in their leaders.

We have argued that a lot of what we know about and practise in leadership is not in fact leadership but MisLeadership. We have outlined the huge difficulties that this MisLeadership creates and have shown how embedded and prevalent it is in our society. This is due to the way we are brought up and educated to see leadership, how we have seen others lead and how we are pressurised to lead. We have argued that MisLeadership is so embedded and prevalent in our psyche that it is Institutional MisLeadership on a global scale. It is very difficult for individuals to break out of this system.

We have emphasised that the situation we are facing is so complex and rapidly changing that our proposals will clearly not resolve all the problems. We argued that it is better to take small steps to resolution and evaluate as we go, rather than do nothing or take major steps that may be in the wrong direction. We believe that our proposals assist this process.

Overall, this book aims to:

- highlight errors and learn from our past

- establish the need for rapid and fundamental change

- encourage everyone to play their part

- make initial suggestions for a way forward.

It looks to achieve this by challenging fundamentals of current thinking on leadership, economic and social theory, thereby encouraging and empowering every individual to think on a vastly different scale, challenge assumptions and take a leadership role.

**POINTS FOR REFLECTION**

1.   What has been your initial reaction as you have read this first chapter?
2.   What has caused you to react in this way?
3.   What does this cause and reaction mean for your learning and future development?
4.   What are the most significant elements to MisLeadership that you have experienced in your life?
5.   What experiences have you had that you would say demonstrated Globally Fit Leadership?
6.   What does Globally Fit Leadership look like?
7.   What would the world look like if Globally Fit Leadership occurred everywhere?

## References

Boush, D.M., Friestad, M. and Wright, P. (2009). *Deception in the Marketplace*. Hove: Routledge.

CIPD (Chartered Institute of Personnel and Development). (2008). *Research Insight – Engaging Leadership: Creating organisations that maximise the potential of their people*. London: CIPD.

Hope, C. (2009). Almost all MPs still facing questions over expenses. *Daily Telegraph* [Online, 16 September]. Available at: http://www.telegraph.co.uk/news/newstopics/mps-expenses/6140802/Almost-all-MPs-still-facing-questions-over-expenses.html [accessed: 16/9/09].

Moore, C.C. (1822). *Twas the Night before Christmas*. [Online]. Available at: http://www.carols.org.uk/twas_the_night_before_christmas.htm [accessed: 17/9/09].

Quinn, J.B. (1980). *Strategies for Change*. Howewood: Richard D. Irwin, Inc.

Rural Poverty Portal. (2009). [Online]. Available at: http://www.rural povertyportal.org/web/guest/topic [accessed: 16/9/09].

Senge, P., Scharmer, C.O., Jaworskil, J. and Flowers, B.S. (2008). *Presence: Exploring Profound Change in People, Organizations and Society*. London: Nicholas Brealey Publishing.

Smircich, L. and Morgan, G. (1982). Leadership: The management of meaning. *Journal of Applied Behavioural Science*, vol. 18, no. 2.

Talbott, J.R. (2009.) *The 86 Biggest Lies on Wall Street*. London: Constable and Robinson.

Yukl, G. (2006). *Leadership in Organisations*. 6th Edition. New Jersey: Prentice Hall.

# 2

# Missing Leadership and the Need for Effective Decision-Making

In Chapter 1 we defined MisLeadership as being any leadership action or inaction which results in less than optimum achievement of objectives, and outlined the four key elements of MisLeadership. This chapter will now examine what may be the most prevalent and far-reaching of these – Missing Leadership. This is where appropriate and necessary leadership does not take place for whatever reason.

In each of Chapters 2 to 5 we use a series of short case studies to illustrate the points being explored. Our first case study in this chapter relates to the sinking of the *Titanic*. It is based on information extracted from the internet encyclopaedia Wikipedia, which will be sufficient for our illustrations of Missing Leadership. In its early days, the Wikipedia site had a reputation for sometimes having facts wrong but this has improved greatly over recent years. Decision makers should always check the reliability of facts they use, with the time and effort devoted to researching them reflecting the importance of their certainty and accuracy. As we shall see a number of times in this book, however, the volume of information available and the extent of deliberate and accidental MisLeadership within it can make this a difficult process, and result in the outcome highlighted in Chapter 1, that we cannot always know which is, or be sure we are working with, the correct information.

## Sinking of the *Titanic*

The *Titanic* exuded quality and luxury, facilities including a swimming pool and gymnasium. She also had the most advanced technology available, including two radios which allowed constant contact with other ships and coastguards, and was popularly believed to be 'unsinkable.'

Even so, shortly before midnight on 14 April 1912, four days into her maiden voyage, the *Titanic* hit an iceberg. Although it took 2 hours and 40 minutes for her to sink, of the 2,223 people on board, 1,517 (68 per cent) died and only 706 (32 per cent) survived.

The ocean was calm and the sky clear but general warnings of icebergs had been received from other ships and Captain Smith had altered his course to the south, that is, toward warmer water and away from the ice shelf. During the evening at least two specific warnings that large icebergs lay in the *Titanic's* path were received but not delivered to the bridge. Passengers were charged for the sending and receipt of messages and were generous with their tips, so the wireless operators were very keen to handle as many passenger messages as possible.

At 23:40 a large iceberg was identified in the ship's path and the lookout raised the alarm. Immediate evasive action was taken by attempting to turn and stop the ship. This was almost successful but the ship's side ran into the iceberg below the waterline as it passed, denting but not severely rupturing the hull. What caused the fatal damage was the fact that rivets meant to hold the metal sheets together started to fail and as the ship continued past the iceberg, there was an unzipping effect such that a 90-metre gash was created for water to pour into.

The ship had been designed with the underwater areas separated into compartments that could be shut off in an emergency by watertight doors such that it would stay afloat even if any four of the compartments were flooded. Several very unfortunate factors now combined: five compartments were filling with water; they were all in the same area of the ship; that area was near the front and on one side. This meant the weight of the water was concentrated in that corner and the ship began to tip sufficiently for water to start coming over the watertight bulkheads and fill more parts of the ship. Inspection and analysis soon enabled Captain Smith to draw the inevitable conclusion.

Further misfortune was the fact that, despite radio distress calls being sent and received by several ships, none of those that received them was close enough to make it in time to be of assistance. One ship, the *Californian*, was nearby having stopped for the night due to the threat of icebergs. Their wireless operator had attempted to warn the *Titanic* that there was ice ahead but been told by the *Titanic's* operator to let him concentrate on sending passengers' messages. The *Californian's* operator reacted by turning off his wireless and going to bed. Later in the night the *Californian*'s officers saw lights and distress signals in the distance and informed their captain who after some debate decided to take no action, not even to wake the wireless operator.

To the passengers, the *Titanic* did not appear to be sinking, so few were prepared to get into the first lifeboats launched. This was particularly true of women and children who clung to the apparent safety of a massive warm ship rather than a small lifeboat on an icy sea. The 'women and children first' philosophy was so engrained that few men wanted to leave first and some of the officers would not allow men on board lifeboats even if they were not full.

The *Titanic* was comfortably within the current regulations although she only had enough lifeboats for one-third (33 per cent) of her 3,547 capacity. The theory was that with so many ships in the North Atlantic if one was in difficulty others would be close enough to help by using their lifeboats too and ferrying the passengers from the stricken ship to the rescuers'. Fortunately only 2,223 people were on board, or else the tragedy would have been even worse.

The majority of deaths were caused by hypothermia in the freezing water. Only two lifeboats attempted to rescue people after the ship sank. There was debate in some of the others about going back but fear of being swamped by people trying to climb aboard overrode their feelings of compassion and desire to help.

Six of the seven children in first class and all of the children in second class survived, whereas only 34 per cent were saved in third class. Four first-class women passengers died and 86 per cent survived in second class, less than 50 per cent in third class. Overall, only 20 per cent of the men survived, compared to nearly 75 per cent of the women. First-class male passengers were four times as likely to survive as second-class male passengers, and twice as likely to survive as third-class male passengers.

The investigators discovered that the *Titanic* had sufficient lifeboat capacity for all first-class passengers, but not for the other two classes. In fact, most third-class or steerage passengers had no idea where the lifeboats were, much less any way of getting to the decks where they were stowed.

Modern analysis has shown that the steel the *Titanic*'s hull was constructed from was not suitable for use in cold locations as it would become brittle. Again very unluckily, the company used strong steel rivets on the central hull where stresses were expected to be greatest, but iron rivets for the stern and bow, where the collision actually occurred. The ship's builder decided to use No. 3 iron bar instead of the higher quality and traditional No. 4 for these rivets, which meant they were weaker still.

There is some debate as to whether the rudders were of sufficient size: should she have been able to turn faster and thereby have avoided the collision? Additionally, the engines were not all capable of being put into reverse: should she have been able to stop quicker? Stopping the engines made the ship less manoeuvrable so the combination of attempting to stop and turn proved fatal – had she hit the iceberg full on, it would not have created as large a hole and she may have remained afloat.

Once the *Titanic* was taking on water, one possible way of saving her would have been to pump it out quicker than it was coming in. Even if the rate of flow could not be matched, more water pumped out would clearly buy more time for help to arrive. Unfortunately the *Titanic*'s pumps were not capable of achieving this.

The conclusion of the British inquiry into the sinking was 'that the loss of the said ship was due to collision with an iceberg, brought about by the excessive speed at which the ship was being navigated'. It is thought that the *Titanic* was at her normal cruising speed of 22 knots which was common practice as it was thought that any iceberg large enough to damage the ship would be seen in sufficient time to be avoided.

Unluckily, there was a flat calm sea with no wind or swell and it was a moonless night. Thus there was no foam from breaking waves or moonlight to help give away the existence of the floating mass of ice.

We stop there with the specific details of this tragic case but will use it throughout the rest of this chapter to consider issues in Missing Leadership.

## Missing Leadership

As stated above, Missing Leadership is where appropriate and necessary leadership simply does not take place. There are a number of reasons why this might occur and before strategies towards a resolution can be considered it is vital that we have an appreciation of what these reasons may be. That is the purpose of the next section.

One common cause of Missing Leadership is the complex and rapidly changing environment leaders operate in and which De Woot (2009) clearly articulates. The issue requiring a leadership intervention may evolve so quickly that people are simply unaware or are operating under the misapprehension that someone else is taking responsibility for that area of activity. We see this in the *Titanic* case where developments in size and speed of ships were too rapid to allow in-depth research into and testing of the strength and suitability of construction materials and methods. The captain may also have been unsure of the handling characteristics and capabilities of the ship. As Talbott (2009:9) identifies with the example of Citigroup, companies, banks and investment banks have become so big and unwieldy that leaders simply cannot control effectively all areas of the business. In these situations it is easy to see some areas suffering from a lack of leadership.

There is great emphasis today on empowerment, that is, the devolution of power as far down an organisation as is practical so as to give more junior staff the opportunity to solve problems and take decisions. This is held to have many advantages such as staff development and freeing senior staff for more difficult or strategic decisions but can result in Missing Leadership if neither party takes responsibility for an issue.

This could be due, say to poor communication, unwillingness by the junior staff to take on the responsibility or fear of the consequences of failure. Poor communication can occur between the senior and middle management tiers of an organisation, for example if the strategy decided is not relayed effectively to those expected to carry it out, possibly due to what we call the 'hour glass effect'.

## THE HOUR GLASS EFFECT

Where communication is limited and information trickles down from above, senior management seeming to assume the middle managers will know what is expected of them.

Poor organisation or communication could also result in an issue falling unrecognised between two people's responsibilities. In the *Titanic* case the radio operators do not appear to have been aware of the importance of their communication role to the safe running of the ship.

Possibly the most common form of Missing Leadership is where the supposed leader just fails to carry out the leadership role, either completely or in part. This could be due for example to incompetence, faulty logic, misunderstanding the expectations of the role, procrastination, being interrupted by other activities or physical absence due to sickness or being on holiday. In the *Titanic* case, the captain of the *Californian* appears to have used faulty logic when deciding to ignore the distress flares from another ship.

Another reason for Missing Leadership closely related to the last two above is where the 'wrong' people carry out the role and decisions are taken and implemented by people who lack the required experience, skills or knowledge to achieve success.

Bakan (2005:164) quotes Oscar Olivia, a union official who led a popular uprising against the privatisation of the freshwater system in Cochamba, Bolivia, who said:

> We live in a world full of fear, people are afraid of the dark, people are afraid of giving their opinion, people are afraid of acting ... It's time that we lose that fear ... [and] develop the capacity to unite, to organise, and to recover our faith in ourselves and in others.

This quotation from Olivia illustrates another reason why leadership may be missing: fear to take a stand and seize the leadership role. Marianne Williamson (1992:190 – although this is often mistakenly attributed to Nelson Mandela's inaugural speech in 1994) also picks up on the idea that fear can cause individuals not to take on a leadership role but provides another perspective:

> Our deepest fear is not that we are inadequate.
> Our deepest fear is that we are powerful beyond measure.
> It is our light, not our darkness, that most frightens us.
> We ask ourselves,
> 'who am I to be brilliant, gorgeous, talented and fabulous?'
> Actually, who are you not to be? You are a child of God.

Williamson's comments suggest that it may not be fear of failure that prevents people from fully stepping into an effective leadership role, but fear of what they might achieve – possibly going beyond their comfort zone.

Leaders may not want to act, take on responsibility, take control or challenge a common trend if it means being out of line with their peers. It may be easier simply to let the situation roll along in common with everybody else. The consequences of such approaches, dubbed 'Groupthink' by Janis (1972) are well illustrated by the recent turmoil in the finance markets. Banks followed each other to expand at unsustainable rates through lending money to individuals less and less likely to be able to repay. Ultimately, all have suffered tremendously and this approach has threatened the whole financial system. The issues connected to the financial markets collapse and groupthink are further developed in Chapters 4 and 6 respectively.

Whether leadership is in fact missing may be related to perception and different expectations of what leadership intervention is necessary. It may be that a leader is using one particular style of leadership, say delaying action until the time is right, when observers want or expect to see immediate action. This mismatch between the leader's actual and expected style may be due to a lack of appropriate training for the leader or observer and is undoubtedly influenced by national cultures. Followers from cultures with high uncertainty avoidance (Hofstede 1980) for instance might look for different leader traits than those from low uncertainty avoidance cultures. It is easy to see that the expectation of a leader's actions in Uzbekistan may be different to that in Sweden for example and if leaders are not aware of these cultural differences in expectation they can easily get it wrong and leadership can be seen as missing.

We have already mentioned the possibility of the leader being physically absent but they may be there in body but not in mind. This can be because they are carrying out other duties and unaware that a problem exists which requires their attention; they are so involved in the other tasks that they neglect the one in question, or are too busy to give sufficient time and focus to both.

> Over 33% of all new incidences of ill health are work related stress – 13,800,000 working days were lost to work related stress, depression and anxiety in 2006/7. Each case of work related stress, depression and anxiety leads to an average 30.2 working days lost.
>
> *Source*: HSE 2009.

Many leaders complain of stress due to work overload and while this may be due to poor time management or delegation skills, it can equally be due to genuine excess workload. This may occur at certain peak activity times of the year or immediately following a period of absence when others assume the leader is back in charge but they are actually still getting back up to speed.

It may also reflect a long-term issue such as poor organisational structure, lack of training, inefficiency or acceptance of other people's problems due to a desire to impress and gain promotion or an inability to say no. Whatever the cause of the work overload and stress the outcome is likely to be poor leadership.

Advent of the internet and emails has meant that it is no longer necessary to be physically present to be 'at work' hence there is confusion over whether the leader is missing or not. Followers may not be sure who is theoretically and practically in charge at any one time, resulting in confusion. Emails encourage leadership in absentia, where the leader is rarely seen but continues to carry out the role. This may be tempting as it helps avoid getting drawn into office gossip and minutiae but is unlikely to work effectively in the long-term as followers feel remote and undervalued. Very often office gossip contains a great deal of value to a leader and communication via email is not always effective as it can be easily misunderstood and lacks the personal touch.

The causes of Missing Leadership briefly outlined above are summarised in Table 2.1

**Table 2.1      Causes of Missing Leadership**

| |
|---|
| Complex, rapidly changing environment |
| Large, unwieldy size of organisations |
| Failed attempts being made to empower another |
| Failed attempt to delegate responsibility |
| Lack of appropriate education related to leadership styles and cultural differences |
| Different cultural expectations of leadership |
| Not taking responsibility for leadership |
| Fear either of failure or great success |
| Group think |
| The leader is preoccupied with other things |
| The leader is overloaded with work |
| Incompetent; faulty logic; misunderstanding process |
| The leader is not there |

## Problem-Solving

Having outlined common causes of Missing Leadership it is useful to consider whether they are underpinned by any recurrent threads or themes. We believe there is such a factor here, namely poor or inappropriate problem-solving. Effective problem-solving is particularly challenging in today's rapidly changing global environment and the process, style and methods adopted must be appropriate for this and guard against group think. Where a number of people are involved, they have to clearly identify who has responsibility for leadership and that responsibility must be recognised and accepted. The remainder of this chapter briefly explores one approach to problem-solving that might be used, then illustrates its use via three short case studies.

Many useful problem-solving frameworks exist but here we use the ASK SIR L model proposed by Rayment (2001) as it covers the full process from recognising a problem exists through to learning from its solution. This is a systematic, logical model as illustrated in Table 2.2

**Table 2.2      The ASK SIR L Problem-Solving Model**

| A | Appreciate | that there is a problem |
|---|---|---|
| S | Specify | its nature and scope |
| K | Causes | identification thereof |
| | | |
| S | Solutions | generation and selection |
| I | Implement | chosen programmes |
| R | Review | whether the problem has been solved |
| | | |
| L | Learn | how to avoid repetition |

A logical, systematic approach helps ensure the leader considers all facets of a problem in a careful, methodical manner. There are potential weaknesses to such a logical approach particularly in a turbulent environment and it does not cover all aspects of effective leadership. Later chapters deal with those issues and introduce three other approaches to problem-solving, namely systems theory (Chapter 3), mind games (Chapter 4) and group dynamics (Chapter 5). An effective leader must understand all of these aspects and approaches and apply those relevant to a particular leadership challenge. In this chapter we therefore only begin the journey into effective decision-making.

We do not have space here to go into detail on the theory of problem-solving and those wishing a fuller exploration are referred to Rayment (2001). Here we briefly introduce and use the mnemonic ASK SIR L then demonstrate its use in the *Titanic* case outlined earlier. We then examine two current issues – global resource depletion and toxic childhood – to see how they reflect Missing Leadership and show how effective problem-solving processes may help these.

## Analysis of the *Titanic* Case

When studying a past event we are able to study the actual causes (K in Table 2.2) so our thinking can become very specific. What we should be doing, however, is attempting to learn from the experience. We have chosen to make most of our comments under the cause umbrella but it is not particularly important which section they are placed in provided they are specified and solutions sought and implemented.

### APPRECIATE – A PROBLEM EXISTS

Before any attempt is made towards making a decision it is vital that as full as possible an understanding of all the issues involved is gained. In the description of the *Titanic* case earlier in the Chapter, the term 'unlucky' was used on several occasions. In truth, however, it is MisLeading to say they were unlucky as it encourages us to think that the people involved were blameless and disaster unavoidable and it can prevent a full exploration of the issues in this appreciate stage. It is fair to say that the people involved in a disaster of this nature are unlucky in that it could have occurred at any time but they just happened to be the ones who were on board at the time. This must not be used, though, to avoid a thorough examination of the causes of the tragedy and the role played by the ship's designer, builder, captain and crew.

Many of those involved in the design, construction and sailing of the ship appear to have been somewhat complacent and to have made little attempt to appreciate the true risks faced by ships using the route. Given the number of cruises taking place and the type of environment they were working in, it is likely that a tragedy of this nature was predictable.

There was general awareness of the possibility of coming across icebergs but assumptions as to how easily they would be avoided appear to have been wrong. Warnings were sent by other ships but the vital ones ignored due to lack of training/awareness of their importance. Lookouts carried out environmental scanning but again invalid assumptions made as to its effectiveness.

## SPECIFY THE PRECISE NATURE AND SCOPE OF THE PROBLEM

The next stage of our model pulls the exploration in the appreciate phase together by encouraging decision makers to specify the precise nature and scope of the problem. Unless the earlier stage of appreciating as many of the issues involved as possible has been completed successfully this specify stage may be incorrect. As pointed out at the start of this chapter, the volume of information available and extent of deliberate and accidental MisLeadership within it can mean we cannot always know which is, or be sure we are working with, the correct information. In the complex and rapidly changing environment faced by leaders today it is not possible to gather every piece of information and some compromise is necessary.

When designing, building and running the *Titanic*, the relevant parties should have attempted to identify, specify and manage all risks faced by them, including, for example, a tsunami, enemy action if a war broke out, piracy, outbreak of disease or illness, collision, engine failure or explosion and extreme weather. We are uncertain as to how many of these risks were considered in detail but obviously not all were. Icebergs, for example, were a known hazard but there appears to have been little attempt made to quantify the risk.

## CAUSES

The next phase of the problem-solving model encourages decision makers to identify the causes of the problem that has now been clearly specified. This continues to build a thorough understanding of the issues before any decisions are made.

In our *Titanic* case, the possible causes of the sinking that have been mentioned in the case include poor design and manufacture (Bassett n.d.) including use of substandard materials, failure to adjust to adverse conditions, possibly wrong evasive action, insufficient lifeboats, failure to properly instruct and train the crew in emergency procedures and the importance of messages to the bridge, inbuilt prejudice in favour of saving women, children and the first-class passengers, and failure of communication between the crew and passengers of the severity of the situation.

Underlying causes that are not necessarily mentioned but can be deduced include a number of invalid assumptions which led to complacency and failure to think, plan and react: the ship would not sink/is not sinking; an iceberg would be seen in time to avoid it; calm sea and clear skies meant no imminent danger; token measures were taken to lessen the risk, leading to more complacency and false security; lives of third-class passengers were of low value; the radio would work and be picked up by other ships; warning messages would be delivered to the bridge; radio operators would realise their importance; having received general warnings it became even easier to assume any urgent specific ones would be delivered; other ships would be alert and close enough to come to assist; their captains would care enough to take action.

Possibly due to the above assumptions, not all risks seem to have been identified accurately, so insufficient attempts were made to avoid or deal with them if they did occur. This includes proper testing of the manoeuvrability of the ship and what actions to take in particular circumstances. Little testing, trials, experimentation or modelling had taken place such that when an iceberg suddenly appeared, basic instinct took over.

The fact that it was her maiden voyage may be relevant here. The captain and crew were inexperienced as to the handling and capabilities of the ship but also may not have gelled together as an efficient and effective team. Assumptions seem to have been made as to the roles people would perform and tasks seem to have fallen between them. Facilities such as the new radio were untried and possibly the operators not brought into the system properly – were they aware of their potentially vital leadership role in the case of an emergency? They appear to have been self-centred and focused on other tasks such as personal financial gain.

Blindly following rules, regulations and customs without checking their validity occurs throughout the case from the number of lifeboats to refusing men access to half-empty lifeboats. There was a general failure to keep systems and procedures up to date with the new technology and changing speed, size and capacity of passenger ships. Escape routes, effective lifejackets, escape drills and training were all missing.

Fear and rumour are common causes of disaster but were only relevant here when some lifeboats failed to return to look for survivors. Complacency seems to have been far more prevalent.

## SOLUTIONS AND IMPLEMENTATION

We now turn our attention in the problem-solving model to solutions. Note the emphasis that has been placed to this point on gaining as full an appreciation of the issues as possible so that the most effective solutions can be developed.

Following the *Titanic* disaster a very wide range of changes were suggested and successfully implemented including improved hull and bulkhead design, open access throughout the ship for passenger escape routes, lifeboat requirements, improved life-vest design, the holding of safety drills, better passenger notification and radio communications laws. It also had an effect on social norms and attitudes although these are much harder to quantify since they are part of a general move toward equality and the First World War started two years after the sinking.

## REVIEW AND LEARN

These are vital stages within the problem-solving process but it is often the case that as soon as solutions have been implemented leaders run to the next problem. By doing this however they do not learn and improve as fully as they could.

The *Titanic* case reveals several common errors in these stages of decision-making. Knowing what happened, it is tempting for us to assume the people involved should have been able to predict and avoid it. It is also tempting to introduce measures to prevent recurrence of the specific event but if the circumstances were genuinely extremely rare it is unlikely to be repeated exactly – what we should be doing is looking to avoid events of this nature.

Possibly the worst error is to focus on who was to blame for the event. This often leads to a blame culture and people trying to avoid taking responsibility – Missing Leadership again.

There are clearly a vast number of facets to the *Titanic* case but we believe the lessons were by and large learnt and implemented such that passenger and other vessels all became much safer. It is also fair to say that at the time little general thought had been given to risk management and problem-solving techniques. Use of approaches such as ASK SIR L is now commonplace and we are sure they help to avoid many disasters. Nevertheless, as will be seen throughout this book, there are many situations in which we believe these techniques are still underused. They could be taken as fundamental to the concept of MisLeadership and particularly Missing Leadership.

The final angle we want to consider for this case is the psychology of the captain of the *Titanic*. It can be useful when trying to learn from a situation to put yourself in the person's shoes and seek to understand the pressures they were likely to be experiencing in order to try to understand their actions. Captain Smith was aware of the danger of icebergs and had received several warnings yet continued at high speed when at least some other ships had completely stopped. Why did he do this?

Was the captain a risk taker who put speed before safety? Had he thought through the logic of the situation properly? Had he checked the conditions to see how hard it would be to see an iceberg in time to avoid it? Was he complacent or brainwashed into believing the ship was unsinkable? Even if he believed that he would surely want to avoid a collision.

It is fascinating to try to put yourself in his position. Was he trying to impress the owners and passengers as to the superiority of this new ship and his ability to get the best out of it? Trying to set a new fast time for the crossing? Were the owners putting pressure on him to do so? Was he cool calm and confident or hot, bothered and bewildered? Was his mind on other things? Was he actually asleep?

We feel the *Titanic* case is a good illustration of the fact that too much of the focus in many attempts at problem-solving tends to be on the middle 'SIR' phase – selecting, implementing and reviewing solutions, while insufficient attention is paid to 'ASK' – appreciate, specify and look for causes.

This chapter so far has looked at what Missing Leadership is and considered the possible reasons why this may be so prevalent in our current leadership approaches. We have analysed these causes and argued that one issue that seems to underpin many of the causes is ineffective problem-solving processes. We have then introduced a mnemonic to assist leaders to follow a more logical approach to problem-solving and have said that this is only the first element to effective problem-solving and that later chapters will build on these basics. This mnemonic has been applied to the *Titanic* case to illustrate the main elements in its use. We now move on to consider these elements of Missing Leadership and effective decision-making in contemporary society. Three Urgent Global Issues – Global Warming, Resource Depletion and Toxic Childhood – are the focuses of our attention.

## Global Warming and Resource Depletion

As we have said earlier, the ASK phase in the decision-making mnemonic we use is the area that is most often overlooked. This appears to be the case also with global warming and resource depletion. As the Global Humanitarian Forum (2009:iii and 1) argue:

> Climate change already has a severe human impact today, but it is a silent crisis … so few people are aware of just how much is at stake.

As identified in Chapter 1, humanity is faced with the urgent issue that the world's resources are rapidly running out, and that current consumption levels require more than the earth can possibly supply. People have been warning of this danger for some time. Judd (2009) quoted from Thomas Malthus's (1766–1834) 'An Essay on the Principle of Population':

> 'The power of population is so superior to the power of the earth to produce subsistence for man, that premature death must in some shape or other visit the human race. The vices of mankind are active and able ministers of depopulation. They are the precursors in the great army of destruction, and often finish the dreadful work themselves. But should they fail in this war of extermination, sickly seasons, epidemics, pestilence, and plague advance in terrific array, and sweep off their thousands and tens of thousands. Should success be still incomplete, gigantic inevitable famine stalks in the rear, and with one mighty blow levels the population with the food of the world.'

In 1998 Fidel Castro (1998:64) said:

> It is a world where nation-states are disappearing, losing strength, as in Europe where they fought each other for so many years and now they are integrating, coming together, suppressing boundaries, nation-states will disappear one way or another, the trend is there … [But] What kind of global world will that be? Will a world with a global economy be sustainable under today's prevailing concepts? Can you imagine, for instance, 1.5 billion Chinese people, each of them with a car at the front door, when they have only 100 million hectares of arable land? Or again, 1.5 billion Indian people, each with cars at their front door? The fact is that capitalism has not only developed the productive forces and created an economic and political system which is predominant in the world

*today, but capitalism has also developed models of life, consumption and distribution of wealth that are unsustainable worldwide.*

Despite many warnings like the above there still seems to be a lack of appreciation of the importance and urgency of the problem. Global population levels are set to grow by 40 per cent by 2050 (Global Humanitarian Forum 2009: iii), resource consumption and waste production are all at levels far above those a century ago, have risen particularly quickly in recent years and continue to do so. The earth simply cannot sustain current activity levels and approaches in the long-term. And long-term may not be long if we are to believe the Japanese Science Council (2008) who in the lead up to the 2008 G8 summit in Hokkaido, Japan, highlighted some significant indicators that could lead us to surmise that by 2050 there may be no human race or living planet left if we continue to be driven by a consumerist, energy-hungry, resource-depleting lifestyle.

---

'Climate change is happening more rapidly than anyone thought possible. Should humankind stop worrying about global warming and instead start panicking? My conclusion is that we are still left with a fair chance to hold the 2°C line, yet the race between climate dynamics and climate policy will be a close one.' Hans Joachim Schellnhuber – Founding Director, Potsdam Institute for Climate Impact Research; Member, Intergovernmental Panel on Climate Change.

*Source*: Global Humanitarian Forum 2009:8.

---

The Global Humanitarian Forum (2009:iii) argue that if we do not reverse current trends by close to 2020, we may have failed. Global warming will pass the widely acknowledged danger level of two degrees by then, since there is an approximately 20-year delay between emission reductions and the halting of their warming effect. This report clearly demonstrates that climate change is already highly dangerous at well below one degree of warming. Two degrees would be catastrophic. The findings of this report (Global Humanitarian Forum 2009:1) also indicate that climate change is already having major effects. Each year they argue it leaves over 300,000 people dead, 325 million people seriously affected, and economic losses of US$125 billion. Four billion people are vulnerable, and 500 million people are at extreme risk.

Focusing on these unsustainable practices, Diamond (2006:509) highlights a worrying lesson from his study of a number of collapsed civilisations in that:

*A society's steep decline may begin only a decade or two after the society reaches its peak numbers, wealth, and power ... The reason is*

> *simple: maximum population, wealth, resource consumption, and waste*
> *production mean maximum environmental impact.*

Of course it is difficult to establish the full facts on things like global warming and resource depletion as there are competing factions, each trying to protect their own interests, get their own points heard or pursue their own ends. A recent book by Taylor (2009), for instance, claims from his studies of satellite data, cloud cover, ocean and solar cycles that we are being fed a distorted understanding of changes in global climate due to the needs of politicians and lobbyists for simple answers, slogans and targets.

Diamond (2006) is also concerned that many of the routes to survival used by civilisations he studied (such as geographical relocation and assistance from outside) are not available to us in the now global village: we must achieve ecological balance ourselves and in situ.

Despite these clear and stark warnings, we seem to have done little to halt the rise in global warming and resource consumption. This seems to indicate Missing Leadership and ineffective decision-making. As the Global Humanitarian Forum (2009:iii) argue:

> *Climate change already has a severe human impact today, but it is a*
> *silent crisis. Weak political leadership as evident today [will be] all the*
> *more alarming then.*

Missing Leadership here stems from the failure to get to grips with the scale of the problem and tackle it in a consistent and comprehensive manner. It seems clear that the majority do not fully appreciate the issues. In the Appreciate phase of the mnemonic in Table 2.2 we might look to establish the major cause of global warming, why it is currently a silent crisis, which resources were under threat of depletion and to what extent, and why many seem reluctant to act. It would also adopt a global outlook. Resources examined should not just be the obvious oil and gas but also all others that could potentially be limited such as wood, fish stocks, fresh water, agricultural land and good quality air to breathe. The situation for each resource would be established including reserve levels, feasibility of making/growing more and current and likely future usage rates.

The causes of resource depletion are fairly clear and are evidenced by all the exponential growth charts that illustrate consumption in various guises (Klass

2007:1, Gore 2006). These basically result from two aspects: increasing population and rising standards of living, particularly in developing countries.

Sustainability can mean different things to people in different circumstances, but the basic facts are straightforward – for a sustainable world we need total worldwide consumption of resources to be equal to or less than the Earth's capacity to replenish them. Many commentators claim we have already moved beyond the point where the Earth can replenish what we use. However, if we assume for a moment that we are still just in balance then there would now have to be zero growth in global resource consumption.

The causes of global warming and resource depletion of course go deeper and are influenced by many factors. BRIC countries (originally Brazil, Russia, India and China but many others could be included), for instance, have spare resources in that they do not use all the wood they grow, oil they extract or, ironically since many of the people in these countries are starving, food they grow. Their view of sustainability is they can expand their economies including developing infrastructure until they reach equilibrium. Given their relatively low current standard of living and that most individuals want to be seen to be successful, based on the same measures of success as used in the West (their own house, car, television and up-to-date mobile phone), who can deny them?

Countries in the West claim to be moving to become sustainable but even the control measures that are taken to reduce global warming are nowhere near enough to reduce carbon levels in the short-to-medium term. Misleading sleight of hand is used such as a figure being counted as a reduction even if it is bigger than previous years' figures so long as it is less than the original prediction for the year in question. This sliding of the true objective means resource consumption in the West will continue to grow for many years.

Most international companies make similar claims about becoming sustainable but often what they mean is that they will reduce their levels of waste, packaging per unit and delivery miles. They are virtually all continuing to look for growth in total sales, profits and market share. It is difficult to imagine a chief executive lasting very long if they told the board their objective was to shrink the business by 10 per cent per annum. They continue to scour the world looking for cheap, unprotected resources to convert into products people in the West will pay high prices for.

So the causes of global warming and resource depletion go deep into people's psyche and are underpinned by the unshakable belief in the strength of the market economy and need for growth. We believe they are misguided in their continued quest for profit maximisation, partly due to being misinformed by the business schools who should be thinking through the problems of modern business and leading business to a new role and approach. These issues are discussed in Chapter 4: Misinformed Leadership and a New Paradigm.

Many individuals in the West profess to be keen on sustainability but tend to focus on fairly small changes like recycling. As prosperity increases, increasing numbers take second and third holidays and buy second homes and cars. Rising population further stokes demand.

In total these approaches clearly add up to increased global resource consumption for many years into the future even if drastic action is taken now.

The financial crisis in 2008/9 is a good example of the embedded thinking on the importance of growth. Instead of using the downturn at this time as a chance to make a concerted global drive toward genuine sustainability and reduction in resource consumption, the knee-jerk reaction by world governments has been to do anything and everything to prop up the system in order to avoid recession. This reveals Missing Leadership both in the build-up to and aftermath of the crisis on the part of the governments and bankers.

Ultimately, the lack of effective action on these life-threatening – possibly even total life-destroying – issues is clear evidence of Missing Leadership. In this example why it is that so few of the people in positions of power and authority are prepared to act? Is it that the rich, powerful or politically aware are not the ones most likely to suffer most from the effects of climate change – an issue we return to in Chapter 5 on Machiavellian Leadership. Is it that they are fearful, are afraid to act or are complying with Groupthink? Is it that the leaders do not know what to do because of the lack of appropriate education for this complex global environment?

The only government to have tackled their population explosion head-on is China's where the approach had been to restrict the number of children people are allowed to produce. According to Moore (2009), though, these restrictions are now being eased in response to concern about economic problems caused by the country's ageing population, which again seems to be underpinned by the growth mindset.

The Chartered Association of Certified Accountants (ACCA) made the following press release to accompany 'Going Concern?' their contribution to the sustainability debate. It contains many strong words – we hope they will be followed with equally strong action.

---

*The 'business as usual' model for organisations worldwide is no longer an option in this sustainable age...*

*The report offers eight key policy areas to be addressed, from corporate governance to audit and assurance. The report also offers a series of recommendations for business, government and the accountancy profession to take on board, including:*

*Businesses should make sustainability a core part of their strategy and include sustainability key performance indicators in their reward and pay systems for senior managers.*

*Small and medium-sized enterprises (SMEs) need help from governments to guide them in measuring their key environmental and social impacts. SMEs should become more proactive in the CSR debate and increase their profile and contribution to the growing number of initiatives, guidelines and standards being developed.*

*Governments should encourage organisations to produce sustainability reports and learn from other governments in this area (e.g., Sweden and Hong Kong) to report themselves.*

*Investors should work to adapt investment practices to account for climate change, integrating them into their investment processes and systems.*

*The International Education Standards Board of the International Federation of Accountants should incorporate SD and CSR matters into its basic education requirements.*

---

**Figure 2.1     ACCA's Going Concern Press Release (Extracts)**

The reference in this ACCA report to basic educational requirements is supported by Scott (2009):

> *The process that we call sustainable development makes no sense other than as a social learning process of improving the human condition that can be continued indefinitely without undermining itself. In this sense, sustainable development doesn't, instrumentally, depend on learning; rather it's inherently a learning process of making the emergent future ecologically sound and humanly habitable, as it emerges, through the*

*continuous, responsive learning which is the human species' most characteristic endowment.*

This fits with our views on the importance of the education process and a fundamental rethink of leadership education so that leaders have the necessary tools to tackle these complex global contemporary issues.

Following Barrett's (2003:349) argument, sustainability must include an organisation's financial viability, but this new mission has to be broader than containing purely financial considerations. As Jim Collins, author of bestselling book *Good to Great* puts it (as cited in Pickard 2009:24):

> *A truly great company realises that growth and making money aren't the fundamental purposes of the enterprise. The enterprise exists to achieve some purpose in the world and with enough discipline will grow and get enough return on invested capital to fulfil that purpose. You may have to resist opportunities for growth that will pull you away from that goal.*

## Toxic Childhood

The phrase 'toxic childhood' refers to the concern that the way children are being brought up is actually harmful to their all-round development. Some of the signs for this might include rising obesity, posture and eyesight problems, lack of reasoning and social-skill development, little outdoor exercise and too much time spent watching television or playing computer games, and consumption of large amounts of junk food. (Children's.org. 2009, Hug-Ammitzboell 2009).

---

Most children not active enough.

*Source*: NHS Choice, 2009.

---

As with resource depletion, the signs are clear but those in power do not seem to be responding to them in a systematic manner nor taking sufficient actions to achieve the necessary changes to achieve holistic development, the term we use for all-round development and explore in the next chapter as part of our Global Fitness Framework.

As with the resource deprecation case above we feel it is an example of Missing Leadership and wonder whether the fundamental difficulties are a lack of a full appreciation of the issues and how significant they are.

Using our problem-solving mnemonic, it is also important to consider the causes of the toxic childhood. Some argue that one causal factor in the UK is the collapse of family life. As an example, an editorial from Initiatives of Change (2008) quoted a senior British judge as claiming family life was in 'meltdown', the effects of which will be as catastrophic as the meltdown of the ice caps, terrorism, street crime or drugs.

> *What is certain is that almost all of society's social ills can be traced directly to the collapse of family life ... I am not saying every broken family produces dysfunctional children but I am saying that almost every dysfunctional child is the product of a broken family ... And what is government doing to recognise and face up to the emerging situation? The answer is: very little and nothing like enough ... It is fiddling whilst Rome burns.*

The article continues:

> *It would be simplistic to lay all our recent troubles at the door of family break-up. But surely the tragic increase in knife-crime among teenagers; what many see as declining academic standards in schools; historically high figures for teen pregnancies; and child health issues such as anorexia and obesity all point to the fact that family life is not what it should be.*

> *Children need to know that they are loved, valued, trusted, respected. They also need to know that they have a contribution to make ... The challenge to those of us who are parents, grandparents, guardians, or even proxy aunts and uncles is that children learn far more by example than from exhortation. 'Do as I say, not as I do' has never been an effective formula for successful child-rearing.*

Another cause of toxic childhood may be the way in which education has become increasingly focused on developing skills for the economy, use of exam-results-based performance measures to judge performance of schools and pupils, and the language used in education policy and implementation. Pring et al. (2009) in the Nuffield 14–19 Review say:

> *The consumer or client replaces the learner. The curriculum is delivered.*
> *Aims are spelt out in terms of targets. Audits (based on performance*
> *indicators) measure success defined in terms of hitting the targets ...*
> *As the language of performance and management has advanced, so we*
> *have proportionately lost a language of education which recognises*
> *the intrinsic value of pursuing certain sorts of question ... of seeking*
> *understanding [and] of exploring through literature and the arts what*
> *it means to be human ... The Orwellian language of 'performance*
> *management and control' has come to dominate educational deliberation*
> *and planning, namely the language of measurable 'inputs', 'outputs',*
> *of 'performance indicators' and 'audits', of 'customers' and 'deliverers',*
> *of 'efficiency gains' and 'bottom lines'.*

In problem-solving, it is often the case that well-meant solutions are implemented quickly, but without first a full appreciation of all the issues and causes involved. Often when this is done the implemented solution creates more problems that it solves. An example of this in the toxic childhood debate is the introduction by the Home Office of new controls over people who regularly drive children for sports or social clubs in the UK. They now fall under the scope of the Vetting and Barring Scheme and have to undergo criminal record checks.

The measures are intended to safeguard children by stopping paedophiles and any other unsuitable people gaining access to them by ensuring those who work with children in a position of trust are indeed trustworthy. It was recommended by the Bichard (2004) report following the Soham murders of Holly Wells and Jessica Chapman by college caretaker Ian Huntley.

This is a valid objective but the approach adopted is likely to discourage millions of people from volunteering, with a total of around 11 million adults affected including doctors, nurses, teachers, dentists and even school governors.

This could result in sports and social clubs and activities closing down, leaving more bored young people on our streets or indoors playing computer games with the adverse effects outlined above. There is also the danger of creating a situation where we assume every adult who approaches children means to do them harm. It is already the case that many parents rarely let their children go out to play in case something untoward happens to them.

The scheme will only catch those people who attempt to register and already have a conviction or other 'soft evidence' against them. Unless the scheme is tightly policed, paedophiles with a record are likely to not register but still gain access. If the scheme is tightly policed even more people will be put off, concerned about people prying into their private lives, wondering whether some entirely innocent activity might be interpreted as valid 'soft evidence' against them and leave then with some kind of social stigma and threat of physical or mental violence from a member of the public deciding to take the law into their own hands – several paediatricians have been assaulted by such people confusing the word for paedophile.

We finish this section on toxic childhood with a brief outline of the terrible abuse of children in Irish institutions throughout the period 1910s–1990s, reminiscent of the abuse that took place at the Haut de la Garenne children's home in Jersey which came to light in March 2008 and is still under police investigation. The latter case may be more horrific in that it involves the murder of several children but the former reveals extremely widespread abuse and failure to act. We believe it summarises the extent to which we have let our children down over many years, includes elements of all four aspects of MisLeadership and illustrates the Institutional MisLeadership throughout every sector of society.

The European Network of Ombudspersons for Children (2009) summarise the Report of the Commission to Inquire into Child Abuse which found that throughout the 80-year period ending in the 1990s, thousands of children suffered physical and sexual abuse in homes run by religious orders in Ireland. They reported that sexual abuse was endemic in boys' homes but hidden by the orders that ran the institutions, offenders being simply transferred to other homes where they were able to continue the abuse. Out of 1,700 witnesses interviewed, 500 men and 300 women claimed they had been sexually abused, the remainder referring to a climate of fear in the homes, with serious injuries including broken bones common; 800 priests, brothers, nuns and lay people from 200 homes were implicated.

Apologies have been made by many senior leaders, including the Pope. The Catholic Archbishop of Dublin, the Most Reverend Diarmuid Martin, said that the organisations concerned should seriously examine how their ideals had become debased by systematic abuse.

The institutionalised abuse of children in Jersey and Ireland forms only two of many such cases, another recent revelation being the UK government in the

1950s to 1970s sending thousands of children from British care homes to work in terrible conditions in Australia. These children were often told their parents had died when in fact many had been forced to give up their children due to financial hardship or being single parents and intended to reclaim them when their circumstances improved.

Each of the four main examples we have used in this section on toxic childhood (collapse of family life, misguided educational reform, criminal-record checks on adults helping in sports or social clubs and abuse of children in homes) illustrates an important aspect of the debate that has not been properly dealt with, but the situation is stark if one takes a broad view. We argue that they all show examples of MisLeadership and particularly Missing Leadership. The environment in which children are growing up has changed dramatically in recent years but our treatment of them has not kept pace with the challenges. Perhaps the key issue is that the ASK element within our decision-making mnemonic has been weak and that leaders have not fully appreciated the issues involved, specified clearly the problem or examined the underlying causes of the difficulties. As a result the solutions implemented have not been effective. They have been piecemeal solutions rather than a coordinated systematic response.

## Summary

This chapter has considered the concept of Missing Leadership which we have said is where appropriate and necessary leadership simply does not take place. Some of the main reasons for this have been highlighted and we have argued that underlying many of these reasons seems to be poor or inappropriate problem-solving.

We introduced the theoretical side of problem-solving by focusing on the systematic, logical approach using the ASK SIR L model. Particular emphasis should be given to the ASK phase as unless we appreciate a problem exists and its scale and scope we will not look for solutions. Practical aspects were introduced through a case study of the sinking of the *Titanic* and a wealth of other illustrations and examples.

The chapter concluded with three case studies focused on the ASK phase of the ASK SIR L model, Global Warming, Resource Consumption and Toxic Childhood.

**POINTS FOR REFLECTION**

1.  How common is Missing Leadership in your experience?
2.  Do your experiences of it fit the descriptions and approaches used in the chapter?
3.  Several causes of Missing Leadership were identified in the chapter. Can you identify any others?
4.  Would effective problem solving have helped deal with the situation?
5.  What other steps would have been necessary?

## References

ACCA Chartered Association of Certified Accountants. (2009). *Recommendations for the sustainable age*. [Online]. Available at: http://direct.accaglobal.com/e_article001168557.cfm?x=bd948lD,bbdjvbwC [accessed: 8/10/09].

Bakan, J. (2005). *The Corporation: The Pathological Pursuit of Profit and Power*. New York: Free Press.

Barrett, R. (2003). Culture and Consciousness: Measuring Spirituality in the Workplace by Mapping Values. In Giacalone, R.A. and Jurkiewicz, C. eds. *Handbook of Workplace Spirituality and Organizational performance*. M E Sharpe Inc: New York.

Bassett, V. (n.d.). Causes and Effects of the Rapid Sinking of the *Titanic*. *Undegraduate Engineering Review*. [Online]. Available at: http://www.writing.eng.vt.edu/uer/bassett.html [accessed: 30/9/09].

Bichard, M. (2004). *The Bichard Inquiry report*. [Online]. Available at: http://police.homeoffice.gov.uk/publications/operational-policing/bichard-inquiry-report?view=Binary [accessed: 10/10/09].

Castro, R.F. President of the Republic of Cuba. (2003). *Cold War Warnings for a Unipolar World*. Cuba: Ocean Press.

Children's.org. (2009). *Leading Causes of Child Obesity*. 1 October. [Online]. Available at: http://childrens.org/health/causes-of-child-obesity/ [accessed: 10/9/09].

De Woot, P. (2009.) *Should Prometheus be Bound?* Basingstoke: Palgrave Macmillan.

Diamond, J. (2006) *Collapse: How Societies Choose to Fail or Survive*. London: Penguin Books.

European Network of Ombudspersons for Children. (2009). [Online]. Available at: http://www.crin.org/enoc/resources/infodetail.asp?id=20289 [accessed: 1/10/09].

Global Humanitarian Forum. (2009). Human Impact Report. *Climate Change: The Anatomy of a Silent Crisis*. [Online]. Available at: http://www.ghfgeneva. org/Portals/0/pdfs/human_impact_report.pdf [accessed: 13/10/09].

Gore, A. (2006). *An Inconvenient Truth*. A Global Warning Paramount Classics, Paramount Pictures DVD. [Online]. see http://www.climatecrisis.net/ [accessed 1/10/09].

Hofstede, G. (1980). *Culture's Consequences: International Differences in Work-related Values*. London: Sage.

HSE. (2009). *Work Related Stress*. Health and Safety Executive. [Online]. Available at: http://www.hse.gov.uk/stress/index.htm [accessed: 14/10/09].

Hug-Ammitzboell, N. (2009). Importance of the Family to the Protection of the Child. *World Congress of Families Report, 10 August*. [Online]. Available at: http://www.worldcongress.org [accessed: 10/10/09].

Initiatives of Change. (2008). *What are Our Children Telling Us?* [Online]. Available at: http://iofc.org/en/resources/editorial/6246.html [accessed: 14/7/08].

Janis, I. (1972). *Victims of Groupthink*. New York: Houghton Mifflin.

Japanese Science Council. (2008). *Joint Science Academies' Statement: Climate Change Adaptation and the Transition to a Low Carbon Society*. [Online]. Available at: http://www.scj.go.jp/ja/info/kohyo/pdf/kohyo-20-s7.pdf [accessed: 1/10/09].

Judd, W. (2009). *GM Food*. [Online]. Available at: http://www.nzgeographic. co.nz/articles.php?ID=289 [accessed: 15/10/09].

Klass, D.L (2007). *Energy Consumption, Reserves, Depletion, and Environmental Issues. Science Direct*. [Online]. Available at: http://www.sciencedirect.com/ science? [accessed: 1/10/09].

Moore, M. (2009). China begins lifting strict one-child policy. *Daily Telegraph* [Online, 24 July]. Available at: http://www.telegraph.co.uk/news/worldnews/ asia/china/5901573/China-begins-lifting-strict-one-child-policy.html[accessed: 8/10/09].

NHS Choice. (2009). *Most children not active enough*. [Online, 29 September]. Available at: http://www.nhs.uk/news/2009/09September/Pages/kids-must-get-more-active.aspx [accessed: 10/10/09].

Pickard, J. (2009). *The Fall Guy: People Management*. London: Chartered Institute of Personnel and Development. 8 October.

Pring, R., Hayward, G., Hodgson, A., Johnson, J., Keep, E, Oancea, A., Rees, G., Spours, K. and Wild, S. (2009). *Education for All. The Future of Education and Training for 14–19 year-olds*. Oxon: Routledge.

Rayment, J.J. (2001). *Decision Making and Problem-solving Using Logic and Magic*. Essex: Earlybrave.

Scott, W. (2009). Director: Centre for Research in Education and the Environment Director: South West learning for Sustainability Coalition http://www.bath.ac.uk/cree. By personal communication, 5 October 2009.

Talbott, J.R. (2009). *The 86 Biggest Lies on Wall Street*. London: Constable and Robinson.

Taylor, P. (2009). *Chill: A Reassessment of Global Warming Theory*. East Sussex: Clairview Books Ltd.

Wikipedia. [Online]. Available at: http://www.wikipedia.org/ [accessed: 30/9/09].

Williamson, M. (1992). *A Return To Love: Reflections on the Principles of a Course in Miracles*. London: Harper Collins.

# 3

# Misguided Leadership and the Need for a Global Approach

In the previous chapter we highlighted how important it is for leaders to ensure they use effective decision-making processes and place sufficient emphasis on the ASK phase of the ASK SIR L model. We now focus on Misguided Leadership, the type of leadership where the adopted solution is invalid in that while the final objective or intention is laudable, the intermediate targets set do not lead toward their achievement, or invalid methods are used. The leadership may be efficient in that it hits its targets but ineffective in that they are the wrong targets.

Hitting the wrong target can be a missed opportunity but otherwise harmless, cause costly delay in terms of money, time or other resources, mean true objectives can never be achieved because the window of opportunity has gone, or have undesirable results that work against achievement of the true objective.

We start this chapter by considering the extent and effects of Misguided Leadership in one of the most important areas of human activity, the business world.

## Misguided Leadership in the Business Environment

Misguided Leadership is often seen and can have some of the most significant effects within the business environment. As scale, complexity and globalisation of business grow, the potential effects of Misguided Leadership also grow such that the worst cases of Misguided Leadership are seen in large-scale, often international, businesses. A focus purely on maximising the business' returns to shareholders is an example of leaders losing sight of humanity's overall objectives and such a target can have the results outlined in the previous paragraph.

Bakan (2005:140) and Lorange (2003:133) are two of the many to suggest that, in general, businesses have a short-term, parochial and finance-dominated focus. We agree that there is currently a widespread presence in business organisations of this short-term, narrow focus on maximising shareholder value – even when organisations publicly espouse the importance of their Corporate Social Responsibility (CSR) initiatives, and despite the limitations of this approach that has been evidenced in the recent financial crisis.

Friedman (1970/1993) argues, however, that the larger issues faced by humanity including the urgent global issues (UGIs) shown in Table 1.1 are of no concern to business since there is only one social responsibility for corporate executives, namely to make as much money as possible for their shareholders. Bakan (2005:35 and 37) reluctantly agrees, arguing that existing international corporate law actually forbids companies from being genuinely socially responsible, since it requires them to maximise their shareholders' returns. In this case CEOs have a duty not to spend what is in effect shareholders' money on larger societal projects that do not have a direct positive impact on the bottom line. He argues that under the *'best-interests-of-the-corporation principle'* (from Dodge v Ford in 1916 according to Bakan, 2005:37) it has become *'universally accepted as a kind of divine unchallengeable truth, that corporations exist solely to maximise returns for their shareholders'*.

Bakan goes on to argue, however, that this *'divine, unchallengeable truth'* is invalid and must not be allowed to continue. Avery (2005:212) and Howard (as cited by Baker, 2008:10) present clear evidence to show that legislation, regulation and financial markets do not have to prevent organisations from operating in sustainable ways that give consideration to the UGIs and their resolution.

We fully endorse the need to 'challenge the unchallengeable' and encourage businesses to expand their horizon from the short-term, parochial and finance-dominated focus to encompass humanity's overall objectives. As shown in our discussion of resource depletion in Chapter 2, if businesses do continue to act purely in their own interests there may not be a habitable world for them to operate within. This is not a difficult concept to grasp and we believe most people, including business leaders, actually recognise it.

More fundamentally, the overriding justification for allowing businesses to operate in a market economy is that it results in optimal utility. If the way businesses operate becomes detrimental to the general well-being of humanity, as it currently seems to be doing, this justification is removed and the market system becomes seriously flawed.

Businesses are not solely responsible for causing UGIs, nor are they the only source for effective resolution: individuals, religions, governments, the United Nations, the World Trade Organization, G8, G20 and many others all have their part to play. Bakan (2005), for example, believes responsibility for resolving UGIs lies with governments and should be enacted through passing and enforcing laws requiring organisations to be socially responsible. We accept that governments do have a crucial role to play, but argue that they cannot do this alone. As De Woot (2005) argues, the most dynamic players in globalisation are corporations and those who control them (investment funds). Corporations hold a great deal of power; for example, 50 of the world's 100 largest economies are not countries but companies and the 10 biggest companies turn over more money than the world's smallest 100 countries (Leopold et al. 2005:281), and their combined power, size, international operation, and global influence mean companies have a crucial role to play in helping to address the UGIs. As Hormann (1990) argues:

> Business, the motor of our society, has the opportunity to be a new creative force on the planet, a force which could contribute to the well-being of many. For that to occur, we must all substantially increase our commitment to integrity and accountability, and courageously make a quantum leap in consciousness: beyond conventional solutions; beyond opposing forces, beyond fear and hope.

## Causes of Misguided Leadership

There are a number of reasons for the type of MisLeadership we categorise as Misguided and this section will briefly outline some of these.

Misguided Leadership in businesses may result from being too exclusively directed at trusting the market. As De Woot (2009:39) suggests:

> A question of too absolute a faith in the efficiency of markets and an almost visceral mistrust of public intervention and regulations ... Everyone knows that the market economy is a successful growth model, but pushed to its limits the model may become an ideology ... for a long time the market ideology has had many supporters ... In the West it still

*appeals to the majority of business leaders and management schools. It*
*is the greatest barrier to the emergence of truly responsible firms.*

The type of thinking that De Woot outlines above may be due to poor, outdated or inappropriate training or education or simply as a consequence of an upbringing within that ideology of thought.

Misguided Leadership could also be a consequence of the huge pressures exerted on leaders from internal and external stakeholders and the media. Much of the pressure on business to focus on shareholder value, for instance, comes from shareholders and the financial markets. Requirement of one- or two-year payback periods is common in the West, whereas much longer payback periods are acceptable in other parts of the world such as Japan.

Misguided Leadership does not just apply to the business world. We demonstrate this in the case studies at the end of this chapter where we first consider the controversy over the grades given to A level students, then review the actions and motives of Henry V at the Battle of Agincourt and the exploits of Christopher Columbus in the Caribbean at the end of the fifteenth century.

With this more general application in mind, Misguided Leadership could result from leaders having too narrow a focus, perhaps just on their own community, project or organisation and not looking sufficiently outwards at the bigger picture. Capra (1997, cited in Kriger and Seng 2005:773) identifies an important problem with this perspective:

> *The more we study the major problems of our time, the more we come*
> *to realize that they cannot be understood in isolation. They are systemic*
> *problems, which means they are interconnected and interdependent ...*
> *There are solutions to the major problems of our time, some of them*
> *even simple. But they require a radical shift in our perceptions, our*
> *thinking, our values ... [However] the recognition that a profound*
> *change of perception and thinking is needed, if we are to survive, has*
> *not yet reached most of our corporate leaders or the administrators and*
> *professors of our large universities.*

The kind of systemic problems to which Capra refers occur because individuals and organisations are all part of a larger system; a system that is itself impacted on, and influenced by, its external environment (Czander 1993:178). Globalisation and advances such as the internet have resulted in

an exponential increase in the complexity of the system in which leaders are required to operate. Feeling they are being pressured to do something which is beyond their capacity to understand and control, the leader may revert to a narrow focus which is easier to cope with and where they feel they are able to fulfil the leadership role. This is termed 'bounded rationality' and Lindblom (1959) claimed, for example, that politicians use bounded rationality when they base their solutions on past positive experiences and attempt to avoid failure rather than seek appropriate solutions.

In order for managers and leaders to be able to cope with this increasing complexity they require education and experiences at that level. Perhaps current leadership models and approaches which emphasise the need to closely control and 'manage' the situation have become outdated and are unable to cope with the rapidly changing, complex and global environment that is the leader's world today.

This moves us to the conclusion that Misguided Leadership is often the result of the environment the leader is placed in rather than their failure as an individual. We believe they are in the most part doing their best to lead effectively in very difficult and challenging circumstances. They are often literally killing themselves through high levels of stress and overwork in the drive to make things work in a system that is increasingly unworkable with the tools currently available to them. Thus Misguided Leadership becomes an embedded part of the system and it is the failure to educate and train leaders to cope with the complexities and scale of the modern world that we are principally calling into question. We call this Institutional MisLeadership.

We have briefly covered some of the main causes of Misguided Leadership and these are summarised in Table 3.1.

## The Global Fitness Framework (GFF)

Many of the reasons identified above point to the need for a fundamentally new approach to leadership which we believe has three key aspects. First, they show the need for leaders to recognise that all individuals, groups and societies in the world are interconnected and interdependent, so leaders must now think beyond traditional organisational, sectoral and national boundaries. Second, leaders' thinking must be holistic in that it needs to consider the physical, mental and spiritual as advocated for some time by many commentators

**Table 3.1      Reasons for Misguided Leadership**

| |
|---|
| Over-reliance on the benefits of the market economy |
| Short-term and parochial focus |
| Lack of appropriate education |
| Pressure from internal and external stakeholders |
| Pressure from the media |
| Complex, rapidly changing environment |
| Inappropriate leadership models |

including Wilber (2001:13) and Covey (1999a:176). As Stephanie Bird, director of HR capability at the CIPD argues (as cited by Arkin 2009:19):

> It's critically important for anyone in business ... to take a holistic look at what it is that business is about,' she says. 'It's not just about tools and techniques. It's looking at the implications of what you are doing for the whole stakeholder community. It's being able to question assumptions, being able to challenge existing dogma ...

Third, leaders should consider the fitness for purpose of the entity they are leading. We view this fitness as comprising three elements: strength, stamina and suppleness. To outline and clarify the above thoughts we have developed the Global Fitness Framework (GFF) shown in Figure 3.1.

The axes of the GFF reflect the above requirement to consider the holistic fitness for purpose of various organic levels. There are clear differences in the factors and attributes that need to be considered by a leader when they are concerned with people as individuals, in groups or part of a society. Similarly the physical, mental and spiritual aspects of such organic groupings are each very different from each other in the ways they can be analysed and assessed. Again, strength, stamina and suppleness are three aspects of fitness that can be usefully considered independently from each other.

While such focused analysis is valid and useful, the underlying requirement for leaders to think holistically and keep in mind the interrelationships between all elements of the framework is crucial. To illustrate, while an individual's physical strength, stamina and suppleness can each be considered in isolation, it is not until they are considered as an overall package or system that a clear indication of the individual's overall physical fitness can be obtained.

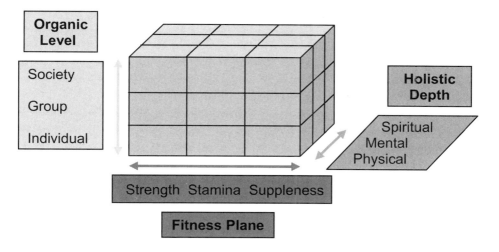

**Figure 3.1    The Global Fitness Framework**

Again, it may be useful and valid to study the people in a large organisation as individuals, groups or a society but their interconnectedness is clear and should be recognised in relevant deliberations. Individuals will be members of many different groups and societies, and conversely a society is made up of groups of individuals. Thus a fundamental decision for the leader will be what organic levels to consider for a particular issue.

The importance of systems theory and being aware of the inter-relationships between objects, actions and information flows has been mentioned earlier in this chapter. In similar vein, the cells in the Global Fitness Framework are all inter-connected, each relying on the others, such that attention should be given to combinations of cells and their interaction and at the meta level to consideration of the whole framework. For example, a leader could focus on:

- The cell representing the physical suppleness of an individual. This would be at the bottom, right front of the GFF and could be referred to as cell H1, F3, O1 in Figure 3.1 There are 27 cells in the model and each represents one such focus.

- The core covering the holistic (that is, physical, mental and spiritual) stamina of a society. This is the three cells running from front to back at the top centre of the model and could be referenced as core H1–H3, F2, O3 in Figure 3.1 There are a total of 27 such cores available, each representing a different group of three cells that form a straight line through the model.

- The slice covering holistic fitness of a group. This is the nine cells that cover all aspects relating to a group, is the middle slice of the model when looked at vertically and could be referred to as slice H1–3, F1–F3, O2 in Figure 3.1 In total, nine such slices exist.

Any combination of the above foci is possible, giving tremendous flexibility while retaining a clear analytical framework. We believe the GFF may help to take the chaos out of theory.

To date, more thought has been given to elements represented by cells toward the bottom front left of the model (individual, physical, strength) than those represented toward the top back right (society, spiritual, suppleness). Reasons for the relative neglect of certain cells in the GFF may be that the aspects covered by them are more complex and contentious or have not been of primary concern to the investigator. For example, people in general are likely to have a clearer understanding of the physical fitness of an individual than they do of the spiritual suppleness of a society. The authors maintain, however, that it is these complex and contentious areas that should be of greater and increasing concern for leaders in the modern world. Many UGIs may, at least in part, be the result of poor spiritual suppleness of one or more societies and neglecting this fact would be MisLeadership.

## SPIRITUAL IN THE GFF

Of all the aspects within the framework, it tends to be the spiritual dimension which is least understood, most contentious and most often avoided. In the GFF we adopt a broad interpretation of spirituality – any aspect of humanity that is not physical or mental is spiritual.

Physical covers an individual's body including their brain, their clothing, house, car and other assets. For an organisation, physical would be its assets such as land, buildings and equipment but also including money, so if we assume an organisation is 'profit-maximising' we are assuming its objectives are purely at the physical level. Societies, including nation states, pay great attention to their physical resources such as land, oil, gas, water and the physical health of their people. Discussions we touched on in Chapter 2 regarding resource depletion can focus mainly on these physical resources.

In order to optimise our physical circumstance, we (individuals, groups and societies) need to solve problems and make and implement decisions. The authors view this as the mental element where use is made of techniques such as those outlined throughout this book.

As discussed at the start of this chapter, it may be, however, that relatively little attention is paid to what the ultimate objectives should be. When this is missing it is Misguided Leadership and this is the focus of this chapter. In our view, setting of ultimate objectives falls within the spiritual dimension and includes such aspects as morality, ethics, team spirit, motivation and morale.

Often objectives that are set, such as to maximise profit, are only intermediate level, often physical objectives not necessarily resulting in achievement of ultimate goals such as increased fulfilment or helping others. There is an implied hierarchy, with spiritual at the top including ultimate objectives, philosophical approaches, values, and inter-relationships, on which the mental processes of decision-making and problem-solving should be based, which then lead to our taking particular physical actions.

In the next section we briefly explain the other terms used in the framework and their contextual meaning.

## ORGANIC LEVEL

This relates to whether an individual, group, or society is being considered.

It is at the level of the individual that most attention has hitherto been focused when considering physical, mental or spiritual fitness. It may be seen as the simplest level in the GFF in that it is only concerned with one person, but there are still nine cells, and numerous possible combinations to consider.

The group level refers to any collection of people working together to achieve a common objective. In an organisational setting, this can be anything from a small work team to the management board. It could refer to a significant part of the organisation, such as a department or division, or the whole organisation. Less formal groups would include sports and social clubs in addition to the family, a very important group in our consideration of Misguided Leadership.

Groups can be of vastly different scales, moving from a minimum of two members to a limitless maximum. At the small scale, group performance will be heavily influenced by each individual, while large groups will be far more reliant on overall characteristics, with only a few of the members having major individual effect. Since groups consist of a number of individuals, to get the best out of a group we need to consider both the fitness of the relevant individuals and how they gel together.

A society will typically consist of many groups, with the individuals in the society each being members of several groups. A particularly interesting type of society is that of the nation state, in the modern world tending to consist of a number of often disparate individuals, groups and sub-societies.

To get the best from a society we need to consider both the fitness of the relevant individuals, groups and sub-societies in its makeup and how they gel together or react to each other.

Some groups may have members from a number of different societies, this being increasingly common as the IT and travel-based environment develops and spreads. Large organisations are often international with potential for conflict and confusion due to the need to integrate individuals and groups from varied societies and their cultures.

## FITNESS PLANE

Fitness relates to an entity's ability to carry out its objectives or purpose and should be considered at all three holistic levels, physical, mental and spiritual. These different types of fitness are also inter-related, physical fitness being ability to physically carry out the desires of the mind, mental fitness the ability to make decisions and solve problems so as to achieve objectives, and spiritual fitness relating to the establishment and achievement of high level objectives that may be in tune with the broader needs and obligations of humanity.

Physical fitness is often considered in terms of strength, stamina and suppleness. Strength is the power that can be applied to a task, stamina is the ability to sustain application of power to a particular task, and suppleness is the ability to bend and flow, and apply or resist power in various ways without injury.

It is our contention that these terms are also relevant to the study of mental and spiritual fitness as is recognised in such phrases as 'a powerful argument'.

## HOLISTIC DEPTH

This considers an entity's physical, mental and spiritual aspects.

*Physical*   At a basic level, physical fitness refers to the attributes of an individual's body, their limbs, torso, heart and lungs, skeletal and muscular strength. When considering an individual's fitness, particularly in a competitive environment, it is also necessary to take account of physical resources at their disposal. Tools, equipment, armour and weapons will all be pertinent here. Physical fitness of a group, organisation or society will, similarly, depend on the resources at its disposal, but also on how well these are combined and used by its constituent parts, that is, the individuals and groups within.

Correct diet plays an extremely important part. Historically, many people in the West suffered from malnutrition, still common in much of the world. They are now more likely to suffer from the effects of excess nutrition, for example by being overweight or taking in too much salt, exacerbated by an unhealthy life-style, drug or alcohol abuse, or the effects of smoking. Overall physical fitness of Western societies has been declining, with average life expectancy of children now lower than that of their parents.

It is impossible and largely pointless to attempt to add together all of these elements to come up with an overall, universally valid measure of physical fitness. Fitness depends on what one is trying to be fit for so it would be very different for example for a racing driver, cyclist, marathon runner and director of an international corporation. What is important is whether the type and level of fitness is right for the individual and the requirements of the roles they play in groups and society. This can be summed up in the phrase 'fit for purpose'.

For general well-being it is important to aim for good all-round fitness. A concern with the current focus on high stamina levels, built up by running long distances, is that it may result in permanent damage to joints and ligaments, with long-term consequences on strength and suppleness. Thus it may be the case that the people who encourage jogging to keep fit are often Misguiding those they advise.

This need to consider general well-being rather than focus on one element is fundamental to understanding the inter-connectedness of elements in the GFF and the potential for leaders to be Misguided or Misguide others. Individuals benefit from good levels of physical, mental and spiritual fitness, as do groups and societies, and from a global viewpoint physical, mental and spiritual fitness of all the individuals, groups and societies that make up humanity should all be of concern.

*Mental*    As with physical fitness, we need to consider what we are trying to be mentally fit for. As a base level, we might look for the ability to control the physical body, which is a link between these two levels of the model, and could be viewed from the other direction: physical fitness is the ability to physically carry out the desires of the mind.

Mental fitness goes further. Leaders need to be able to make decisions and solve problems, but also judge whether such decisions and solutions are correct, implying a need for an objective, which is where the link to the spiritual dimension lies. Physical strength, stamina and suppleness will all be important in enabling the entity to achieve its objectives, but efficient and effective use will depend on mental fitness, and the objectives themselves will depend upon the entity's spiritual fitness and stance.

As with the physical dimension, there are many different types of mental strength, such as good memory, ability to solve complex problems and handle large amounts of information, application of numerical and verbal analytical and reasoning techniques, working in a logical, structured manner, and being resilient to attack. Influential factors include depth and breadth of knowledge, conviction and commitment, clarity of thought, concentration and focus, innate ability and training.

Mental stamina is required in circumstances where an instant solution to a problem cannot be found. This can be because the problem is complex, requires several stages in its solution or is of an iterative or cyclical nature such as an annual budget.

Stamina could be assessed in terms of ability, over a substantial period, to:

- maintain effort and belief in ability and approach

- continue to act in a consistent manner

- remain determined to succeed

- keep arguing for a cause

- yet be willing to debate and discuss issues repeatedly without becoming frustrated, annoyed or demoralised.

Such qualities will often enable success in the long-term, but there are potential disadvantages in having too much mental strength or stamina. The entity may be or seem to be dogmatic, rigid and stiff, tending to use traditional methods and solutions when circumstances may warrant change, unwilling to compromise, and slow to act. Winning an argument by attrition does not make the decision correct, so could easily lead to the wrong solution being implemented. This is particularly concerning where the outcome is of a 'win-lose' nature, when a more flexible approach may have found a 'win-win' solution. This is where suppleness is particularly important.

Mental suppleness includes openness to new thoughts and ideas, varied attitudes, approaches and beliefs, and a willingness to rethink one's own views as change occurs to the environment, knowledge, or personal circumstances. It fosters the ability to listen to other's views with an open mind, consider their validity, reflect upon their consequences and implications, and change one's own views accordingly. Robustness, flexibility and resilience are other positive aspects, some negative ones being a tendency towards indecisiveness, prevarication and inclusion of unnecessary factors.

*Spiritual*   We have already given a simple definition of spirituality, that is, anything that is not physical or mental. Nevertheless, there is a great deal of confusion surrounding spirituality and its role, many people seeing it as closely bound to religion.

Our view is that a focus on just the forms of spirituality that revolve around a relationship with a higher power or being can be divisive and discourage those who do not have such belief from involvement in development or consideration of a spiritual aspect to their life, work and society. This may, in our opinion, also discourage working together to solve common problems, despite the whole of humanity being faced with similar issues which require a solid decision framework and integrated solutions.

This led us to the following positive (that is, saying what spirituality is as opposed to what it is not) definition of spirituality:

> *Spirituality is a state or experience that can provide individuals with direction or meaning, or provide feelings of understanding, support, inner wholeness or connectedness. Connectedness can be to themselves, other people, nature, the universe, a god, or some other supernatural power.*

'Inner wholeness' means feeling complete and that all aspects of a person – mind, body, and soul – are valued. Groups and societies are made up of individuals, and ultimately it is the spirituality and well-being of individuals which determines the spirituality and well-being of groups, societies and humanity as a whole. This highlights the inter-connectedness of elements not only within the GFF, but also in the real world, and is a factor behind our giving connectedness such high prominence in the above definition.

Ethical and moral decisions such as 'what should the role of families be in modern society?', 'Should I care about the AIDS situation in Africa?' and 'Was invading Iraq justified?' cannot be answered by mental process alone, but must be based on ultimate objectives, philosophical approaches, values and inter-relationships. All such aspects of humanity are viewed by us as spiritual, making spirituality of relevance and concern to all individuals, groups and societies. As decisions grow in importance and effect, the importance of spirituality in achieving valid solutions grows.

A further aspect that drives our concern over the need to increase the attention paid to spirituality is its complex nature. Physical and mental fitness can only be positive, the level depending on how well strength, stamina and suppleness have been developed. We believe that spirituality, in addition to being at the top of the holistic depth hierarchy, can also be negative or non-existent.

Positive spirituality implies overall objectives, philosophies and values focusing on 'we', not 'I'. Such an approach leads to fair treatment of others, searching for common ground and enlightenment, open discussion of beliefs and philosophies, success measured in terms of happiness and fulfilment, corporate social responsibility, ethical altruistic behaviour, self-belief, confidence, friendship, honesty, trust, collaboration, and search for opportunities to grow and develop.

In order to achieve such objectives, individuals and leaders must be brave, make tough decisions and follow them through. They must be prepared to make and accept fair criticism and challenge themselves and the validity of their beliefs, philosophies and values. They must be determined to succeed and hard to tame – like a spirited horse. Such attributes require an inner drive, motivation and 'spirit', a term often used when referring to a team or group, but we would contend it is equally applicable to individuals and societies.

Negative spirituality includes deliberate exclusion of other faiths, philosophies and values; misconstruing other's beliefs or demonising their followers; being selfish, excessively competitive, exploitative, prejudiced, parochial, nepotistic, corrupt or hypocritical; measuring success purely in terms of money; allowing continuation of inequalities of resource distribution; reluctance to acknowledge or correct past injustice; and adopting a 'might is right' or 'not in my back yard' attitude. People adopting such approaches may not be aware that they are doing so or may justify them to themselves and others as being valid due to special circumstances so as to not regard them as negative. Traits like being selfish or competitive may not be easily classified as positive or negative or their classification may depend on circumstances and scale.

Non-existent spirituality is the failure to accept the existence and importance of spirituality and its role. This may result in decisions being made without a set of coherent objectives, values and philosophical approaches in place by which choices can be assessed and such decisions justified and tested. Issues in these areas are likely to be either missed or misunderstood and where they are recognised and attempts made to tackle them, decisions are likely to be inconsistent. Even when valid decisions are taken, without a strong spiritual framework the factors necessary to implement tough decisions are also likely to be at too low levels for success.

Leaders must recognise the crucial role of spirituality (positive and negative) if their decision-making is to be effective. This is true whether they are acting as individuals or leading groups, societies and humanity at large. Leaders must be brave, make tough decisions and follow them through. They must be prepared to make and accept fair criticism and challenge themselves and the validity of their beliefs, philosophies and values.

*Spiritual fitness*    The word spirit connotes breath or 'life force' and we believe the latter term is particularly useful when considering spiritual fitness. Life force represents the things most crucial to an entity's existence, the foundation of its motives, and its ability and determination to achieve them. This is in line with our view that the spiritual dimension is on a higher level than the physical and mental dimensions.

The term well-being conveys some of what we mean by spiritual fitness but we feel it has a connotation of passivity. Wellbeing may encourage concern about the whole being, that is, physical, mental and spiritual, but implies a focus on not being ill or undernourished rather than the more positive idea that there are objectives and missions to fulfil and life force or spiritual fitness is required to do so.

Turning to the three elements of spiritual fitness, spiritual strength reflects such factors as depth and breadth of conviction, commitment, influence and power, clarity of beliefs and the ability to resist attack on them. To some extent this may be influenced by knowledge, but upbringing and culture will also tend to play a major role.

An entity's spiritual stamina is its ability to maintain beliefs and act accordingly in the long-term, be consistent, willing to debate and discuss, but ready to stand up for its cause and beliefs. As with mental strength and stamina possible negative aspects of high spiritual strength and stamina include dogmatism and rigidity, being unwilling to compromise and slow to act, all potentially lessening the prospects of a 'win-win' solution to a problem being found.

Spiritual suppleness considers the ability to listen to other views on spirituality with an open mind, consider their validity, reflect upon them and change one's own views where relevant to allow for new thoughts, ideas and changes to the environment or personal circumstances. It requires the ability to understand and accept that there are very many attitudes, approaches and beliefs each of which may contain some truth. Excessive spiritual suppleness can, however, cause problems of apparent indecisiveness, lack of a firm foundation to beliefs and low levels of conviction.

Spiritual fitness is a useful concept when considering societies and nation states. Do countries (both individually and collectively) still have a strong 'life force', or have their reasons for existing (geographic; defensive; exploitive; maintain law/order/monarchy) declined due to environmental changes to such an extent that they may no longer serve a valid purpose and the individuals and societies within (and humanity in general) may cease to support their existence? It is interesting to consider how short-lived many nation states have been and the GFF could be used to analyse why, including why some last longer than others.

Perhaps globally we are now at the stage that the United States was at in the period leading up to its civil war, with individual nations recognising the need for a global approach but each still wanting to be able to control its own future including its own defence and suspicious of the motives of others.

## EMOTIONS

The above section has considered physical, mental and spiritual facets as representing holistic depth, but many researchers include emotional as a fourth facet, often relating physical to the body, mental to the mind, emotional to the heart and spiritual to the soul. The term 'Emotional Intelligence' (Goleman 1995) has been used to describe the extent to which individuals understand and control their emotions.

We agree that emotions are an important consideration in the holistic depth of individuals but argue that those elements of personality typically referred to as emotions can best be considered as having two separate aspects, short-term and long-term, and that both are contained within our framework.

Emotions are displayed and we work with them through our physical, mental and spiritual states. An event such as being made redundant often causes strong emotional feelings that could result in an initial physical or mental over-reaction which Goleman termed the 'Amygdale hijack' (according to Freedman 2002). Short-term emotions influence immediate reactions to events including the 'fight or flight' response that may be necessary for survival. Such extreme feelings tend to be short-lived, however, with more considered mental reactions taking over once there has been sufficient time to reflect upon their meaning and importance. Our view is that these considered reactions build to form our spiritual stance.

Thus we argue that the long-term aspects of emotions, such as love, faith, determination and fear, are part of the spiritual dimension, while short-term emotions and their handling depend on the entity's physical, mental and spiritual fitness. From this viewpoint, emotional intelligence may in part reflect the mental process by which we handle the short-term aspects of emotions and make long-term adjustments to our spirituality, thus altering our spiritual fitness.

Emotional Intelligence is also used to refer to awareness, concern and sensitivity to other people's emotional states. We would again argue that this often reflects the observer's spirituality. Note that if the observer has negative spirituality they may use their emotional intelligence to exploit weaknesses in others, a well-known illustration of this being emotional blackmail.

While emotion is experienced directly by individuals, it still affects groups and societies, and can play a significant role at those levels if the individuals involved allow their emotions to influence their actions. Reactions at various organic levels to '9/11' are a good example. One concern here is that while allowing short-term emotions to influence actions that can give added determination, it may result in excessively aggressive behaviour. If such behaviour is exhibited by several parties to a debate it can lead to a spiral of increasingly damaging words and actions and ultimate adverse effects on spirituality, possibly even turning it negative long-term. This can be related to The Embedded Values Cycle in Figure 1.1 and may require the same kind of deliberate reversal of the process: challenging the negative elements of spirituality and related values and habits to return to free behaviour and thinking. This is what the 'Truth and Reconciliation' approach adopted in South Africa post-apartheid was based on.

Having set out the GFF framework and related terminology as a way of tackling Misguided Leadership, the next section considers its practical application in the business world. We then move to use it in regard to the topical debate of the grades awarded to A level students in the UK, to an assessment of the fitness of King Henry V at the Battle of Agincourt and Christopher Columbus' exploits in the Caribbean at the end of the fifteenth century.

## Helping Business Leaders

This chapter commenced with an analysis of the prevalence of Misguided Leadership in modern business, which we argued was largely a result of Institutionalised MisLeadership. Increasing complexity in the environment means leaders require education and experiences at that level, but current leadership models and approaches emphasise the need to closely control and 'manage' the situation which may be impossible in the new global environment therefore leaving the leader unable to cope.

Our Global Fitness Framework and the other models developed in this book are designed to help managers and leaders gain the new order skills and approaches now required so that they can begin to find global solutions to global problems. We argue that important elements here include the provision of a framework for them to build their thinking around; the flexibility of being able to focus on particular cells, cores, slices and combinations thereof; the inclusion, in addition to the common mental aspects, of physical and spiritual aspects of their own and followers' lives; the different organic levels available and the focus on fitness for purpose. The value of the model here was demonstrated by considering one possible cell, that which relates to the spiritual suppleness of society. Proper consideration of the ramifications of issues in that cell would add significantly to a leader's understanding of the complexities of the global business environment.

Spirituality is an area which is taboo in many businesses and other organisations. We accept that it is complex and contentious but believe that failure by leaders to consider and adopt valid stances and approaches in the areas it embraces is a root cause of many global and local issues. It can mean that vitally important elements of business life including motivation, ethics, mission and culture are paid scant attention and rarely discussed. We believe our broad and inclusive definition of spiritual will facilitate leaders bringing such issues to centre stage, where they belong. A focus on the spiritual and societal aspects includes raising leaders' awareness of issues that are bigger than their current organisation and specific role, including connectedness (to self, others, nature or some higher being), meaning and purpose, global equality and the very role of business in society.

Ability to flex the whole framework is another valuable facility. At one level an individual department of a large organisation could be seen as the society with sections being the group element and staff being the individual, to the opposite extreme where society is the whole animal kingdom, humanity is one of the groups and particular nations, ethnic origins or age ranges could be the individuals.

A leader could use the GFF to help analyse virtually any business situation. This might include the effects of a potential merger on group and individual spiritual fitness elements such as motivation, benchmarking of physical assets to those of a competitor, causes and costs of work-related stress, and managerial issues related to use and abuse of emails at work.

The recent crisis in global financial markets is discussed as the major case study in Chapter 4. The focus there is on Misinformed Leadership and the need of a new paradigm but it could also be analysed using the GFF.

Having outlined ways in which the GFF can be used in the business world, we now turn to its use in helping analyse two very different situations to further illustrate its global fitness. The first is a topical issue in the UK. the grades awarded to A level students, the second being a historical application, the role of King Henry V at the Battle of Agincourt.

## A Level Grades in the United Kingdom

A levels are the main qualification taken by pupils in their final year at school in the UK so form the main measure of their success and ability at that stage. Objectives of the grades awarded are manifold but basically laudable, covering the spiritual, mental and physical needs of stakeholders including to test students' ability; give them, their schools and other interested parties an independent performance measure; assist future students, parents and teachers to select which school to attend; allow the Government to decide how to treat the school – as failing, average or successful; enable universities and potential employers to select the right students; allow students to decide their best future including which university if any to attend, and which career to follow.

The assessment process itself seems to be fair, equitable, flexible and thorough. It is tried and tested, accepted and understood. Mistakes have been made but the underlying system has been sufficiently robust to cope with them in an acceptable way. As we would put it, from the mental aspect the assessment process has been fit for purpose.

What has caused a vast amount of debate and concern is the fact that grades awarded to candidates have shown a continuous upwards trend over the last 25 years or so such that recent sittings have so many students receiving top grades that it has proved to be increasingly difficult to use the results for many of the objectives stated above. In particular, highly ranked universities have struggled to identify which students to admit to their programmes because they rely heavily on A level grades to identify the top students.

Students, schools, examining boards and the government all have a vested interest in seeing high and rising grades as they can be used as evidence of improving standards of education, teaching and hard work. These are all positive spiritual aspects and to be encouraged.

Many commentators have, however, claimed that a continuous rise over such a long period must be due to the standard required for a particular grade falling. This focuses on the physical result and assumes it is more valid and reliable than mental and spiritual aspects which are more the focus of those who counter by claiming that students' performance has indeed been improving due to better teaching methods, hard work by the students and advances in IT. They also argue it would be unfair and demoralising to artificially lower the grades just to facilitate easy selection of students by universities.

## COMMENTARY AND ANALYSIS

We believe the above debate misses the point as to what A level grades are meant to do and as such is Misguided Leadership. Identifying whether student performance is improving year on year was NOT one of the original objectives of the grading system and it is poorly equipped to achieve that. It is almost certainly the case that students are able to do much more than they were able to years ago, when there was no internet, word processing or computer spreadsheets. They may well be generally worse at certain tasks and skills including those most easily performed using IT, but equally generally better at others. Thus the whole debate over whether standards are falling or performance rising is impossible to determine objectively.

The system aims to rank a particular year's students as to their relative ability compared with their peers. One approach that would achieve this is to have a fixed percentage of students awarded the top grade, the next band the next grade and so on. Thus the top say 5 per cent could be given an A grade, the next 10 per cent a B, the next 15 per cent a C and so on. This would mean all interested parties would be able to see who the top performers were each year.

This would have several additional advantages, first that the percentage of candidates given a particular grade could be varied in any particular year or by a particular examining body if it was felt desirable for whatever reason (possibly to reflect economic conditions or reward those students studying programmes that are viewed as particularly difficult or desirable). A second advantage would be that in practice there is far more variation in the difficulty of assessments between years and examining bodies than there is between the mass of students taking the exam each year and the suggested approach would automatically cope with such variations.

Our suggestion would not allow comparison of standards between years but that is not the main objective and in any case, for the reasons stated above, neither does the existing approach. By adopting our approach much of the confusion over what A level results can and should be used for would be removed and achievement of all the main objectives of the tests facilitated. If there was a desire to establish relative performance between years, measures could be sought that would achieve that aim.

Having used the A level grading debate to illustrate the value of focusing attention on the ultimate objective rather than intermediate often recently introduced targets, we now turn our attention to the global fitness of an early fifteenth century king. It will be enlightening to consider whether the concept of, attitudes to and extent of Misguided Leadership have changed over a long period.

## King Henry V at the Battle of Agincourt: Leadership or MisLeadership?

The quoted sections in the following description and commentary on the Battle of Agincourt are summarised from Beckster (n.d.). Our commentary should not be assumed to represent the views of the author.

> On 11 August 1415, a fleet of ships carried Henry V with a force of 8,000 archers and 2,000 men-at-arms with accompanying horses, baggage train and camp followers across the English Channel to France in an attempt to substantiate his claim to the French throne, which he had been persuaded was his lawful birthright.

Henry is exhibiting high spiritual fitness, his advisers having used historic spiritual claims and strong mental arguments to persuade him of the validity of his claim of sovereignty over a neighbouring country. Being king, he has a great deal of personal and societal power and seems to have strong support of those close to him – organisational power. He thus seems to be 'fit for purpose'. He intends to force home his spiritual claim partly through mental persuasion but mainly through physical force, which shows at least an element of negative spirituality. Through modern eyes, the whole concept of domination by force tends to be viewed negatively. Thus Henry and his followers believed they were seeking a valid objective in a legitimate way but we might view it as Misguided Leadership.

A sizeable army has been persuaded to join him but at this stage it is difficult to tell the extent to which this is based on agreement with the claim, fear of refusal, opportunism or other factors. Whether an army of the stated size is sufficient remains to be seen as does whether its make up of four archers to one man-at-arms – armoured soldiers with swords, some on horseback – is suitable.

> They landed near Harfleur, a strongly fortified town defended by several hundred men-at-arms. The besieging Englishmen were forced to sleep mainly on the ground drinking contaminated cider, wine and water

*which resulted in dysentery and disease such that by the time Harfleur surrendered one third of Henry's army were sick. Henry decided to abandon thoughts of conquest and instead stage a token battle with the French army before returning home via Calais, leaving an occupation force in Harfleur.*

This was a very disappointing and demoralising start which could be blamed on lack of physical and mental preparations. Why pick a strongly fortified town, particularly if your army is dominated by archers who presumably fight best in the open? Shouldn't more consideration have been given to the physical aspects of a siege such that he didn't lose so many men to illness? Much of this may be the fault of Henry's advisers as it may be unreasonable to expect Henry to have planned such operational details himself. Perhaps Henry was too strong spiritually such that he believed God would give him victory without much effort on his part, so became careless and over confident. He seems to assume the French army will be happy to let him escape without a major battle.

At least the initial target was achieved, even if it was poorly selected – misguided. It did give Henry a fall-back position and bargaining tool and would have boosted his army's morale. Personally he must have felt a failure in that he had not made any real headway towards his true objective.

*Henry took just 900 men-at-arms and 5,000 archers with him but ran out of food while searching for a viable route and being harassed by the French, who were determined to engage the English, their heralds informing Henry:*

*'Our lords have heard how you intend with your army to conquer the towns, castles and cities of the realm of France and to depopulate French cities. And because of this, and for the sake of their country and their oaths, many of our lords are assembled to defend their rights; and they inform you by us that before you come to Calais they will meet you to fight you and be revenged of your conduct'*

*Henry simply replied 'Be all things according to the will of God.'*

Henry is in an extremely precarious situation, again largely the result of poor planning. His continued occupation of a French town was very provocative and served to unite and enrage the French while also meaning he had a small army to fight with. Perhaps he had a good idea of the severity of his situation and did not want to place too many men in danger with him – if so it shows very strong and positive personal spiritual fitness. The spirit of an army tends to be greatly influenced by whether it is fighting on home or foreign soil. The small and bedraggled nature of Henry's force must have further encouraged the French as they envisaged a rout. Henry proclaims his continued faith which was probably genuine but in any case a necessity if he were to retain any respect and thus solidarity and determination from his men. If they cracked he was certainly doomed.

> *Ultimately the main French army outflanked the English to block the way to Calais. Henry realised he was heavily outnumbered and his army were sick, exhausted and starving so offered to return Harfleur and pay for damages in return for free and safe passage to Calais but would not renounce his claims to French soil and the French not surprisingly refused to agree.*

The French are playing cat and mouse, knowing they have the English trapped they seem in no real hurry to finish the sport and are probably enjoying the suffering of the English. Henry continues to pay the penalty for poor planning and his men are becoming physically and presumably mentally unfit, only being held together by their faith in their leader and his cause. Very many examples exist of armies being defeated by hunger and illness rather than their human foe and the writing is on the wall. If Henry was too spiritual in his initial approach, he is now very realistic and willing to give up his earlier gains and make amends if it will buy his freedom. He does still retain his fundamental faith and belief in the justice of his claim to such an extent that he is not prepared to barter with them

> *It rained for most of the night before the battle, turning the ground sodden with ankle deep mud in some places. The English army of 5,000 archers and 900 men-at-arms faced more than 20,000 French. The French were so confident of victory that they knowingly took up a position that was disadvantageous to them as the armies were separated by a recently ploughed field making use of cavalry difficult, while on each side was a forest that greatly restricted the scope for the French to exploit their far greater numbers by outflanking and enveloping the smaller force.*

The French become over-confident, complacent and extremely unprofessional. They ignore important physical factors and fail to prepare mentally for the battle both in terms of having a well thought plan and correct frame of mind.

> *The English formed into a single line of men-at-arms with no reserves. The archers were positioned on the flanks, 2,500 to a side, angled forward to allow converging fire on any attack to the lines centre.*

The English have been allowed to adopt the only formation that holds any real hope of success. They have been heavily reliant on their archers throughout the campaign and now more than ever. Their plan should have been very clear to the French.

> *The French formed three lines but every French nobleman wanted to be in the first line with his banner prominently displayed, leading to jostling for position and mounting confusion.*

Completely convinced of an easy victory, the French do not take the coming battle seriously. They have no clear and accepted leader (Missing Leadership), no shared plan and no discipline. Individuals are more concerned with their own personal glory than that of their country (Misguided even Machiavellian Leadership) so they are rapidly turning into a mob rather than an army.

> *The two sides faced each other for four hours, each waiting for the other to attack. The French could have forced the English to either attack, which would be very difficult with so few men-at-arms and vastly outnumbered, or starve! Henry knew that they would have to fight that day as his troops, without food, would only get weaker so ordered the English advance.*

The French were at least sufficiently disciplined to hold back and force the English to make the first move, which they were evidently keen to avoid since in addition to the effects of illness on their mobility, it meant giving up their established positions. The archers were all on foot and very lightly clad so any attack would have to be extremely slow, effectively attempting to drive the French back with arrow fire – directly attacking a force of 20,000 with 900 fighting men would have been suicidal.

It is difficult to see how the English could win. What strategy with any real prospect of success was available to them? When he ordered the advance, did Henry have a plan in mind or was it out of pure desperation?

*The English slowly advanced to about 250 yards/220 metres from the
French – just within longbow range but too far for the French bowmen
to reply. Henry had ordered each archer to carve an eight foot long stake,
pointed at each end and on reaching their position, the archers drove
their stakes into the ground at such an angle as to impale a horse as it
charged. They commenced a barrage of arrow fire, their skill being such
that they could fire an arrow every 6 seconds.*

Henry's only advantage was that his bowmen could fire further than
the French. By stopping the right distance from the French lines they could
therefore rain arrows down on the French army at leisure. This is an excellent
example of fitness for purpose, or perhaps purpose for fitness – finding the
right situation for the fitness you possess. The French could stay where they
were and hope the English ran out of arrows, retreat, or attack.

*In the confusion and cries of outraged Frenchmen, the French cavalry
on the flanks charged, followed by the first line of dismounted men-at-
arms.*

The French discipline cracked. They would have won the war by either of
the other two actions, particularly the latter as it would have forced the English
to keep advancing when they would have quickly become exhausted and lost
the protection/weapon of their sharpened stakes. Retreating may have been
unthinkable to the French given their overwhelming odds and it is easy to see
that forcing the soldiers to remain under a hail of arrows with no means of
retaliation would have been hard to achieve even with a well disciplined army.
Besides, the French were keen to out-shine each other in the coming glorious
victory so as individuals were very keen to attack, having waited so long.

*Due to the woods on either side they were unable to outflank the archers
necessitating a frontal assault. Those who reached the lines of archers
crashed straight into the thicket of spikes and were unable to breach
the lines. As the survivors retreated in disarray, they were followed
by further volleys of arrows. Horses crazed and uncontrollable by
injury and fright, with no space to manoeuvre, crashed directly into the
advancing men-at-arms breaking their orderly advance.*

It is now the turn of the French to rue their earlier lack of planning and
professional approach. They have not taken due note of the English defences, are
uncoordinated and naïve in their attack, hemmed in by the physical layout of the

battlefield and even their superior numbers starts to count against them as they are squashed together and unable to fight freely. Vastly superior physical fitness is being countered by superior mental fitness – due to complete ineptitude on the part of the French who are scoring say $^1/_{10}$ for that element at this point. Their self-centred approach also means they score poorly on spiritual fitness, so lack determination to win what has suddenly become a very tough fight.

> With the press of numbers, the French were unable to attack or defend effectively meaning that the English would win in a one on one contest. As the attackers fell, they presented obstacles to those following and a tumbling effect would have developed where the French were pushed forward from behind but also back by the English. Within half an hour, the first two French lines were annihilated.

> Vast numbers of prisoners were being taken and a French counter attack took place. They also still had one-third of their army in reserve, having seen what was happening to their comrades they had kept well out of it.

Henry was faced with a dreadful choice: kill the prisoners or risk defeat if: the French rally was successful; their reserves entered the fray or the prisoners broke free. Physical and mental arguments pointed to the former choice but spiritual aspects such as morality and chivalry to the latter. Perhaps Henry was so convinced of the legitimacy of his spiritual claim that he placed that above all other factors.

> Henry ordered killing of prisoners to commence. The rally faltered and the French reserves retreated, whereupon Henry ordered the killing to stop.

Modern estimates of French losses range from 7,000 to 10,000 killed and a further 1,500–1,600 taken prisoner. English losses may have been as low as 100.

The scale of Henry's victory was astounding and from that viewpoint he can be seen as a great leader, having trained, disciplined and deployed his army to maximum effect: very high physical and mental fitness at all levels. He had, however, led his army into an extremely risky situation with no food or chance of retreat, following very poor planning and reconnaissance. Had the French not thrown the battle away, he was doomed.

In addition to doubt over the legitimacy of killing prisoners, a further question remains whether the war was justified in the first place. Henry was seeking control over lands he had very dubious claim to but was prepared to allow so many deaths to try to physically force his position.

Historically, it was generally accepted that kings had the right to rule, other lands were legitimate targets for invasion and conquest, 'our' nation was superior to 'other' nations, 'our' religion superior to 'other' religions and the Earth's resources were there to be exploited – including humans, defeated enemies often being killed as above, sold as slaves or ransomed if they were lucky enough to have rich friends or family prepared to pay to get them back.

## Christopher Columbus

Another example of assumed superiority of one nation over another comes from the Spaniard Christopher Columbus and his exploits in the Caribbean at the end of the fifteenth century. Columbus has traditionally been portrayed in the UK at least as a brave and heroic figure who 'discovered' the new world. According to Shreve (1991:703), some argued for his official sainthood within the Catholic Church, he was listed among the top of the most influential persons in history worldwide, and it was claimed that Columbus did more to direct the course of history than any person since the Emperor Augustus.

Columbus' voyages were around the Caribbean islands. He did not 'discover' these, though, as there had been groups of people (often now known as the Caribs and Arawaks) living there for many years. According to 'The Indigenous people of the Caribbean' guide (2004) though, none of the indigenous peoples of the Caribbean actually referred to themselves as Caribs or Arawaks. These names and the term Caribbean were a white European invention that ignored the fact that these groups belonged to an extended cultural lineage stretching throughout the circum-Caribbean. The indigenous peoples are and were more complex than the early Europeans wanted to admit, which is another example of Misinformed Leadership.

According to many commentators, the Arawaks were a peaceful and gentle tribe of American Indians who inhabited the entire Caribbean archipelago. They were generous and guileless, embraced the Spaniards when they arrived and provided every comfort for them. The Spanish (followed by the French and British in the eighteenth century in other parts of the world) carried out slave raids and mercilessly slaughtered the Caribs and Arawaks so that within a few decades they were extinct. As Shreve (1991:710) writes:

> Edgar Lee Masters [in his epic 'The New World'] pulled no punches about the effect that the arrival of Columbus had upon the unfortunate natives: 'In twelve years from the day Columbus kneeled Upon San Salvador, and gave thanks to God A million natives perished at the hands of the Spaniards.'

This account reveals the extent to which Machiavellian and Misguided Leadership dominated Western thinking at the time of the great discoverers. Fellow human beings were treated worse than animals: murdered, their riches plundered and their lands stolen – how much of today's land and mineral rights 'ownership' can be traced back to such thefts?

In terms of the GFF this can be seen as the leader exhibiting high holistic fitness but negative spirituality, resulting in Misguided Leadership. If the leader is strong and has strong support, this combination can be extremely damaging to achievement of the global objectives of humanity as pointed out by Drucker (2003:102):

> No century has seen more leaders with more charisma than our twentieth century and never have political leaders done greater damage than the four great charismatic leaders of this century. Stalin, Mussolini, Hitler and Mao. What matters is not charisma. What matters is whether the leader leads in the right direction or misleads.

Great Britain was extremely successful throughout the period from the 'Middle Ages' to the start of World War II by which time it was a valid claim that 'the sun never sets on the British Empire'. Canada, Australia and the United States of America had, however, already gained their independence and the War solidified feelings against the validity of the attitudes outlined above and toward the growing recognition of the equality of humanity and need for a global approach that goes beyond organisational and national boundaries.

## Summary

This chapter has considered Misguided Leadership as where the leader's ultimate intentions are valid but inappropriate or invalid objectives are set or methods used. It then introduced the Global Fitness Framework as a model for assessing the physical, mental and spiritual fitness of individuals, groups, societies and humanity as a whole.

Illustrations have been provided of ways in which this framework could be used in helping leaders ensure they are not misguided in their thinking and actions. Spirituality was viewed as covering the ultimate objectives, philosophical approaches, values and inter-relationships on which the mental processes of decision-making and problem-solving should be based, thus it is spiritual fitness which is the key to ensuring decisions are on the right track to achieve ultimate intentions.

The idea that spirituality can be positive, negative or non-existent was introduced and the importance of establishing strong positive spirituality explained. This broad approach to spirituality is viewed by the authors as crucial to valid decision-making, particularly at the societal and humanity levels. Without such an approach, valid solutions to global issues are unlikely to be achieved.

Emotions are viewed as having two distinct elements, short-term and long-term. It is argued that long-term emotions, such as love, faith, determination and fear, are part of the spiritual dimension, while short-term emotions and their handling depend on the entity's physical, mental and spiritual fitness.

Fitness is used to highlight the need for individuals, organisations and societies to be 'fit for purpose'. It can also be related to 'well-being', encouraging organisations and societies to consider the holistic well-being of all those whose lives they influence. We are optimistic that humanity will solve the global problems it faces but agree with Diamond (2005:522) that this requires the correct choices to be made:

> *Two types of choices seem to me to have been crucial in tipping their outcomes towards success or failure: long-term planning and willingness to reconsider core values.*

## POINTS FOR REFLECTION

1.   Do you think modern leaders do generally try their hardest?
2.   Is the world becoming too complex for leaders to cope?
3.   Does the GFF help?
4.   Is there an issue you intend to analyse using the GFF?
5.   In Chapter 1 we related how one of the authors suddenly saw the truth about 'Cowboys and Indians'. How does that truth fit with the attitudes of Henry V and Columbus?
6.   Was the decision by the USA and UK to declare war on Iraq justified?
7.   How would you analyse it based on the GFF?

# References

Arkin, A. (2009). School for Scandal. *People Management*, 8 October. London: CIPD.

Avery, G.C. (2005). *Leadership for Sustainable Futures: Achieving Success in a Competitive World*. Northampton: Edward Elgar.

Bakan, J. (2005). *The Corporation: The Pathological Pursuit of Profit and Power*. New York: Free Press.

Baker, M. (2008). 'Battling the master builders of the balance sheet'. *Daily Telegraph*, Thursday 23 October.

Beckster. (n.d.). *Battle of Agincourt* [Online]. Available at: www.geocities.com/beckster05/Agincourt/AgCampaign.html [accessed: on 5/10/09].

Castro Ruz, F. (2003). President of the Republic of Cuba. *Cold War Warnings for a Unipolar World*. Ocean Press, in association with the office of publications, Cuban Council of State.

Covey, S.R. (1999). *The 7 Habits of Highly Effective People*. London: Simon and Schuster.

Czander, W.M. (1993). *The Psychodynamics of Work and Organizations*. London: Guilford Press.

De Woot, P. (2009). *Should Prometheus be Bound?* Basingstoke: Palgrave Macmillan.

Diamond, J. (2005). *Collapse: How Societies Choose to Fail or Survive*. London: Penguin.

Drucker, P.F. (2003). *The New Realities*. New Jersey: Transaction Publishers.

Freedman, J. (2002). *Hijacking of the Amygdale*. [Online]. Available at: http://www.eqtoday/archive/hijack.html [accessed: 11/12/06].

Friedman, M. (1970/1993). 'The Social Responsibility of Business is to Increase its Profits'. *New York Times*, 13 September.

Goleman, D. (1995). *Emotional Intelligence*. London: Bloomsbury.

Hormann, J. (1990). *Creative Work: Constructive Role of Business in a Transforming Society*. Knowledge Systems Inc.

*Indigenous People of the Caribbean: A Guide*. (2004). [Online]. Available at: http://www.geocities.com/teresitasi/caribevibes.htm [accessed: 16/9/09].

Kriger, M. and Seng, Y. (2005). Leadership with inner meaning: A contingency theory of leadership based on the worldviews of five religions. *The Leadership Quarterly*, 16, 771–806.

Leopold, J., Harris, L. and Watson, T. (2005). *The Strategic Managing of Human Resources*. Harlow: FT Prentice Hall.

Lindblom, C.E. (1959). The science of muddling through. *Public Administration Review*, vol. 19, no. 2, 79–88.

Lorange, P. (2003). Global responsibility – business education and business schools – roles in promoting a global perspective. *Corporate Governance*, vol.3, no.3, 126–35.

Shreve, J. (1991). Christopher Columbus: A Bibliographic Voyage. *Choice*, January, vol. 29, 703–11. (On line) Available at: http://www.millersville.edu/~columbus/data/bib/SHREVE01.BIB [accessed: 16/9/09].

Wilber, K. (2001). The *Eye of Spirit: An Integral Vision for a World Gone Slightly Mad*. London: Shambala.

# 4

# Misinformed Leadership and the Need for a New Paradigm

Misinformed Leadership is where the leader is unaware of important information, skills, techniques or consequences, misunderstands their importance, or misunderstands how to use them.

We start this chapter with a review of the recent near-collapse of the entire global financial system. This has been a tremendous crisis which is still to be resolved and will have repercussions for many years to come as the fallout from Wall Street impacts on Main Street. Generations will be affected. For these reasons it is the major case study in the book.

## Global Financial Markets

Banks are in an extremely advantageous position. Traditionally, they have received deposits from investors and lent the money to borrowers at a slightly higher interest rate, the difference being their 'margin' to cover the banks' costs and give a 'fair' return on the bank owners' capital. They act as a financial intermediary matching those with money to save or invest with those who need money to pay expenses and refinance maturing loans. This role is crucial to the smooth operation of the whole financial system and thence to the well-being of the global economy.

Most of the money they lend out is used by the borrower to pay their creditors, who pay the money into their bank. These deposits can be lent to another borrower, whereupon they go round the circle again. Known as the banking multiplier effect, this 'merry-go-round' results in the amount of money in the system increasing dramatically. The extent to which there is no underlying physical backing is known as 'fiat money'. If a bank started with

£100 (million, billion or whatever denomination fits your scale of thinking) it may be able to move this round the system so as to multiply it by say 10 times and result in the balance sheet shown in Table 4.1:

**Table 4.1    Balance sheet showing multiplier effect**

| Assets | | | Liabilities | |
|---|---|---|---|---|
| Loans made | 1,000 | | Deposits received | 1,000 |
| | | | | |
| Cash held | 100 | | Owners funds | 100 |
| | | | | |
| Total | 1,100 | | Total | 1,100 |

The bank would be required to keep a certain percentage of the money it lent in the form of reserves so that it had some money available to cope with some of the deposits being withdrawn before the equivalent-sized loan was repaid. This is very important because one of the problems banks have to cope with is that the majority of their loans are long-term, whereas the majority of their borrowing is short-term so if there is a lack of free money in the system for any reason, they can very quickly be in a situation where they run out of cash themselves. The traditional reserves ratio has been 10 per cent which is in line with the illustration in Table 4.1, its original funds of £100, held as cash, being 10 per cent of the total loans/deposits of £1,000.

If the bank charges say a 2 per cent margin it will have £1,000 × 2 per cent = £20 to cover its costs (say £8) and give a return (£20 − £8 = £12) on the original £100. This would be a return of 12 per cent on owners' funds. Potential ways to increase this return are clear: increase the multiplier effect, increase the margin, or both. If the bank was able to multiply its original funds by 20 times and charge a 3 per cent margin, assuming its costs were unaltered, the situation would become £2,000 × 3 per cent = £60. Take off £8 costs leaves £52, that is, a 52 per cent return on the original £100.

The corollary to the multiplier effect is that banks have very high gearing (UK) or leverage (USA). This term refers to the relationship between owners' funds and liabilities. As can be seen above, these two represent where the money has come from to finance the assets. In most industries an organisation would be said to be low geared if liabilities were a small fraction of the total financing, say 20 per cent with owners' funds being the other 80 per cent. If it were the other way round, with liabilities 80 per cent and owners' funds only 20 per cent, the organisation would be said to be highly geared.

The benefit of high gearing was demonstrated above, with the bank making its margin on a higher level of activity. The same result would occur if the bank used some of the deposits to buy assets and they increased in value – the increase would all go to the owners, so the higher the gearing, the more assets could be bought and the higher return made for the owners. With extremely high gearing if a positive margin is maintained and asset values rise, the owners make vast profits. The converse is true; if a negative margin occurs and asset values fall the owners make big losses. With 95 per cent gearing, the assets only need fall by 5 per cent in value for the whole of the owners' funds to be wiped out.

Thus highly-geared banks are extremely vulnerable to relatively small fluctuations in asset values or any move by depositors to withdraw their funds. They must be very careful to avoid becoming excessively highly geared or giving cause for alarm, so must be ultra cautious in their activities. This would apply if banks were a typical business sector attempting to ensure their long-term survival. We are often told that finance is the lifeblood of business, the oil that keeps the wheel moving, vital to the smooth running of the economy. If that is so, banks have an extra duty of care to the whole of society to act responsibly and it is a fundamental task of the government (via their appointed regulators) to ensure their smooth operation by tight control.

The other way in which banks can make extremely high returns was also demonstrated above that is by increasing the margin between the interest rates they charge borrowers and pay on deposits. While this is good news for the banks, it is bad news for their customers. If banks are able to charge a wide margin, the cost of finance to industry will increase discouraging investment and making suppliers charge higher prices for their goods and services. Again the banks are in a privileged position, vital to the economy and must be tightly controlled.

This tight control could be done automatically in a 'perfect market' where there were many banks all competing with each other to provide loans at low rates and pay good returns on money deposited with them, so as to increase their market share. The logical borrower and investor, having perfect knowledge of the market, would also be aware of the extent to which each bank was using the multiplier effect and avoid those where it was being used excessively.

In practice, the banking industry is far from a perfect market. It is dominated by a few very large banks who have tremendous power; they consult with each other as to what interest rates they will apply; the borrowers and investors do not necessarily act logically as will be shown below; there is not perfect market knowledge; and few people understand the banking industry so as to be able to accurately assess such aspects as risk levels. Prior to the recent financial markets crisis, most people would not have even contemplated how risky it was to deposit their savings in a particular bank.

This meant the control should have been enforced by government. But instead of keeping them tightly controlled, governments around the world gave banks increased freedom under the free market philosophy that has been in vogue for the past 30 years. In particular, governments of countries with a major financial centre wanted to encourage banks and other financial market players to trade in their market. One of the difficult issues facing the world is that corporations have become international but countries, by definition, have not. This means corporations can outflank the governments that we rely on to control them – if they do not like the regime in one country they can move to another offering better terms. As long as there are countries prepared to undercut the market, the corporations will always win. Individual countries can attempt to enforce their own tighter controls but then often find themselves up against free market and competition rules. Before becoming Prime Minister in the UK, Gordon Brown was the Chancellor of the Exchequer and very much in favour of 'light touch regulation' as he believed the markets should be given a very high degree of freedom. During his time in that role, the finance markets and economy boomed and he claimed it was 'the end of boom and bust' meaning that markets would keep on rising for the foreseeable future, without the downturn that had historically always followed a period of growth.

In the UK, as part of the drive to free up the finance market, building societies were encouraged to become private companies, known as demutualisation. Building societies had originated when groups of individuals pooled their savings so as to provide loans for their members to buy houses. They were owned by their members and tended to operate at relatively small margins thus acting as a brake on the width of margin banks could operate. As they privatised, the brake on margins started to weaken. (It is interesting to note that none of the building societies that demutualised still exist as individual entities.)

Given this new freedom, banks started to act in an increasingly competitive market style, looking to maximise return to owners as any company is obliged to do by law. Failing to do so would in any case have left their shareholders looking to sell their shares and buy those in a more venturesome bank – the vast majority of investors were by now caught up in the drive for higher returns. To attract the best managers, able to market their services most effectively, banks started to compete with each other in paying extremely high salaries and bonuses justified by the mantra that there was a shortage of high-quality people and if they were not paid that much, they would go elsewhere.

These highly paid, highly competitive, market-focused fund managers searched for new ways to make profits through innovation – coming up with new types of deals and transactions. But in an efficient market, high returns equal high risk. This is a crucial point as 'modern' banks were able to persuade investors they had found ways of lessening risk but still make high returns. They did this by changing the model under which banks operated. Traditionally, if a bank made a loan it held on to the debt and had a long-term relationship with the borrower. The new model was such that the banks now packaged various loans together then sold them on to other financial operators, this becoming known as securitisation. Clever packaging of debts often persuaded the buyers to take on more risk than they realised.

Before looking at the financial market collapse of 2008/09 it is important to recognise that while it was far larger than any other threat to the financial system, it was not an isolated, one-off 'once-in-a-life-time' 'impossible-to-predict' event. Over many years there has been a vast array of scandals in the financial markets, 23 major ones being outlined on the website:

projects.exeter.ac.uk/RDavies/arian/scandals/classic.html

Each of these is a massive scandal in its own right but together they reveal systemic failure to prevent and detect global grand scale corruption and the fact that all four categories of MisLeadership were endemic in the financial system to such an extent that they may have become the accepted norm. The Embedded Values Cycle in Figure 1.1 illustrated how this process can lead to the brain becoming reconditioned such that these ways of thinking and acting become hard-wired habits and ultimately values.

We will briefly review two of the above scandals, the Bank of Credit and Commerce International (BCCI) which was one of the first warnings that the financial system was becoming hard-wired with inappropriate processes and structures, and Nick Leeson and Barings Bank as it was the first to reveal the extent to which an individual could wreak havoc across the financial system and commit their organisation to ruinous transactions.

## BANK OF CREDIT AND COMMERCE INTERNATIONAL (BCCI)

BCCI was set up in 1972 and for its first 15 years traded without major concern, although in 1987 the Bank of England, with other regulatory bodies, established a 'college of regulators' which suggests some concern. In the following 4 years BCCI was vilified for money laundering, false and deceitful transactions, colluding to mis-state or disguise the real purpose of significant transactions, massive and widespread fraud and a criminal culture.

The Bank of England ultimately closed BCCI in Britain, the governor stating that the culture of BCCI was 'criminal'. Other central banks followed suit, including the US, despite subsequent revelation by the CIA (the Criminal Investigation Authority in the US) that it had used BCCI 'as a way to move money'. This might highlight Machiavellian Leadership by the CIA and also shows how difficult it is to step away when the partner to collusion is revealed. Naturally, the CIA would claim they have to use such tactics to achieve the greater good, that is, they are not being Machiavellian, rather they are showing Globally Fit Leadership. The Embedded Values Cycle in Figure 1.1 shows the danger of having our values corrupted by exposure to corrupt behaviour.

An official inquiry held in the UK found the Bank of England had failed to be inquisitive and alert enough to spot widespread fraud in BCCI (Missing Leadership and poor decision-making). The Bank denied this, but set up a special investigations unit to prevent further fraud – better late than never, but the number of major scandals since then shows that this unit was ineffective. To us this is an example of using old tools to tackle new problems. Perhaps the Bank needed to have been thinking on a more global and systemic level rather than focusing on the prevention of individual frauds.

A case was brought against the Bank of England, claming it had failed to carry out its supervisory duties, but this was ultimately dropped. It has been 18 years since the closure of BCCI yet the argument continues as to whether the Bank was guilty of negligence. As stated above, we believe that even before the recent financial markets collapse the number and scale of scandals in these markets is proof in itself of systemic failure to prevent and detect global grand-scale corruption. Whether that role is the responsibility of the Bank of England is arguable but the inability to hold particular individuals or organisations responsible for fundamental and catastrophic weaknesses in the system is in itself a serious flaw.

We believe the Bank was in an impossible situation such that while it may have been slow to act, it was not entirely to blame. The whole regulatory system was still based on national level control whereas the market and therefore scope for fraud had moved to the global level which required a global response. Attempts made to move toward such an approach were piecemeal and selective and as subsequent events proved, ineffectual.

## NICK LEESON AND BARINGS BANK

This case, summarised in the film *Rogue Trader*, reveals a frightening and sad story, starting with the 1980s financial markets scene in which vital strategic decisions were being taken by young and greedy individuals determined to make their name and fortune (Missing Leadership and Machiavellian Leadership which is covered in Chapter 5). It ends with Barings Bank, the UK's oldest merchant bank, being sold for £1 and Nick Leeson getting a six-and-a-half-year prison sentence, suffering from colon cancer and being divorced.

Rapid promotion was based on success, so those who took the biggest risks and were lucky soon found themselves in positions of great authority often without any formal education in banking theory (Misguided and Misinformed Leadership). Nick Leeson worked in the far eastern currency markets and quickly became Barings Bank's star performer.

As the markets were new, expanding very rapidly and operating at the global level, these incredibly successful individuals, who had made fantastic profits for their organisations were often accepted as being ahead of the theory experts (Misinformed Leadership). The more profits they earned for the bank, the more bonus they were paid such that they led a very high lifestyle as well as having tremendous kudos and being held in esteem by their fellow workers and most of society. Naturally they wanted this to continue so took increasingly high risks – with other people's money. Nick Leeson's bonuses were more than double his already high basic salary. Machiavellian Leadership is discussed in Chapter 5; Chapter 6 will discuss how power corrupts.

Sooner or later every gambler has a run of bad luck. In 1994 Nick Leeson's luck ran out when the markets turned against him and there was an earthquake in Kobe, Japan, leaving him with losses of just over £200 million. Due to poor internal controls (Missing Leadership) and the bank's strong faith in their star performer, Leeson was able to hide the true position by using several trading accounts. He attempted to recover by taking out more, even riskier, deals but these also went badly and ultimately increased his total losses to over £800 million.

The result was disaster at the individual, group and societal levels with all parties involved finishing far worse off than they would have been if they had acted as Globally Fit Leaders.

City chiefs were shocked (Misinformed Leadership), made changes aimed at ensuring it could never happen again, but further scandals revealed that the new systems were not working (Missing Leadership). Ten years ago the bubble that ultimately collapsed in 2008 began to grow and many commentators feared a repeat of the Leeson affair as rewards were still being linked to short-term performance and the level of bonuses was rapidly increasing. No action was taken and 10 years on the bonus culture is now recognised as one of the major causes of the 2008/09 turmoil in financial markets. Banks are, however, already moving back into paying massive bonuses based on very short-term performance.

Failure to act decisively on such a clear and massive problem over a long period is clear evidence of long-term and continuing Missing Leadership and Institutionalised MisLeadership.

These cases, all the others mentioned and the many smaller ones that also occurred show how the scene was set for the financial markets collapse of 2008/09. While the perpetrators may have genuinely believed they had mastered risk, in fact extreme risk-taking, weak controls, complacency and arrogance were clearly still rife in the finance markets, despite repeated system failures and attempts at patching it together using outdated tools. A great deal of concern had been expressed over the governance of large organisations and new regulations brought in requiring directors of private companies to conduct annual reviews of the effectiveness of internal financial, operational and compliance controls and systems, and risk management – but these were clearly ineffectual as regards the finance markets and did not prevent the financial markets collapse. The well-documented issue of high bonus on short-term performance had not been tackled.

## BUILD UP TO THE CRASH

As discussed earlier banks were increasingly competitive, looking to maximise return to owners and paying extremely high salaries and bonuses to those making the highest returns. To keep their edge, these people had to find new ways to keep those profits growing. Derivatives, hedging, swaps and futures are some of the innovative approaches used.

The term 'derivatives' refers to financial instruments derived from underlying transactions with returns dependent on the outcome of those transactions. Hedging is a transaction whereby the parties attempt to lower their risk by entering into an agreement which removes some or all of the uncertainty they face. Swaps can be used as a hedge by the parties swapping, say, fixed and variable interest rates with each other so as to match their own exposure profile, while futures are agreements to buy an asset at an agreed price at an agreed future date.

All of these instruments can be used defensively in an attempt to reduce exposure to risk but also offensively to deliberately take on more risk if the players believe they can out-perform the market, that is, predict outcomes better than other players. Use of terms such as players indicates the attitude of those participating and it has been estimated that 97 per cent of transactions on the London Stock Exchange are of an offensive nature.

Deliberately taking on risk in this manner is known as speculation but is effectively gambling and has similar results. For every winner there must be a loser but the vast majority of gamblers overstate their winnings and understate their losses. The people who win long-term tend to be the bookmakers (in this case the banks) because they either make a margin on every transaction or are able to fix the odds to virtually guarantee that they win. The bookmaker's costs and profits are all taken from the gamblers, thus there are in fact many more losers than winners. Many relatively poor and uninformed people are keen gamblers so it can be viewed as a way of stripping them of the little wealth they have and returning it to the rich (Misguided Leadership).

## The Housing Bubble

In addition to the above ways of increasing their profits, banks started to look at how they could make more from loans to homeowners.

Traditionally, banks and building societies would only provide say 80 per cent of the market value of a house, expecting the buyer to have saved or inherited the other 20 per cent. This gave the bank a cushion in case house prices fell. Over a period of several years house prices continued to rise such that many people started to believe they would continue to do so indefinitely. This made the above lending policy seem over-cautious and the highly paid, highly competitive, market-focused fund managers saw the opportunity to capture a larger share of the market by lending a higher proportion of the value. They started to compete with each other, lending higher and higher proportions of the value until they were lending more than the current market value of the property. The situation became so extreme that banks in the USA began to lend to 'NINJA' borrowers, that is, ones who had 'No Income, No Job or Assets', while those in the UK made what came to be termed 'Liar Loans', that is, allowing the borrowers to self-certify their earnings without any proof.

## ILLUSTRATION OF THE HOUSING BUBBLE

A bank lends £100,000 to a person buying a house worth £90,000 who uses the extra £10,000 for decorating and furniture. The interest rate is at a relatively low 5 per cent, so the borrower has to pay £5,000pa interest. This is relatively easy to pay, no higher than the cost of renting a similar property, and most people want to own their own house so there are many buyers willing to take up the offer. This forces house prices up and the bank sees no real risk so is willing to lend.

As prices are rising the borrowers are gaining (on paper) a more valuable asset than they bought. If prices rise faster than the interest being paid, the borrowers are effectively getting free housing. The market value of the house soon exceeds the lent/borrowed £100,000 so the bank becomes even more confident that it will get its money back if the borrower decides to sell or they have to repossess due to the borrower failing to pay the interest.

Over time, house prices double and earlier loans look very secure indeed, so now the bank is very happy to lend £200,000 to a person buying a house now worth £180,000 and using the extra £20,000 for furniture and a new car. If the person selling the house bought it originally for £90,000 and spent £10,000 on decorating as above, they will have made an £80,000 capital gain which may be tax free and would have been made without investing any of their own money.

Interest may have risen to 6 per cent (more demand for cash so its price rises too) so the annual interest charge would be £12,000pa. While this is not as easy to pay as the £5,000pa above, prices are still rising so buyers see at least part of the interest cost as being off-set by increased capital value. House prices have been rising continuously for many years now so the banks see no real risk and continue to lend. House prices are forced up still further so the borrower is still gaining (on paper) and the bank is also happy since the market value of the house now exceeds the £200,000 lent.

Prices rise further so a similar house now costs £270,000. The bank has earned tremendous profits on previous loans so is very keen to lend the borrower £300,000, the extra £30,000 being for furniture, a new car and a flash holiday. Both the bank and borrower are very happy and the person selling the house has received £270,000 for an asset maybe bought only a few years earlier for a fraction of that amount. Everyone's a winner. Roll up, roll up!

## Prick – The Bubble Bursts

BUT some borrowers are now unable to pay the £21,000 annual interest, the rate having risen to 7 per cent, and £300,000 × 7 per cent = £21,000. They have to sell, so more houses appear on the market and other buyers start to become wary so less willing to buy. Prices stabilise so borrowers are now no longer gaining any capital appreciation and annual interest cost looks too high to be justified by just the annual occupancy value. More owners look to sell, prices start to fall which means the effective annual cost is now the £21,000 interest plus a loss in sales value.

Banks start to worry that the underlying value of the property is below the amount lent and moving downwards, so they start to panic and take measures such as requiring lenders to pay back some of the loan so that what is left is less than the falling market value. Those who can't do this may have their house repossessed and in the UK be sued by the bank for the shortfall. In the USA, the borrower can just post the keys back to the bank and walk away which may discourage the bank from foreclosing but means they are in an even worse position if the householder does decide to get out. Banks start to require borrowers to have a 10 per cent deposit before they will lend to them as a safeguard against further falls in house values. All these measures put further downward pressure on the market, forcing a downward spiral of prices.

Those who borrowed more than their house is now worth are in a difficult position. The new car loses value very quickly, particularly as few people can afford to buy it, and the luxury holiday is just a memory. If they sell, they will have nowhere to live and (in the UK) still owe the bank the difference between the selling price and the outstanding loan. If they stay put, the value continues to drop so their paper loss becomes greater by the day but provided they can meet the repayments at least they have somewhere to live and will eventually own the house.

People who became landlords (that is, bought houses and rented them out) during the boom time made a theoretical fortune as the money borrowed to buy the houses was soon far less than the market value of the properties, but now these values begin to tumble. Those alert enough to see what is happening and quick and brave enough to sell at prices that are now falling are able to convert their theoretical gains into (slightly diminished) real gains, but those who delay start to be faced with real, rapidly growing, losses.

As people begin to default, banks are also in a quandary. If they push too hard, more people will default, lowering both the bank's revenue and asset values, the latter because the banks will have to take back the houses and attempt to sell them to other buyers, adding yet more pressure to the downward spiral. If they do not put pressure on, arrears levels will increase which again reduces revenue and true underlying value of their assets, although it may be possible for the bank to keep that hidden for some time.

With all the above pressures on their revenue and asset values, those banks that were particularly venturesome in their lending are likely to come under unsustainable pressure because their high levels of lending are likely to have resulted in very high gearing levels, thus even a very small fall in asset values would threaten their owners funds. Further, to drive their growth particularly quickly, they are likely to have lent money to borrowers who are less able to repay either the interest or the loan. These are people with low or no incomes who were effectively reliant (as was the bank that lent them the money) on continued rises in house prices to finance their borrowing. They have become known as sub-prime borrowers, the loans to them being sub-prime loans. They are likely to be among the first to default, hitting the bank's liquidity (that is, cash flow) and asset values.

In most industries, a gearing level of 50 per cent (defining gearing to be borrowing as a percentage of total long-term finance) would be viewed as becoming quite high but each £1 of borrowing would be matched by £1 of owners' finance, so asset values could fall by half before the owners funds were wiped out. At the beginning of this case study we illustrated the extremely high financial gearing banks can become exposed to. Total assets of £2,000, financed by deposits received of £1,900 and owners' funds of £100 gave gearing of 95 per cent so asset values would only need to fall by 5 per cent for all owners' funds to disappear.

Actual gearing ratios of some of the world's biggest banks prior to the financial markets collapse are shown in Table 4.2.

**Table 4.2     Gearing ratios of banks**

| Bank | Assets | Shareholder equity | % |
|---|---|---|---|
| Bank of America | $1,715B | $146.8B | 8.6 |
| Citigroup | $2,187B | $113.6B | 5.2 |
| JP Morgan | $1,562B | $123.2B | 7.9 |
| Wells Fargo | $575B | $47.6B | 8.3 |
| Deutsche Bank | €2,020B | €38.5B | 1.9 |
| UBS | Fr2,272B | Fr42.5B | 1.9 |
| Credit Suisse | Fr1,360B | Fr59.88B | 4.4 |
| Fortis | €871B | €34.28B | 3.9 |
| Dexia | €604B | €16.4B | 2.7 |
| BNP Paribas | €1,694B | €59.4B | 3.5 |
| Barclays | £1,227B | £32.5B | 2.6 |
| RBS | £1,990B | £91.48B | 4.6 |
| HBOS | £667B | £22.2B | 3.3 |
| Lloyds | £353B | £12.4B | 3.5 |

*Source*: Adapted from Langthorne (2008).

The sheer scale of these figures is staggering in itself – the three big US banks have balance sheet totals equivalent to 40 per cent of US GDP. The level of gearing is even more incredible. These are banks, with special roles, very privileged positions and one would have thought responsibilities to act cautiously so as to provide a safe deposit for peoples' savings. To have gearing so high that a 2 per cent – 3 per cent fall in asset values wipes out all shareholders' funds is self-evidently a very high-risk strategy. It is MisLeadership in the extreme.

Ultimately the plight of the venturesome banks became clear to those lending them money and they began to withdraw their funds, putting even more pressure on liquidity. Such banks were forced to sell assets in an already rapidly falling market, so the disposal value was likely to be well below that shown in the balance sheet, again hitting the owners' fund values.

Banks became reluctant to lend each other money as they were not sure whether it would be safe. Those unable to refinance their debt (both banks and all other businesses and individuals) found themselves in difficulty. On

14 September 2008 Lehman Brothers collapsed and on 29 September 2008 the whole system came extremely close to collapse. Wall Street fell by 777 points, the biggest fall in a single day, and banks announced to the regulators that they were preparing to stop allowing withdrawals through cash points later that day! Governments felt they had to step in.

## Cost to the Government, that is, the People

As previously stated, money is the life blood of the business world so governments could not allow a situation to exist where perfectly sound organisations could not borrow money to pay their staff and trade creditors and individuals could not obtain cash from cash points. It was evident that non-payment of people's wages and lack of cash in people's pockets could quickly lead to riots and anarchy, collapse of both private and public sectors and no hope of re-election for the government.

Thus they were effectively forced to support the banks even if they felt the banks were to blame for their own difficulties and in a true market economy would have been allowed to fail. This was very difficult for proponents of a true market economy to stomach. The banks had been given freedom to act competitively but had been so cavalier to have threatened not only their own existence but that of the whole financial system and with it society.

The scale of the collapse and requisite bail out was shocking to most observers, Figure 4.1 showing the major financial rescue packages provided in the period September to November 2008.

In Figure 4.2, Thatcher (2009) argues that the UK Prime Minister attempted to avoid informing the public of the extent of reduction that would be required to public sector spending but was forced to do so following the leak of a Treasury document.

Figure 4.2 gets to the heart of what this chapter is all about – Misinformed Leadership. If facts were being kept hidden by the government, all other leaders in the country were being Misguided and therefore unable to make informed decisions. If this was being done deliberately, it would be Machiavellian Leadership.

Misinformed Leadership was defined at the beginning of this chapter as where the leader is unaware of important information, skills, techniques or

| 26/11 | European Commission unveils an economic recovery plan worth 200bn euros |
| 25/11 | International Monetary Fund (IMF) approves a $7.6bn (£5.1bn) loan for Pakistan The US Federal Reserve announces it will inject another $800bn into the economy |
| 24/11 | UK government announces a temporary cut in the level of VAT - to 15% from 17.5% - in its pre-Budget report |
| 23/11 | US government announces a $20bn (£13.4bn) rescue plan |
| 20/11 | IMF approves a $2.1bn (£1.4bn) loan for Iceland |
| 9/11 | China sets out a two-year $586bn economic stimulus package |
| 6/11 | IMF approves $16.4bn Ukraine loan to bolster its economy |
| 30/10 | Federal Reserve cuts its key interest rate from 1.5% to 1% |
| 20/10 | Sweden's government offers credit guarantees to banks and mortgage lenders worth £117bn |
| 19/10 | South Korea announces a $130bn financial rescue package to stabilise its markets The Dutch government injects 10bn euros ($13.4bn; £7.7bn) into the banking and insurance company ING |
| 14/10 | US government unveils a $250bn (£143bn) plan to purchase stakes in a wide variety of banks |
| 13/10 | UK government plans to pump £37bn into three UK banks |
| 8/10 | UK government announces details of a rescue package for the banking system worth at least £50bn and £200bn in short-term lending support |
| 6/10 | Germany announces a 50bn euro ($68bn; £38.7bn) plan to save one of the country's biggest banks |
| 3/10 | US House of Representatives passes a $700bn (£394bn) government plan to rescue the US financial sector |
| 30/09 | Dexia becomes the latest European bank to be bailed out |
| 29/09 | UK mortgage lender Bradford & Bingley is nationalised. The government takes on its £50bn mortgages |
| 25/09 | Washington Mutual, a mortgage lender with assets with a book value of $307bn is closed down by regulators and sold to JPMorgan Chase |

**Figure 4.1     Major financial rescue packages: September to November 2008**

*Source*: Adapted from Langthorne (ibid).

consequences, misunderstands their importance, or misunderstands how to use them. Trillin (2009) claims that the reason why the financial system nearly collapsed can be summarised in one sentence: *'because smart guys had started working on Wall Street'*. He argues that these people thought they were clever enough to change the financial market model as described above and that their top managers, *'didn't have the foggiest notion of what a credit default swap was. All our guy knew was that they were getting disgustingly rich, and they had gotten to like that. All that easy money had eaten away at their sense of enoughness.'* We argue that neither the government nor many of the players in the finance market properly understood how the free market approach would operate in modern financial

---

**The truth hurts, by Mike Thatcher**

Truth and politics are not easy bedfellows. But misleading the public, whether actively or by omission, is a dangerous tactic for any politician.

Gordon Brown has flirted with this dilemma in recent months. His refusal to acknowledge that cuts are inevitable verged on the ridiculous.

Sense prevailed at the TUC conference, and the prime minister finally used the C-word. However, he was undone the following day when the extent of the necessary cuts became clear.

A leaked Treasury document showed that departmental budgets are likely to fall by 9.3% in real terms over the four years from 2009/10 to 2013/14.

Debate immediately ensued over whether these were real, planned cuts or just projections. But either way, the Whitehall mole has exposed some big issues.

Unemployment – now at a 14-year high – will inevitably rise further. By 2013/14, social security spending will be approaching £200bn and debt interest will have climbed to almost £64bn.

Having been dragged kicking and screaming to the honesty box, it's clear that Brown still has some way to go. Public service cuts are going to be painful and long term.

It's a grim future and the consequences cannot be ignored or played down. Labour has bad form in this regard, but the Conservatives also have some work to do … He has made some specific proposals – including scrapping identity cards and the children's database – but this would not scratch the surface of what would be required.

Only the Liberal Democrats have attempted to address the public finance black hole. Treasury spokesman Vince Cable published a pamphlet this week offering annual savings in excess of £14bn. We may take issue with some of Cable's ideas, but he at least acknowledges the enormity of the problem.

Labour and the Tories need to take the same approach. The government has an early opportunity with the impending Pre-Budget Report, when it has promised to identify priority areas for future spending. All the parties should offer detailed breakdowns of planned departmental spending. Only then can voters make an informed choice come election day.

---

**Figure 4.2      The Truth Hurts article**
*Source*: Thatcher, 2009.

markets, where few if any of the requirements of perfect competition existed and the banks were extremely powerful and too important to be allowed to fail.

We believe that knowledge and understanding were at such a low level that participants were unable to recognise that the market was acting in an unsustainable manner, unacceptable risks were being taken and a massive bubble being created. This was despite the number and scale of scandals in the financial markets over a long period which revealed systemic failure and the banks' inability or unwillingness to take sufficient steps to achieve a sustainable system – Institutional MisLeadership.

The senior bankers and regulators, feeling they were being pressured to do something which was beyond their capacity and control, reverted to a narrow focus which they felt able to cope with (as discussed in Chapter 3). Thus they attempted to solve the problems as if they were of the old familiar type (local, minor, controllable) using traditional methods and ignored those elements of the problem (global, scale, speed, risk, complexity) that were outside their comfort zone and capacity. Keynes (1920) summed up the problem as 'The *market can stay irrational longer than you can stay solvent*' and it is extremely hard to stand against the tide when people acting in what you believe is an irrational manner are making massive profits over a run of several years.

Even if the top bankers and regulators had been aware of their personal leadership shortcomings and the potential for unprecedented disaster, it would have taken tremendous mental and spiritual courage to confess and call in outside help. They were, after all, the top people whose responsibility it was to understand and control their organisations and the environment they operated in. In any case, to whom could they turn for help? If our argument is correct, possibly there was no one who truly understood because no one had the right tools.

Failure of the senior bankers and regulators to carry out the leadership role left a leadership vacuum, quickly filled by whoever was willing to step in. Big and immediate rewards were available to those achieving sales growth, so a headlong rush in that direction ensued, with results that should have been predictable had the lessons been learned from previous 'bubbles' such as the South Sea Bubble, that preceding the 1939 stock market crash, and the housing boom in the UK in the 1980s.

> Gordon Brown admits he was wrong to claim he had ended 'boom and bust'
>
> *Source:* Kirkup 2008.

Unfortunately, as is the case with many gamblers including those whose scandals were reviewed above, these leadership usurpers had early success in that their actions seemed to be working and the economy booming. This encouraged them to believe in their approach and exploit its apparent benefits. They started to believe they were invincible and when things went wrong poured more money in, thinking it was only a run of bad luck and they would soon be back to winning ways.

## Causes of Misinformed Leadership

Having studied the financial markets crash in some detail, we now turn our attention to a more general assessment of the causes of Misinformed Leadership.

An important cause of Misinformed Leadership is the attitude toward the telling of lies that results from the operation of the Embedded Values Cycle as shown in Figure 1.1. As highlighted in Chapter 1, from birth we are subjected to a deluge of information and misinformation from those around us including our parents and others closest to us. This forms a vast jumble of myths, legends and hard facts but we become hardened to the situation such that misinformation becomes an expectation which is fulfilled by the wide range of seemingly inconsequential and benign communications that can be described as everyday interpersonal 'little lies' about one's beliefs, feelings or autobiography.

There is widespread misunderstanding of how significant these 'little lies' are in gradually building an environment that is insensitive, tolerant and accepting of MisLeadership. Drawing on two studies as examples (DePaulo et al. 1996 as cited in Boush et al. 2009:8), college students reported lying in approximately one out of every three of their social interactions, and people drawn from the larger community said they lied in one out of every five social interactions. These results also illustrate how widespread the practice of Machiavellian Leadership may be since many of these lies will be told to obtain some kind of hidden advantage.

A leader may be misinformed through a lack of ability, time, motivation or training. As discussed above, it may also be as a result of the rapidly changing and increasingly complex environment such that the leader may be relying on a knowledge base, world view and paradigm of thinking that may be outdated and irrelevant.

Misinformed Leadership may also occur because the leader is working with information that is out of date or wrong because of the MisLeadership acts of another. Talbott (2009) identifies 86 lies on Wall Street. His lie number 1 is:

> *Going into the current crisis, the American economy was the strongest and most resilient in the world*

He shows (2009:15) that nothing could in fact be further from the truth, pointing out that while consumption by citizens, big businesses, banks and the government have all exploded, causing a dramatic increase in GDP, much of this consumption and government spending was fuelled by borrowing. He claims that the US government is expected to have a \$2 trillion deficit in 2009 alone, with the total amount of all debt outstanding in the United States being over \$60 trillion – which excludes unfunded liabilities in social security, Medicare, retirement and health-care plans. Most of this deficit is financed by China, the basic cycle being US markets buy goods from China, then China gives the money back by buying US bonds and other forms of debt. This will only work for as long as China continues to spend less than it generates. Thus, leaders who believed the economy was fundamentally strong were being misled, so likely to make invalid decisions.

We have now considered some of the main causes of Misinformed Leadership and these are summarised in Figure 4.3.

| Lack of appropriate education |
|---|
| Complex, rapidly changing environment |
| Using outdated knowledge, world view or paradigm as the basis for making decisions |
| Poor decision making models |
| Wrong information resulting from the MisLeadership acts of others |

**Figure 4.3     Causes of Misinformed Leadership**
*Source*: The Authors.

## Mental Fitness

In many instances, the information relied upon by leaders when making decisions is not based on fact or logical analysis, but on handed-down wisdom, commonly held beliefs and viewpoints. While there is a role for such sources, it can be seen as MythLeadership! This is particularly the case when those passing on the wisdom claim it to be infallible and therefore unchallengeable, expecting the recipient to accept it without question. Those passing on such wisdom are very often the elders of the society, viewing themselves as guardians of the faith and possessing special knowledge and relationships with ancestors and god(s), so it is their duty to ensure the wisdom is passed on intact.

Ancient civilisations had myths and rituals they passed on in this manner, most commonly referred to in Europe are those of the Greeks, Romans and Norse, but indigenous peoples the world over still pass on stories to their children, Australian Aborigines being famed for their rock paintings depicting the Dream

Time and their continued desire to 'go walkabout' in search of their ancestors and roots. At the start of Chapter 1 we outlined some of the myths and stories typically passed on by Western parents to their children and the confusion they can cause.

Changes to knowledge and skills are relatively easy to achieve but it is the innermost beliefs and values that are hardest to change as has been illustrated with The Embedded Values Cycle in Figure 1.1. To free up our thinking and thus behaviour we must reverse the cycle by deliberately challenging our habits including habitual ways of thinking and behaving. This is part of Mental Fitness, particularly mental suppleness as discussed in Chapter 3 under the Global Fitness Framework model.

In Chapter 2 we made use of the ASK SIR L model for problem-solving (Rayment 2001). The same book contains a section on Mind Games which has a number of suggestions of how we can challenge our mental fitness. Some of the issues that may need challenging are anticipation, artificial boundaries, analysis paralysis, bias and prejudice, limited attention span, and excess focus on looking for causes of problems.

To illustrate this last point, when we discussed the ASK SIR L model in Chapter 2 identification of causes was taken for granted as an important step in the process. If we don't know the cause of a problem, how can we tackle it? In many situations, however, trying to establish causes may make the problem worse because it will become or be seen to be an attempt at establishing blame, the next step being assumed to be some kind of punishment or ridicule. If this becomes the expected and accepted way that problems are dealt with, a 'blame culture' can result such that people will deliberately disguise the real cause of a problem, putting forward causes they know are not valid, then going along with implementing solutions to those phantom causes.

An unfortunately common situation where this often applies is in marriage counselling. If too much time is spent attempting to establish the cause of friction in the marriage it can easily turn into an attempt by both parties to show how they are the innocent party while their partner has been unreasonable. Relationships deteriorate and the situation is aggravated. If a reconciliatory approach is adopted, focusing on solutions rather than causes, this can help put current issues into perspective and the partners may solve the problem without having to agree what the problem was or whose fault.

In the work environment the same applies and can even be worse as there may be a group of people who side with each other to blame another person who is innocent. Focusing on the solution rather than precise cause at the individual level can move the problem closer to resolution. It may be impossible or extremely difficult for the leader to establish the truth when several individuals or groups were involved in a situation that went wrong. In a criminal case it may be necessary to seek to establish guilt so that the judicial system can take effect but with more typical work problems we have the requirement to find an approach that will facilitate the parties working together effectively in the future.

Rayment (2001) goes on to suggest a variety of approaches to tackling these issues by improving mental suppleness and all-round mental fitness. These approaches include treating the problem as a game; having fun playing with it; looking for different angles to approach it from; flexible thinking; challenging assumptions; problem reversal; removing dominant ideas; focusing on crucial factors; suspending judgement; generation of alternatives; using different analogies; involving children or people with completely different viewpoints, attitudes and experiences; deliberately adopting an unconventional approach such as widening the problem instead of attempting to narrow it down; using mental imagery and maps; and group approaches such as brainstorming – this last being covered in Chapter 6 of this book.

While these approaches will help improve our mental fitness they will also help to keep or improve our spiritual suppleness which was an important aspect of the Global Fitness Framework discussed in Chapter 3.

One of the causes of Misinformed Leadership identified above was that of the leader using an outdated worldview or paradigm to base their thinking on. The following section goes deeper into this, firstly by considering the format of the current economic and social paradigm, then which aspects of that paradigm may be outdated. It then outlines some of the attributes a new economic and social paradigm might require.

## The Current Economic and Social Paradigm

While there are numerous explanations and causes of the type of Urgent Global Issues (UGIs) identified in Chapter 1, many have pointed to the negative impact businesses have on these issues because of the way they operate. Lorange (2003:133) highlights, for example, that many businesses have a short-term, parochial and finance-dominated focus, and that the current way of operating is based on what Covey (1999b:176) describes as a Scientific/Authoritarian paradigm of thought. According to Covey (1999a:67), the word paradigm is from the Greek word paradigma: a pattern or map for understanding and explaining certain aspects of reality. He says:

> *While a person can make small improvements by developing new skills, quantum leaps in performance and revolutionary advances in technology require new maps, new paradigms, new ways of thinking about and seeing the world.*

This gels with our concerns over the extent of Institutional MisLeadership and need to develop new maps, new paradigms, new ways of dealing with the new complex global environment. The current economic and social paradigm has the type of attributes shown in Figure 4.4.

These attributes were established over 250 years ago by such luminaries as Adam Smith, when trade levels were nowhere near as high as they are now, resource consumption far lower, size and influence of individual organisations far smaller and controls over their actions much tighter. In particular, globalisation and information technology had not taken hold and it was generally possible for individual governments to regulate economic activity within their borders.

The validity of the attributes relied upon underlying assumptions, including a large number of competing firms supplying goods and services

| |
|---|
| Individuals should act in their own self interest |
| This also applies to organisations and nations |
| Competition is a good thing |
| Market forces will result in optimisation |
| The public sector can deal with any adverse aspects |
| Market gaps and weaknesses should be exploited |
| Poor competitors should be driven out of the marketplace |
| Businesses should be rewarded for taking the risks inherent in the market place |
| Natural resources are there to be exploited - animal, vegetable, mineral....human |
| Business (and population) growth is desirable |

**Figure 4.4     Attributes of the current economic/social paradigm**
*Source*: The Authors.

to a large number of competing customers; each supplier and buyer having negligible influence on the overall market such that they are price takers; perfect knowledge; perfect flexibility; fair rules and enforcement; and rational actions. If these assumptions applied, the market would be competitive, and only organisations providing a quality product at a competitive price would survive. This would lead to the ultimate objective of optimum utility for humanity to be achieved without the need for regulation.

Risk is an inherent part of business activity, thus it is right that those people taking legitimate business risks should be rewarded, this being automatically achieved through the pricing mechanism.

## ASPECTS UNDERPINNING THE CURRENT PARADIGM THAT MAY BE OUTDATED

Many of the above assumptions are no longer valid in that:

- large sectors of the economy are now dominated by a few organisations who often collaborate with each other and are thus price-fixers

- market knowledge is often kept hidden, being used as a strategic tool

- large-scale investment at individual, organisation and national level has reduced flexibility

- rules are often seen as not being enforced fairly, particularly at the global level.

This last point led to the development of the Fairtrade Foundation in 1992 with the vision of transforming trade in favour of the poor and disadvantaged, thereby helping to provide justice, with sustainable development being at the heart of trade structures and practices such that everyone, through their work, can maintain a decent and dignified livelihood and develop their full potential.

Incidence of risk is another area in which the assumptions are no longer valid. Limited liability means that business owners reap the benefits of risk when they are successful but are able to avoid most of the losses that accrue when the risk fails.

In the typical large corporation of today, owners no longer run the business but rely on managers to act on their behalf. These managers often have their own objectives and hidden agendas which can lead to goal conflict. Thus the risks taken by Nick Leeson and other players in the financial markets were excessive but when vast amounts of money were lost the individuals involved clearly could not be forced to repay it out of their private finances.

When business scale was small, the owner tended to be the original entrepreneur and genuinely cared about their 'baby'. Most shares in modern corporations are held by institutional investors using a portfolio fund management approach with no commitment to individual firms. Thus money has become far more volatile and a short-term focus predominates.

Fund managers rarely use their voting power at AGMs to change the management or have much influence on their approaches, preferring to move their funds around if not satisfied with performance. This means that the supervisory role of AGMs is lost, thus Missing Leadership abounds. The prevalence of poor accounting and monitoring procedures was one of the recurring themes in the analysis at the start of the chapter.

Driving for ever higher, and increasingly efficient, production levels may have seemed desirable when demand exceeded supply and natural resources seemed limitless, but now such an approach is seen to encourage production and marketing of goods and services in such a manner, and to such an extent, that it is not sustainable long-term nor, many would argue, even medium-term. This situation can only worsen as increasing numbers of countries, including China and India with their massive populations, strive for similar standards to those in the West, a point discussed in Chapter 2.

An assumption that underpins the current paradigm and is still prevalent is that humans naturally have a self-regarding, self-focused way of thinking. Wilson argues, however, (1993, cited in Ghoshal 2005:82) that an 'other-regarding' attitude is far more prevalent. The key issue according to Ghoshal (2005:82) is that the self-regarding position adopted by many leaders might have been taught to them by business schools as the correct way to lead and do business. Even though this may have been a wrong assertion by business schools initially it has become accepted as right as managers adapt their behaviour to conform to this doctrine. Our Embedded Values Cycle in Figure 1.1 is pertinent here.

As an example, according to Kennedy (as cited in Avery 2005:9) the focus on maximising shareholder value was initiated by academic accountants and only became popular in the 1970s. The concept was picked up by US investment bankers, and boards began to align managers' compensation to their success in raising the company's share price. Managers began to focus on their own self-interest, and began restructuring their businesses to maximise share price.

Ghoshal argues (2005:76) business school teaching actually created inappropriate management practices through the adoption of a scientific model of teaching which has denied any moral or ethical considerations – fundamental if leaders are to embrace their part in resolving UGIs. This denial of moral or ethical considerations by UK-based management academics is evidenced by Dunne et al. (2008:273), who also highlight that little concern is evident from the majority of management academics with the type of UGIs discussed here.

## CONSEQUENCES

The result is that many leaders are now operating from an outdated paradigm of thought and using knowledge and information which may also be wrong or out of date. Knowledge and information can be relatively easily updated but unless the underpinning paradigm is addressed the leader will still base decisions on invalid attitudes and assumptions – Misinformed Leadership.

Talbott (2009) illustrates the prevalence of this invalid decision-making. His lie number 21 is:

> *Diversification is the key. If everyone held a broadly diversified portfolio, the markets and society would be much more stable, efficient and productive. If you learn but one thing at Business School it is that investors should always diversify. Investors can minimize their risk exposure and maximize their portfolio returns through diversification.*

In addition to being an invalid strategy for achieving an optimum risk/return position (Misguided Leadership) Talbott (2009:66) argues diversification also leads to other problems. When shareholders adopt a diversification strategy it is impractical for them to police activities of individual companies, resulting in Missing Leadership. One manifestation of this is excessively high executive pay, the typical 'Fortune 500' company paying their CEOs 350 times what their average worker earns. How can such a discrepancy be justified from a humanitarian viewpoint? If it is a result of the existing economic paradigm, that paradigm is clearly unacceptable.

Perhaps the most alarming claim Talbott (2009:45) makes is that all the investment and commercial banks in the world are insolvent but:

> They have refused to admit it. They over-inflate the value of their assets and understate their liabilities in order to mask how serious a problem they face.

In other words they misinform us. If this is true they are also displaying Misguided Leadership because their actions are focused on short-term parochial targets rather than longer-term global ones. By hiding the problem they are preventing a search for effective solutions – Missing Leadership, and if any of this is done knowingly they are also being Machiavellian by acting in their own short-term selfish interest while putting all our finances at risk. Thus all four categories of MisLeadership are in evidence. Talbott's (2009:221) final conclusion is:

> There is much lying and cheating going on in the system, both on Wall Street and in Washington, but very little progress will be made until the root causes of this crisis are uncovered and corrected.

Many business leaders have not recognised the changing circumstances that make the current business paradigm unworkable and unsustainable as a long-term strategy. As Lorange's (2003:128) argues:

> Companies are facing today's global challenges with yesterday's national capabilities.

We conclude that UGIs of the type identified in Table 1.1 are of such number, significance and proportion, and business of such scale, power and influence that continued adoption of the paradigm outlined in Figure 4.4 will lead quickly and decisively to catastrophic global disasters. Many businesses have accepted this view and even taken it a step further by recognising that acting in a sustainable manner is a crucial part of their long-term strategy. As Collier and Esteban (2007) suggest:

> Tensions exist between commercial opportunities on the one hand and potential social impacts of their exploitation on the other, and sometimes hard choices have to be made. The activities of legitimate global business create havoc with climate, environment, biodiversity and the very basis

*of life on the planet ... Businesses themselves increasingly recognise that their future profitability and 'licence to operate' depend on their willingness to assume responsibility for the social and environmental consequences of their global footprint.*

## Attributes of a New Paradigm

The number and significance of urgent global issues (UGIs) present clear evidence that the current economic and social paradigm has not coped with the quantum leap in issues facing our world and is unsustainable in the long term. New maps, paradigms and ways of thinking are required in which consideration of UGIs and their resolution are a natural part of the purpose of business and society. This new paradigm may be along the lines illustrated in Figure 4.5. This is closely related to our view of mental and spiritual fitness, our focus on the importance of connectedness and purpose, on the paradigm Capra and Pauli (1995:5) call Holistic World View, and on the paradigm Covey (1999b:176) terms Principle-Centred Leadership.

| Organic Level | Attribute |
|---|---|
| **Leaders and decision-makers** | Act ethically, honestly and with integrity |
| | Are aware of global issues |
| | Recognise their role in shaping the future of humanity and the planet |
| | Work with the whole person and recognise that all aspects of their followers' lives are important, and need to be valued and nurtured |
| | Recognise that people are spiritual beings that want meaning and a sense of doing something that matters |
| **Organisations** | Co-operate with customers and suppliers, and collaborate with other businesses |
| | Actively minimise their use of natural resources and impact on the environment |
| | Focus on measures of performance other than financial and economic |
| | Contribute to the development of the local community and wider society |
| **Nations and Societies** | Recognise each others' basic humanity, value, rights and needs |
| | Act together to tackle issues |
| | Share resources fairly |
| | Steward natural resources and repudiate exploitation of people |

**Figure 4.5    Attributes of a New Business Paradigm**
*Source*: The Authors.

The emphasis in this paradigm is on a global view, treating each member of humanity as of equal value and all part of the same family such that the inequalities in the world illustrated at the start of Chapter 1 are reduced and the location of birth has less effect on a child's prospects.

This global view also encourages a more cooperative and collaborative approach. Competition has many advantages but is inherently wasteful in that the resources and effort put into competing by those who lose do not end up in a final product. We need to find ways of obtaining the benefits of both approaches. Again, thinking globally encourages stewardship of resources which is an important element given current level of consumption, as discussed in the case study in Chapter 2.

While we agree with Wilson's (1993, cited in Ghoshal 2005) point highlighted earlier that more people have an 'other-regarding' attitude than is generally accepted, we recognise that many currently do have a self-regarding, self-focused way of thinking. Ways must be found of protecting us and them from their own greed, so the new paradigm should discourage selfishness but at the same time guard against it.

Greed is a manifestation of negative spirituality which leads us to consider the other aspect of a global approach – being aware of and caring about the physical, mental and spiritual fitness of individuals, groups and societies, ultimately all of humanity and other life forms. We believe adoption of the GFF as a way of thinking about and analysing issues will help leaders cope with the complexities of the new environment as well as improving the effectiveness of their problem-solving. Paying attention to their own spiritual fitness should also help give them the courage and conviction to take some of the more complex decisions and carry them out. Our Embedded Values Cycle highlights the difficulty faced when we attempt to change our innermost beliefs and values to become more mentally and spiritually supple.

Chapter 8 will investigate how we can move toward adoption of such a paradigm. Whilst talk of the need for a new paradigm has been taking place for some time, the above discussion highlights why our exploration of it makes a significant contribution. A new paradigm on its own will not be sufficient but needs to be embedded in a whole system of reform, a reform that first recognises that a lot of current thinking and education have been built on ideas founded on MisLeadership thinking.

## Summary

This chapter introduced the concept of Misinformed Leadership. This is where the leader is unaware of important information, skills, techniques or consequences, misunderstands their importance, or misunderstands how to use them.

The potentially disastrous consequences of Misinformed Leadership were demonstrated by analysis and commentary on the parlous state of the financial markets.

Potential causes of Misinformed Leadership were summarised as lack of appropriate education; complex, rapidly changing environment; using outdated knowledge, world view or paradigm as the basis for making decisions; poor decision-making models; and wrong information resulting from the MisLeadership acts of others.

General approaches to tackling Misinformed Leadership were suggested including improved mental and spiritual suppleness, and specific applications illustrated.

Weaknesses and fundamental flaws in the existing paradigm that underpins current economic and social thinking were exposed and an outline of the attributes required in a new paradigm provided.

---

### POINTS FOR REFLECTION

1.   When an individual is able, by exploitation of system weaknesses, to cause billions of pounds worth of damage, who is to blame and who is carrying the risks?
2.   What other elements do you feel are important in a new paradigm?
3.   What is required to facilitate this paradigm shift in our thinking?

---

## References

Avery, G.C. (2005). *Leadership for Sustainable Futures: Achieving Success in a Competitive World*. Northampton: Edward Elgar.

BBC News. 22/07/99. *How Leeson broke the bank*. [Online]. Available at: http://news.bbc.co.uk/1/hi/business/375259.stm [accessed: 15/10/09].

BBC News. 22/07/99. *Leeson scandal 'could happen again'*. [Online]. Available at: http://news.bbc.co.uk/1/hi/business/the_economy/375184.stm    [accessed: 15/10/09].

Boush, D.M., Friestad, M. and Wright, P. (2009). *Deception in the Marketplace*. Hove: Routledge.

Capra, F. and Pauli, G. (1995). *Steering Businesses Towards Sustainability*. Tokyo: United Nations University Press.

Collier, J. and Esteban, R. (2007). Corporate Social Responsibility and Employee Commitment. *Business Ethics: A European Review*, vol. 16, no. 1, January.

Covey, S.R. (1999a). *The 7 Habits of Highly Effective People*. London: Simon and Schuster.

Covey, S.R. (1999b). *Principle-Centred Leadership*. London: Simon and Schuster UK Ltd.

Dunne, S., Harney, S and Parker, M. (2008). The Responsibilities of Management Intellectuals: A survey. *Organization*, vol.15 (2), 271–82.

Ghoshal, S. (2005). Bad Management Theories are Destroying Good Management Practices. *Academy of Management Learning and Education*, vol. 4(1), 75–91.

*Guardian*. (2005). Timeline for Bank of Credit and Commerce International. The *Guardian* [Online, 2 November]. Available at: http://www.guardian.co.uk/business/2005/nov/02/bcci.money1 [accessed: 15/10/09].

Keynes, J.M. (1920). [Online]. Available at: http://www.maynardkeynes.org/keynes-the-speculator.html [accessed: 19/10/09].

Kirkup, J. (2008). Gordon Brown admits he was wrong to claim he had ended 'boom and bust'. *Daily Telegraph* [Online]. Available at: http://www.telegraph.co.uk/finance/financetopics/recession/3497533/ [accessed: 19/10/08].

Langthorne, S. (2008). Strategic Financial Analysis of the takeover of HBOS by Lloyds TSB. Submitted as part of an MBA at Anglia Ruskin University.

Lorange, P. (2003). Global responsibility – business education and business schools – roles in promoting a global perspective. *Corporate Governance*, vol. 3, no. 3, 126–35.

Rayment, J.J. (2001). *Decision Making and Problem Solving Using Logic and Magic*. Essex: Earlybrave.

Talbott, J.R. (2009). *The 86 Biggest Lies on Wall Street*. London: Constable and Robinson.

Thatcher, M. (2009). *The Truth Hurts*. [Online]. Available at: http://opinion.publicfinance.co.uk/2009/09/the-truth-hurts/ [accessed: 10/10/09].

Trillin, C. (2009). *Wall Street Smarts*. [Online]. Available at: http://www.nytimes.com/2009/10/14/opinion/14trillin.html [accessed: 19/10/09].

# 5

# Machiavellian Leadership and the Need for a Contemporary Mission

Our final category of MisLeadership is the only one that we say is deliberate. It is where the leader attempts to achieve hidden personal objectives and does this by exploiting the trust, friendship, loyalty and ignorance (of the leader's true objectives) of other human beings. Cohen et al. 2001, (as cited in Boush et al. 2009) offer a definition of deception which we feel closely relates to Machiavellian Leadership:

> Deception is the set of acts that seek to increase the chances that a set of targets will behave in a desired fashion when they would be less likely to behave in that fashion if they knew of those acts.

This definition emphasises the pivotal role of the follower (employees, for example, in an organisational context). If followers suspect they are being misled, the leaders' objectives may be ruined or undermined, and their credibility reduced. Trust, friendship and loyalty – some of the most positive aspects of being part of humanity – will also all be threatened. Sometimes the follower is aware of the MisLeadership but willing to go along with or condone it for reasons we explore in Chapter 6.

In our view, this combination of deliberate deception and exploitation for personal gain makes Machiavellian Leadership the worst form of MisLeadership. We commence our study of Machiavellian Leadership with a review of the baby-milk industry.

## The Baby-Milk Industry

Save The Children is a UK-based charity set up in 1919 to help children suffering as a result of the First World War and it has been working in the area of child protection ever since. Its website outlines how some companies violate the baby-milk code, despite around 1.4 million children dying annually due to lack of mother's milk.

According to their website, Save the Children (n.d.) has found that despite a UN approved code to regulate the marketing of baby milk and food, manufacturers still vigorously promote their products unethically, in ways that flout the code, and rarely face any sanctions. These manufacturers market food and drink to babies from four months – contravening World Health Organization (WHO) guidance, which recommends exclusive breastfeeding until six months – and use telephone support lines and websites to contact mothers, which is banned by the code.

Government campaigns promoting breastfeeding are dwarfed by marketing campaigns for manufactured baby food, Save the Children claiming that in Bangladesh, the total value of baby milk and food imports is almost £16 million per year – 100 times more than the government of Bangladesh can afford to invest in supporting breastfeeding promotion.

Milk powder marketing illustrates many of the issues in Machiavellian Leadership. Companies are making good profits out of a product they claim to be beneficial and within the law, while a charity with no obvious reason to undermine such a product is claiming foul play. The situation is muddied because there is genuine debate as to whether breast feeding is preferable and under what circumstances; environmental conditions, prosperity and literacy levels are very different in various parts of the world; the product itself seems to be fine if used in the correct way and for babies of the right age; international agencies have taken lukewarm action and failed to enforce even that.

Save the Children claim use of infant formula instead of breast-feeding causes thousands of unnecessary infant deaths every day. The deaths are caused indirectly, that is, the actual product is fine but access to pure water to mix the powder into milk is limited in many countries, particularly for poor parents whose children are often the most needy, so the milk can become contaminated. Breast milk is particularly important in the early months as it contains nutrients and antibodies which help the infant grow and develop its own immune system, hence the World Health Organization recommendation that it is used exclusively where possible for the first six months.

## Causes of Machiavellian Leadership

Having outlined the scope and extent of Machiavellian Leadership, we turn to its underlying causes. These can be summed up as leaders attempting to achieve hidden agendas and feeling they must do so secretively because they know, or suspect, their followers would rebel in some way if they knew the truth. As stated previously, they are exploiting the trust, friendship, loyalty and ignorance (of their true objectives) of other human beings. Not surprisingly, if they are found out all such positive aspects of being part of humanity are threatened.

As argued in Chapter 4, at an individual level, we see Machiavellian Leadership as a natural result of the Embedded Value Cycle operating as it does in a world where the infant is exposed to a mixture of truths, half-truths and lies from birth and is forced to accept that even those closest to them behave in this manner. There are so many social circumstances where we do not want to be told or tell the truth for fear of being upset or unnecessarily upsetting another person that we fall into habitual lying. In Chapter 4 we quoted two studies that revealed how commonplace lying may be.

This style of leadership may be due to jealousy, fear or ignorance. In each of these cases, the perpetrator tends to be looking at the short-term, one-off aspect and hoping to get away with it. Very often a particular managerial style can dominate an organisation such that it becomes the expected norm. Such indoctrination in the workplace can leave one feeling it is the only way to get on, everybody does it, and if those using the approach are seen to be successful, it becomes the right way and recognised as good management practice. Linked to these causes are a macho leadership style which is often based on arrogance, blind faith in one's own ability and a genuine feeling of superiority and the right to rule and exploit other people.

Those who have worked in the same organisation for a long time tend to discover ways to cheat the system, thereby obtaining extra resources or easing their workload. They may view this as a loyalty perk, particularly if it is shared between all the old hands.

McGregor (1960) found that there were two clearly distinct management styles, which he referred to as theory X and theory Y styles. A theory X manager assumes workers are lazy, will try to avoid work where possible and need constant supervision. From this mindset a manager will attempt to control employees, force them to work hard and be constantly on the lookout. A theory Y manager assumes work is natural and people will want to do it if they find it interesting, challenging and rewarding, thus they will look for ways to keep people involved, interested and motivated. Both theories tend to be self-fulfilling but for our purposes it is probably more likely to be theory X managers who adopt Machiavellian Leadership and expect a similar response from their staff.

Lickert (1967) identified four basic management systems: authoritarian exploitive, authoritarian benevolent, consultative and participative. Authoritarian exploitive is where the leader has a low concern for people and uses threats and other fear-based methods to achieve results. Authoritarian benevolent is where leaders do have concern for people and may use rewards to encourage effort but are still authoritarian in that they do not consult with their staff. Consultative is where the manager attempts to listen to subordinates but does not involve them in important decision-making. Participative is where the leader fully involves subordinates in decision-making and encourages them to adopt a team approach. On the face of it, it would seem that a Machiavellian leader would prefer an authoritarian exploitive system but it may be possible for such a leader to take on the disguise of one of the other three.

Machiavellian Leadership may follow from one of the other forms of MisLeadership in that the leader may recognise their failure but attempt to conceal it so as to avoid the personal consequences. This was the case, for example, in the latter stages of the Nick Leeson affair, when he knew he had lost a vast fortune but attempted to hide it while he frantically sought a lucky break to recover the position. This kind of behaviour may be seen as natural in that from his viewpoint the game was lost unless he pulled off the required masterstroke. From the wider picture, his continued desperate throes were the killer blows to the whole organisation. Another variation on this theme is where managers know they have to carry out an action that will be unpopular with their staff and attempt to do it secretively so as to retain their trust, friendship and loyalty. This is an understandable, possibly even laudable, approach but very risky because if they are found out the very things they are trying to retain will be severely threatened.

## Scale and Scope of Machiavellian Leadership

Machiavellian Leadership is so commonplace that it is what many people initially assume we mean by the term MisLeadership. This type of leadership could be about increasing the leader's own wealth, power, reputation, standing in the community, publication record, annual business results or shareholder value. It could have the objective of getting rid of trouble makers in the organisation, or people with an opposing view to the leader, or someone whom the leader considers to be a threat.

The pervasive nature of Machiavellian Leadership can be illustrated by listing some of the phrases readily associated with it. Theft, fraud, collusion, duress, excessive force, abuse of power, secret deals, bullying, threatening, confrontation, conflict, escalation, war, sabotage, subterfuge, posturing, brainwashing, slavery, entrapment, 'might is right', unethical, selfish, cheating, professional foul, rule bending, lying, hiding of information, corruption, exploitation, nepotism, glass ceilings, sticky floors, constructive dismissal, harassment, hidden agendas, bias, prejudice, murder, uncaring, manipulative, political manoeuvring, excessive competition and rivalry, industrial espionage. It is very likely you have some additional phrases you associate with this kind of leadership.

An immediate difficulty with Machiavellian Leadership is where the dividing line is between this form of MisLeadership and the other three we have discussed. We believe it is important to recognise that MisLeadership is only Machiavellian in our view when the leader deliberately attempts to achieve personal objectives; these are hidden from the people being misled; and the leader does it by some kind of exploitation.

This definition is loose and there is plenty of room for debate in specific instances. This is to be expected because of the very nature of Machiavellian Leadership: hidden and exploitive. The perpetrator will want to keep their actions and motives secret so will be inclined to deny their true nature. Often their actions will have involved some form of illegal, immoral or disciplinary offence, in which case they will be even more determined to avoid admission.

To illustrate the complex nature of this topic, consider a situation where a manager denies promotion to someone with a particular characteristic which the person involved assumes to be prejudice. To be satisfied that it was a Machiavellian action we have to make judgements about whether the person should have been given the promotion; whether the process undertaken was fair; was it correctly operated; was the decision so clear that failure to promote the person was definitely due to irrelevant factors? Even if all of this is accepted, we still have to be sure the managers did it in an exploitive manner and for their own benefit. Perhaps they genuinely believed that the characteristic in question was a valid reason for rejection, which might reflect ignorance on their part. They may have misunderstood the situation or just made a mistake or error of judgement.

Machiavellian Leadership could be thought of as a misnomer in that it is deliberately leading people in the wrong direction – to somewhere they do not want to be. Nevertheless, we believe it is still leadership as much as any of the other forms of MisLeadership – they all lead followers astray to some greater or lesser extent.

In many instances, a particular decision and course of action by a leader will contain elements that are good leadership, others that are accidental MisLeadership and some that are deliberately aimed at the leader's own ends. This could happen in, say, deciding whether to locate to a new building – the decision to move may be beneficial but the wrong location selected, and the manager may obtain an unnecessarily large and well-appointed office. Psychology is such that it may be impossible for even the leaders to know for sure whether or not they have included an element in the decision aimed specifically for their own benefit. If you give a promotion to a close friend, you may genuinely believe they are the best person for the job.

All genuine instances of Machiavellian Leadership have adverse consequences in that they fail to optimise global objectives. Where the action achieves the objectives of a particular organisation or nation to the detriment of humanity, we see this as placing personal objectives above global ones so fitting our definition.

Embedded values result in it being commonplace for there to be a tacit expectation that individuals will act in a Machiavellian way, so the other party to the transaction assumes this to be the case and responds accordingly. This is extremely common in budget setting and control. The expectation is that budgets will be cut by 10 per cent so you ask for 15 per cent more than you really need in the hope of having 5 per cent extra after the cut to allow some flexibility in case things go badly. You are promised a bonus if you achieve all of your targets but you know that your manager deliberately set one too high for you to achieve so you agree with a colleague that they can count some of your sales as theirs and you will share their bonus. Your manager knew you would do that but at least has only had to pay one lot of bonuses between the two of you. All the time and effort spent doing this kind of subterfuge is wasted and anyone who does not know the game or is too naïve to play it loses out. Use of words such as 'game' and 'play' undermine the serious nature of these activities.

As the scale and complexity of businesses has grown and globalised their leaders have become ever more powerful and the scope for them to act in a Machiavellian way to maximise the profits of their organisation has increased. As discussed in Chapter 4, there is a fine line between legitimate exploitation of market opportunities and weaknesses, which is an important element of the current economic/social paradigm, and acting in an unacceptable way. This issue is exacerbated by the facts that many national governments are corrupt so prepared to pass laws which facilitate exploitation of their natural resources and even citizens, and corporations have been far more successful at globalisation than have nations, inhibited as they are by geographical boundaries. In many respects individual nations have a vested interest in NOT globalising as it weakens their national identity.

Managers in large organisations may be more concerned about their own jobs and prospects than those of the organisation so act in their own self-interest. For example, in takeovers they ensure they have a good position in the new company or gain a high severance package thus they insist on clauses in their contracts which guarantee them such payoffs even if they have underperformed. These contracts may also include provision of performance bonuses again payable even if they have in fact underperformed. Boards may be dominated by executive directors, non-executive directors often being weak and not truly independent. Top-level executives tend to be on the boards of several companies such that there is effectively a club whose members all have vested interests in ensuring that each other's pay and prospects are protected. They naturally argue that their high pay is justified.

One well-known example of the Machiavellian type of MisLeadership in business is the tobacco industry. For decades the industry has conspired to hide the addictive and deadly nature of cigarettes. Michaels, 2008 (as cited by Boush et al. 2009), identifies an interesting point here when he draws from a notorious memo in which a tobacco industry executive said that doubt is the company's real product since creating doubt about the health risks from smoking is the essential corporate marketing strategy. It is often this doubt that inhibits people from challenging a leader's actions and which allows the MisLeadership to continue. The tobacco industry is one of the cases we explore in more detail in Chapter 7.

A helpful exploration of Machiavellian Leadership within marketing and marketplace deception skills is provided by Boush, Friestad and Wright (2009: 1–3) who argue:

> *Deception pervades human social life (p. 1) … the American marketplace has a cancer, and that cancer is deception (p. 2) and … deception is a central and inevitable part of marketplace interaction (p. 3).*

We agree but broaden their assertion to claim that Machiavellian Leadership occurs in every aspect of public and private life, and in every country.

Boush et al. (2009:7) go on to suggest:

> *In marketplace communication, all deceptiveness is intentional. All marketing communications are consciously planned, designed, and executed by communication professionals. In our view, a marketer is always responsible for any action or inaction that has a reasonable likelihood of misleading and deceiving consumers.*

The above quotation explains why we have included the misleading marketing activities of organisations in our Machiavellian, conscious MisLeadership category. Organisations clearly adopt this approach in order to increase their sales and profits, but we say it is Machiavellian because it is unlikely to be in the best interests of the consumer or wider society.

Boush et al. (2009:5) provide a useful list of deception (Machiavellian Leadership) examples which include:

- Deceptions that are rooted in the careful choice of words, and the construction of prose texts to imply things without stating them

- The strategic alteration of photos, videos, and other visual representations

- Misrepresentations via numerical information and calculations, statistical information, and research results

- The artful omission, masking, camouflage, and obfuscation of information

- Incomplete and misleading framing of comparisons, risk information and decision problems

- Exaggeration, puffery, and marketing bullshit

- Blatant outright lying about product attributes and usage consequences.

Social animals tend to have leaders and followers and that applies to humanity. In ancient times, tribes tended to be led by an individual recognised by the rest of the tribe as being best equipped for the role. This would have been based on a combination of physical and mental fitness of the individual, coupled with support of allies. Such an individual/group would be able to make and enforce decisions that would generally lead to best outcomes for tribe members.

Many followers are content with their position but others are ambitious and want to take over leadership. At its most fundamental this would be via physically challenging the existing leadership, which is clearly dangerous so tends to be planned in secret and executed quickly, by surprise and with a hopefully pre-emptive stroke. In more civilised circumstances a challenge to power may tend toward such mental aspects as logical debate and negotiation but even so often backed by threat of physical force – 'might is right'. This attitude still dominates today.

Niccolò Machiavelli in his text *The Prince* written in the early sixteenth century outlined how leaders could achieve personal objectives, rather than those of their followers, through building and taking advantage of personal power and the ignorance of their followers. Jay (1967) outlined how such approaches are still used in modern organisations. By extension, this Machiavellian Leadership can be taken to include an organisation achieving its objectives rather than those of society, by exploiting its power and influence. On the global scale, it could be an individual nation putting the needs of its people before those of aliens (as the US immigration authorities refer to non-US citizens).

We will start this discussion at the society level then move through organisations to groups. At all levels, much of the power seeking and attempts to hold on to it are done by individuals but we leave exploration of the types of power and why people attempt to hold on to it to Chapter 6. Even so, it is important to recognise here that people in power do usually try to hold on to it even when it is clear that they are no longer the best equipped to make and enforce optimum decisions. They often initially attempt to achieve this by creating alliances but as their personal power wanes further or their ambition increases, may attempt to ensure power passes to those with similar attitudes and beliefs to theirs and ultimately to their physical descendants.

At the societal level, ways by which this search for permanent power was attempted historically include invention and exploitation of such concepts as royal families and religions, with the leader either claiming personal leadership of both aspects (for example, Moses) or power being shared between their leaders as was the case in ancient Egypt. These two power bases are now discussed from a Machiavellian viewpoint so while we believe what we say here the reader should be aware that it is deliberately written from a particular angle, and comes from a particular cultural influence in terms of the Embedded Values Cycle. It may therefore be MisLeadership to some extent – possibly even Machiavellian – so read it with an open but wary and critical mind.

In large nations where there are both royal families and religions, they have tended to be most successful when they have had separate leadership and structures from each other but acted in mutual support. This has enabled them to focus on their own area (secular and spiritual respectively) and provide apparently independent verification of each other's claim to power. Thus the religious leaders found ways to add their authority to the claims of the royal family to be the legitimate leaders of the tribe or nation, including crowning them in a religious service. The royal family supported the religious leaders and enhanced the importance of the faith by being ardent followers and giving generous physical support perhaps by way of finance or land, but also military at times of religious conflict. The root of the power of religions is their claim to be representatives of a god (or some other higher power) on earth, which clearly relies on followers believing in such a god. Support of secular leaders is highly valuable here.

While royal families and religions may be mutually dependent on each other, each wants to optimise their own power level so there is a tendency for conflict between them. Social unrest and power battles have tended to occur at times when one or other of these power bases has been weak and/or they have fought each other in an attempt to alter the balance of power.

Both have created formal structures to their organisation, enabling them to also create hierarchies to reflect the role, status and power of individuals and reward good and faithful service by promotion. As with all such structures, promotion is given partly on ability but also as a reward for past effort and to ensure the people climbing toward the top of the organisation have similar views and attitudes to those higher up. Thus it tends to be that promotions and other appointments at a particular level can only be made by people at a more senior level and the panel is often chaired by someone even higher up the hierarchy. The more senior the appointment, the more the selection processes tend to concentrate on the candidate's long-term objectives and strategy – helping those appointing to ensure they only appoint people with the desired values, character and approach.

## ROYALTY

Establishing the concept of royalty and royal descent seems to be the ultimate achievement of the power hungry since it theoretically ensures their line will continue to occupy the seat of power forever – or at least until someone else establishes a counter-claim and installs themselves and their heirs as the new royalty. To protect against such an event, the current royal dynasty must attempt to show their legitimate claim to the crown, based on descent from … whom? Or what?

It is a long tradition that royalty marries royalty; thus the ruling houses of Europe are closely related to one another and all current European monarchs are descendants of William I of England. Thus royalty can be seen as an exclusive club but so what? Do members of that club actually possess any characteristics that make them superior to the rest of us so as to legitimise their leadership role? Why should descent from William the Conqueror confer such special privileges, particularly in countries where he was not the king and probably never set foot there? If such descent had any true value or meaning, surely it would apply to all descendents and not be passed on to the eldest surviving legitimate male offspring, as is the norm – although not always the case, which casts further doubt on its legitimacy.

The extent of this MisLeadership has been extreme and of great consequence. At its peak in the UK the Crown claimed rights over all land in the country and the right to grant and withdraw occupancy, appointed lords and lesser ranks. Defying the monarch or rebellion was treason and punishable by death. The monarch lived such a lavish lifestyle that it could not be sustained in one location, so the whole court travelled the country forcing the gentry to act as their hosts, often ruining them in the process.

Since the position held so many perks, there were many people who coveted it. Some felt they had legitimate claims due to unclear inheritance, doubtful legitimacy of heirs and similar arguments, which is why so much attention is paid to the position in line of royal descendants. This clear setting out of relative position meant, however, that those fairly near the top realised that if they killed everyone with a higher claim than theirs they became the rightful ruler. This resulted in frequent bouts of blood-letting, particularly of close relatives. Inter-marriage between royal families resulted in many claims and counter-claims as to being the rightful ruler of neighbouring kingdoms, and the added power and glory from occupying another country led to constant disputes over borders and ownership resulting in plots, treason and war. All based on the doubtful concept of royal descent, backed up by the even more doubtful 'might is right' attitude.

The Crown sat at the top of a hierarchy of subservience with robber barons trying to increase their power base using similar tactics to those of royalty, and all ultimately living off the hard work of the farm labourers, known as serfs. Chapter 3 included an appraisal of the role of King Henry V at the Battle of Agincourt – do you feel he was a great leader for his time, Misguided, Machiavellian or a mix of all three?

## RELIGION

Catholic and other Christianity-based religions have been widespread across the world and have had tremendous influence. This section focuses particularly on these forms of religion but many of the points apply equally well to other forms of religious and spiritual belief.

Religious leaders created the church as their formal structure with individuals mainly being dealt with by their local priest, only being referred higher up the hierarchy if they themselves were powerful or there was an important point at stake.

In the case of religion it was not usually their physical descendents that the leaders were trying to keep in power but those who had the greatest faith in the teachings of the church. To gain promotion one had to show true dedication and subservience to the will of God, as expressed by senior church officials.

This may have included celibacy, thereby precluding the passing of power to a direct descendent. In some religions it was forbidden for those not ordained as a church minister to attempt to contact God directly; they had instead to either ask a priest to do so on their behalf or ask for assistance and intervention from a lesser spirit.

As you will recall from Chapter 3, our definition of spirituality is much broader than religion and one of the difficulties we have with some religions is the fact that they tend to have usurped the term and concept of spirituality as having to be based on belief in some form of god(s). This chapter has only very briefly touched on the topic of religion to consider it as a means of taking and keeping power through establishment of a hierarchy. Chapter 7 includes a deeper exploration in which the focus is broadened to a general review of the actions of religions and extent to which they could be viewed as MisLeadership. An important point to make here is that, providing they were acting in genuine faith and belief that their actions were valid and aimed at a higher purpose, religious leaders were not being Machiavellian by our definition. That would only be the case if they did not themselves believe but used the cover of religion to obtain their own ends.

## REPUBLICS

At various stages of history and in different countries instead of a royal family assuming the right to run the secular side of the nation's affairs, it has been run through the will of the people. On first thoughts one might assume that this kind of approach is a clear advance from the idea that a royal family should rule based on a highly dubious claim of lineage. It should be recalled, however, that both Greece and Rome operated as republics for centuries long before royalty took hold in Europe, but also that the Arab world, including the Egyptians and Israelites, had operated with a royal family for thousands of years before that and to a large part still does today.

Where a republican approach is adopted, the people vote on who should be in power for a given period. In all but the smallest nations, the voters are divided into areas and each area elects one or more representative to the central decision-making body. There are many variations to the structure including whether the top position is voted for separately from that of individual seats, is chosen by a free vote of all the representatives, or where there is a party system in operation, just by members of the party in power. Being in power is clearly preferable to being in opposition, so it is tempting for those seeking election to use Machiavellian methods. Seats may be sold; voting rigged; certain people may have more than one vote, others no vote; seat boundaries may be drawn to favour a particular party.

Possibly the most extreme version of a party using Machiavellian methods to win power was that of Nazi Germany. In many ways Hitler could be seen as a great leader. As Drucker (2003:102) identified, Hitler had a great deal of charisma, excellent oratory power and a clear vision. Unfortunately this vision was not for the common good and is a classic example of our Machiavellian category. Hitler also used many horrific Machiavellian strategies to try and achieve his vision: opposition supporters were threatened and several murdered; and 'enemies' were created via myths, rumours and propaganda for people to unite against.

## HIDDEN AGENDAS

It is extremely difficult to guess what hidden agendas a person or organisation may have when taking part in a particular decision. They might be looking for promotion or an easy life, to increase their own importance in the organisation or be made redundant, to get you sacked or give you a secret helping hand. Equally, they may have what from their stance are valid fears about a possible change such as whether they can cope, will their existing lifestyle be threatened, or will they have to admit to knowing nothing about the internet or a new product.

In all of these situations one can improve the chances of success by listening carefully, paying particular attention to phraseology and body language; thinking carefully about the situation from a number of angles; attempting to put yourself in their place to see how it would feel; asking open questions and giving the opportunity for them to ask questions. Many of these may be seen as just good leadership/management practice, or perhaps they could be thought of as using emotional or spiritual intelligence.

Missing, Misguided and Misinformed Leadership are widespread but relatively simple to start to tackle as we have shown in the last three chapters:

- Missing – examine and improve decision-making

- Misguided – encourage and develop a global perspective

- Misinformed – develop a new paradigm by using mind games to search for truth.

Machiavellian is the only one where the leader is knowingly working against the ultimate goals and bigger picture. Resistance to change is likely to be far greater in this form than for the other three because the leaders may well believe theirs is the right approach in that all they are doing is following natural evolution-based instincts for survival, domination and growth; they may see it as naïve to act in an open manner when all around them are achieving their own hidden agendas – and anyone suggesting otherwise is clearly naïve too; the leaders will see the immediate personal benefits gained by their actions, and they may fear that if they do not act in this way they will be exploited themselves.

It is pertinent to note that much of the behaviour outlined above is in line with free market theory and philosophy. The managers are purely acting in their own self-interest, exploiting market weaknesses to maximise their own positions.

The ethical component to MisLeadership was identified in Chapter 1. The focus on ethics has received a new vitality since the financial crisis. It is clearly an important element in effective leadership, and a lack of ethical motivation and practice may be another reason for a Machiavellian approach. This is clearly articulated by Daly, Speedy and Jackson (2007:91):

> The distinguishing feature of leadership ethics is the profound relationship that exists between ethical leadership and effective leaders. Ethics lies at the very heart of leadership and that without ethics there can be no leadership only mis-leadership of the kind exemplified by Adolf Hitler.

Table 5.1 summarises the possible reasons for Machiavellian Leadership discussed.

## Results of Machiavellian Leadership

By our definition, Machiavellian Leadership fails to optimise global objectives. This type of leadership will, however, often remain undetected for some time until the leader becomes over-confident and increases the scale of deception. The study of the financial markets revealed many instances where initial minor irregularities went undetected and grew into major frauds. This is one reason why it is important to detect and end such activities as quickly as possible.

**Table 5.1        Possible reasons for Machiavellian Leadership**

| |
|---|
| Attempting to achieve hidden agendas |
| Ambition |
| Clinging on to power |
| Spill-over from social life |
| Selfish small-mindedness |
| Accepted management style |
| Knock-on effect of accidental MisLeadership |
| Leaders having too narrow a focus |
| Natural element of existing paradigm |
| Unethical leadership practices |

Once discovered this kind of activity is likely to have very detrimental effects on the spiritual aspects within the organisation. Trust, friendship and loyalty will all suffer, with consequent effects on morale, motivation, dedication, willingness to cooperate, collaborate and share knowledge openly.

If those carrying out the acts are left in leadership roles there could be open hostility or more subtle friction and resistance. Depending on the type of act that took place, people may feel unsafe, insecure and physically or mentally threatened. Future leaders may regard the lack of disciplinary action as tacit approval and that it is the expected way for leaders to behave. This can become a culture of bullying and exploitation.

'Tragedy of the commons' is an expression used to represent the situation where a limited resource is shared by several people. Providing individuals only uses their fair share, all can have a reasonable standard of living, but once some start to use more than their share all will tend to follow, with potentially disastrous results. The classic illustration is where several people share common land and each has one cow on it. Any individual would be better off by placing a second cow on the land but if all do so, there will not be enough grass for all the cows so they all may starve to death. Much Machiavellian Leadership is of this nature and can have similar results, particularly if it becomes an open secret such that everyone is acting in this selfish way.

Followers who suspect a leader may have hidden agendas may spend a great deal of time and effort attempting to 'second-guess' what the hidden agendas are, whether to go along with or challenge them, how to minimise their negative affects and so on. This can lead to stress, burn-out or retaliation, particularly when the staff are insecure due, say, to a downturn in the market or rumours of a takeover. Where Machiavellian Leadership is practised rumours tend to multiply because much of the information is kept secret and people naturally want to be aware of as many hidden agendas as they can so as to protect their own position.

The approach adopted by much of the media is in our opinion a major cause of Machiavellian behaviour in the UK. They condone the misleading advertising placed in their publications and seem to be prepared to stoop quite low in order to sell copy to make money. Their approach is typically hostile and negative and often includes xenophobia. Stars are created then knocked down. Cameras with extremely powerful lenses are used to obtain photographs deliberately designed to show the person in the picture in the worst possible light. Facts in stories are often massaged to provide a particularly damaging headline. Many people who are bombarded with this kind of message will find it enters their value cycle and becomes the embedded accepted way to behave.

The prevalence of deception in marketing has been mentioned above with reference made to Boush et al. (2009:5) and their list of deception types. This kind of approach can result in worthless, even harmful, products being marketed and advertised as beneficial and useful. This may at least in part be the case in the baby-milk industry as discussed at the start of this chapter. It is certainly the case with the cigarette industry to be studied in Chapter 7 as part of the asbestos industry case study. When adopting this approach to the market place, companies may be following the letter of the law rather than its spirit.

Palliative treatments and drugs may be developed rather than curative ones so the patient has to keep buying drugs instead of getting well. Development of drugs for baldness and erectile malfunction may be given priority over those for HIV/AIDS since that is where the money is. Health and safety standards may be kept at the minimum possible level and only actually implemented if forced, which may be rarely. Vehicles may be manufactured with obsolescence deliberately built in. Pressure groups, cartels and trade associations may be set up to lobby for weak rules and controls as happened in the financial markets collapse, when the senior bankers all agreed that it was not their fault and they should continue to be paid their contractual bonuses. In the extreme, this style of leadership also underpins prostitution, drug- and people-trafficking and consequent degradation and loss of self-esteem.

'Market forces' are sometimes used to justify this kind of product but also cost reduction via such approaches as starvation wages, disgusting conditions and terms of employment by companies who base their manufacturing in low cost parts of the world, while at the same time the company is making huge profits. These international corporations are able to avoid tighter standards in their home market in such areas as work hours, minimum wages, age limits, holidays and health and safety conditions and are also able to sell products in ways banned there as was seen in the baby-milk case and will be shown in Chapter 7 in the cigarette and asbestos market studies. They may also locate their offices around the world and use transfer pricing mechanisms to minimise the tax they pay and take maximum advantage of any subsidies.

Much of the pressure for this kind of exploitive behaviour comes directly from the market system and its incessant clamour for more profit. The more profit that is made, the more people buy the shares, so the price goes up and they demand more profit. Bakan (2005) illustrates this when he shows how Ford was forced to keep the price of his cars higher than he would have liked by shareholders wanting their maximum return on investment. Küffner (2009) looks at the actions of the major international corporation Chevron against residents in the Amazon jungle of Ecuador.

## Ways to Address Machiavellian Leadership

We now turn to three ways in which Machiavellian Leadership might begin to be tackled. As we have seen this is one of the most difficult of the MisLeadership elements to address and our proposals will clearly not resolve all the issues. As we have argued in Chapter 1, however, we encourage a logical incremental approach and we hope our approaches will assist in getting started on what may be a long and difficult journey. The first proposal relates to education, the second to actions which followers can take to reduce the effects of Machiavellian Leadership – we head this section 'Group Dynamics'. The third, headed 'Contemporary Mission', encourages the leader to adopt a completely different mission.

### EDUCATION

The ideal solution to Machiavellian Leadership is fundamental to the purpose underlying this book. It comes back to helping leaders challenge the embedded values that result in MisLeadership focus and re-educating them to recognise their true role as a global leader and encourage them to move towards Globally Fit Leadership as will be outlined in Chapter 6. Chapter 7 includes case studies illustrating the moves already being taken by many organisations towards such an approach and Chapter 8 sets out our action plan for the initial steps in this process.

## GROUP DYNAMICS

Leaders can only lead if followers follow. As a result, the approach adopted by a leader can be influenced by followers and so they play an important role in tackling general Machiavellian Leadership.

Formalising procedures can be an immediate way of reducing the ability of the leader to achieve hidden agendas. Such formal procedures cost time and money, and may stifle creativity and use of mind games approaches. They are, however, useful ways to help ensure valid decisions are taken and people feel involved, consulted and valued.

Followers might also encourage their leaders to take part in open discussion of problems and their solutions to ensure they are aware of all the issues and consequences. When they hear the arguments of their followers and see their commitment it may cause them to reflect on whether their hidden agenda is justified – even from their own perspective. In open discussions the leaders may find it difficult to justify the intended approach which can cause them to reveal what is behind it, thereby giving followers the chance to react. Taking a more positive view, the leaders' intentions may not have actually been Machiavellian and they may have just been struggling with one of the other forms of MisLeadership, particularly Misinformed. Once they are aware of all relevant points, they may be happy to change their view and approach.

## CONTEMPORARY MISSION

All of the examples of Machiavellian Leadership discussed above, particularly when related to the urgent global issues we are faced with, illustrate that for the good of humanity and all other life forms, objectives now need to extend an individual's focus from purely self-interest to one which considers the interests of humanity at large. This must then be applied at all levels such that organisations lose their fixation with their own short-term performance (often maximising shareholder value) to becoming more of what Bartlett and Ghoshal (as cited in Manville n.d:2) term a social institution. This is an institution whose centre of gravity is its people, their working relationships, and their sense of meaning and purpose in the workplace, and where the organisation recognises amongst other things its role in addressing the larger social issues facing our planet.

This means that leaders must recognise these wider aims and include them within the scope of their role. The importance of people within organisations is now widely recognised also, with phrases like 'Our People are our most important asset' being common. As discussed in Chapter 3, if these people are to be motivated and fully engaged all aspects to their well-being have to be considered – physical, mental and spiritual – in a holistic approach. If followers are not happy, content and fulfilled, their leaders must surely have failed in an important element of their task. The idea that people can be expected to work for eight hours or more a day, feeling unhappy and undervalued, must be challenged.

Leaders need to establish a mission and objectives for their organisation which take into account changing circumstances and include consideration of UGIs. In order to have the right values to be able to achieve this, they will need to reverse the Embedded Values Cycle by challenging their current ways of thinking. This may be through personal reflection, education, exposure to the effects of their actions, and analysis and discussion of complex scenarios similar to those faced in their world. It is likely to involve the type of whole person learning advocated by Taylor (2007).

At the national level, the contemporary mission becomes one of leaders integrating their own nation with all others in the world so that we can move toward a genuinely global approach.

Those individuals, organisations or nations who respond to this call positively and are looking to adopt a global-facing mission will have to decide how to deal with those that fail to respond in that way. Disciplinary action and prosecution will almost certainly play a role but should be regarded as the final rather than first solution. It is much better and there is more likelihood of long-term success if such people can be persuaded to change their view and attitude through education and discussion.

The Globally Responsible Leadership Initiative (GRLI 2009), a partnership between the European Foundation for Management Development and the UN

Global Compact aims to promote understanding of what constitutes responsible leadership by focusing on three key areas:

- The need to change how people learn

- A new definition of the purpose of business

- The need to embrace concepts of globally responsible leadership in every aspect of education.

One of the GRLI's proposed actions for leaders, which matches our suggestions here for a contemporary mission, is the need to re-visit the raison d'être of the firm. The GRLI stands for formulating the purpose of the globally responsible business in the following terms: 'Create economic and societal progress in a globally responsible and sustainable way'.

Our own proposal for a mission statement which we believe is suitable for all organic levels of humanity worldwide is:

> *Developing a sustainable, just and fulfilling human presence on the planet.*

## Summary

Machiavellian Leadership is the only form of MisLeadership that we say is deliberate. It is where the leader attempts to achieve hidden personal objectives and does this by exploiting the trust, friendship, loyalty and ignorance (of the leader's true objectives) of other human beings. MisLeadership is only Machiavellian in our view when the leader deliberately attempts to achieve personal objectives, these are hidden from the people being misled, and the leader does it by some kind of exploitation. All genuine instances of Machiavellian Leadership have adverse consequences in that they fail to optimise global objectives. Where a secret action is taken that achieves the objectives of a particular organisation or nation to the detriment of humanity, we see this as placing personal objectives above global ones and thus fitting our definition.

If a follower suspects they are being misled, the leader's objectives may be undermined and their credibility reduced. Trust, friendship and loyalty

– some of the most positive aspects of being part of humanity – will also all be threatened.

Milk-powder marketing illustrates many of the complexities in Machiavellian Leadership. Companies are making good profits out of a product they claim to be beneficial and within the law; a charity is claiming foul play; the situation is muddied; there is genuine debate; environmental conditions, prosperity and literacy levels are very different in various parts of the world; the product itself seems to be fine if used in the correct way; international agencies have taken lukewarm action and failed to enforce it.

In our view, this combination of deliberate deception and exploitation for personal gain makes Machiavellian Leadership the worst form of MisLeadership. It is so commonplace that many people assume initially that it is what we mean by the term MisLeadership. Machiavellian Leadership is like a pervasive cancer and occurs in every aspect of public and private life, and in every country. The extent of this form of MisLeadership has been extreme and of great consequence. As the scale and complexity of businesses has grown and globalised their leaders have become ever more powerful and the scope for them to act in a Machiavellian way to maximise the profits of their organisation has increased. Managers in large organisations may be more concerned about their own jobs and prospects than those of the organisation so act in their self-interest.

Causes of Machiavellian Leadership can be summed up as a leader attempting to achieve hidden agendas and feeling they must do so secretively because they know, or suspect, their followers would rebel in some way if they knew the truth.

It includes an organisation achieving its objectives rather than those of society, by exploiting its power and influence. On the global scale, it could be an individual nation putting the needs of its people before those of others. At the societal level it includes invention and exploitation of such concepts as royal families and religions. Both of these have created formal structures to their organisation, enabling them to also create hierarchies to reflect the role, status and power of individuals and reward good and faithful service by promotion. Establishing the concept of royalty and royal descent is the ultimate achievement of the power hungry since it theoretically ensures their line will continue to occupy the seat of power – forever.

We have argued that Machiavellian Leadership is a natural result of the Embedded Value Cycle operating in a world where the infant is exposed to a mixture of truths, half-truths and lies from birth and is forced to accept that even those closest to them behave in this manner. Other causes of this style of leadership include jealousy, fear and pure ignorance due to a selfish small-mindedness

Indoctrination in the workplace can leave one feeling it is the only way to get on, everybody does it, and if those using the approach are seen to be successful, it becomes the right way and recognised as good management practice. Linked to these causes are a macho leadership style which is often based on arrogance, blind faith in one's own ability and a genuine feeling of superiority and the right to rule and exploit other people.

Resistance to change is likely to be far greater than for the other three because the leader may well believe theirs is the right approach. By our definition, Machiavellian Leadership will fail to optimise global objectives.

Education, group dynamics and a contemporary mission are suggested as three ways in which Machiavellian Leadership can be tackled.

The urgent global issues we are faced with illustrate that for the good of humanity and all other life forms, objectives now need to extend an individual's focus from purely self-interest to one which considers the interests of humanity at large. In order to have the right values to be able to achieve this, they will need to reverse the Embedded Values Cycle by challenging their current ways of thinking through obtaining relevant education and exposure to the effects of their actions and analysis and discussion of complex scenarios similar to those faced in their world.

At the national level, the mission becomes one of integrating their own nation with all others in the world so that we can move toward a genuinely global approach.

**POINTS FOR REFLECTION**

1.  Which aspects of Machiavellian Leadership have you experienced?
2.  When we discussed the origination of religions and royal families, we warned that it was from a Machiavellian viewpoint so may be MisLeadership to some extent. We encouraged you there to read it with an open but wary and critical mind. Were you able to do this, or were you sucked in to the flow of the argument such that you lost the challenging, critical edge?
3.  To what extent did you agree with the thrust of the argument? Were there any particular points that you could not accept?
4.  If so, did they cause you to dismiss the whole idea or were you able to stay with the general debate?
5.  Were you able to come up with your own viewpoint at the end?
6.  How different was this from your original position?
7.  One of our main concerns in the book is that it is very difficult for us as individuals, groups or societies to reverse the Embedded Values Cycle. Do you agree? What do you think is the best way of doing it?
8.  How do you feel you can begin to overcome Machiavellian Leadership?

## References

Bakan, J. (2005). *The Corporation: The Pathological Pursuit of Profit and Power*. New York: Free Press.

Boush, D.M., Friestad, M. and Wright, P. (2009). *Deception in the Marketplace*. Hove: Routledge.

Daly, J., Speedy, S. and Jackson, D. (2007). *Nursing Leadership*. New South Wales: Elsevier.

Drucker, P.F. (2003). *The New Realities*. New Jersey, USA: Transaction Publishers.

Globally Responsible Leadership Initiative (GRLI). (2009). *The globally responsible leader – A Call for Action*. [Online]. Available at: http://www.grli.org/images/stories/grli per cent20manifesto per cent202008 per cent20final.pdf [accessed: 10/10/09].

Jay, A. (1967). *Management and Machiavelli*. New York: Holt, Rinehart and Winston.

Küffner, S. (2009). *Ecuador v Chevron: Do the Videos Implicate the Judge? Time* magazine [Online, 3 September]. Available at: http://www.time.com/time/world/article/0,8599,1920104,00.html

Likert, R. (1967). *The Human Organisation: Its Management and Value*. New York: McGraw-Hill.

Machiavelli, N. (2003). *The Prince*. Translated by George Bull. London: Penguin Classics.

McGregor, D. (1987). *The Human Side of Enterprise*. London: Penguin.

Manville, B. (n.d). *Competing on Human Capital: Chris Bartlett and Sumantra Ghoshal on a book in progress*. [Online]. Available at: http://www.linezine.com/7.2/articles/cbsghcbip.htm [accessed: 10/10/09].

Save The Children. (n.d). [Online]. Available at: http://www.savethechildren.org.uk/en/41_955.htm [accessed: 1/10/09].

Taylor, B. (2007). *Learning for Tomorrow. Whole Person Learning*. West Yorkshire: Oasis Press.

# 6

# MisLeadership and the Need for Globally Fit Leadership

In Chapter 1 we said that one way of looking at the leadership crisis is through the lens of the Leadership Fitness Continuum shown in Figure 6.1. In this figure Globally Fit Leadership (GFL) is our term for the best possible leadership that humans are capable of, while Diabolical Leadership would be the worst possible. Actual Leadership Fitness represents the quality or fitness level of leadership currently taking place. The gap between actual and globally fit leadership is the room for improvement and that between actual and diabolical leadership the extent to which we should be pleased with the leadership we have.

In this chapter we look more closely at this continuum, explore its validity and tease its meanings and implications.

## Leadership Fitness Continuum Expanded

The first aspect we consider is the extent to which leadership is 'everything'. Figure 6.1 might give the impression that leadership fitness level is the only thing that determines the level of achievement of our objectives such that if we had GFL the world would be perfect, with diabolical leadership it would be unbearable and wherever the leadership fitness level happens to be at a particular time is the extent of current fulfilment and overall well-being. In practice, there are many factors that will influence the degree of fulfilment and we have depicted this in Figure 6.2.

In Figure 6.2 the ultimate goal of humanity is shown as 'Heaven on Earth' (a proposal from Rutte 2005), with the opposite extreme being 'Hell on Earth'. Even if you do not believe in either place, we hope you can understand the vision. The non-leadership factors that affect our fulfilment, or whatever our

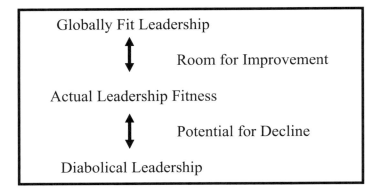

**Figure 6.1     Leadership Fitness Continuum**

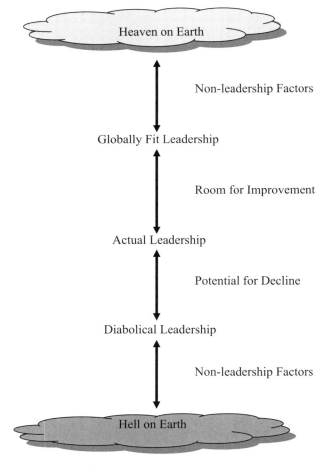

**Figure 6.2     Leadership Fitness Continuum (expanded)**
*Source*: The Authors.

objective is, include fitness and motivation of followers, their willingness to go against the orders and wishes of their leaders, extent to which the leader is accepted, demand and supply of resources, expectation level and natural disasters. Recognition of this linkage but mismatch between leadership fitness and achievement of objectives is crucial to understanding some of the complexities examined in this chapter.

Reasons why followers follow apparently bad leaders are discussed later in the chapter but it is worth pointing out here that heaven on earth can be a vision but never reality for everyone. Even if there were infinite resources there would still be jealousy; there will always be cases of unrequited love; people will be born with physical and mental imperfections; we all get old and die. We can have a vision of what heaven on earth would be though and keep striving for this. This vision is a very useful way of considering whether humanity is making progress and also for weighing up the validity of a great many individual actions whether global or on a small scale. Fortunately, hell on earth also has limitations – there will always be someone who is happy!

Actual leadership represents the quality or fitness level of leadership currently taking place, with actual fulfilment and well-being linked to it. The gap between actual and globally fit leadership is the room for leadership improvement. Put another way, this gap is MisLeadership and the focus of this book. The gap between actual and diabolical leadership is the extent to which we should be pleased with the leadership we have but also be a warning of the consequences of backsliding.

The reason behind the crisis in leadership is that the fitness level of current leadership is not sufficiently high to cope with the challenges of the modern environment. The key question is where are we on the continuum? If we are further from heaven on earth than we were it may reflect a decline in leadership fitness, increased difficulty of the leadership challenge or rising expectations. It could be that the gap between actual and globally fit leadership is large and growing but this is due to increasing complexity and expectations rather than a lowering of leadership fitness per se. This comes back to the concept of fitness for purpose – the leadership may be fitter but the standard required to be a Globally Fit Leader may have risen even more. Thus it would be Misguided to assume that if there is a large gap between actual and globally fit leadership it must reflect falling quality of leadership. We come back to these points later in the chapter but turn our attention now to the categories of MisLeadership and elements of GFL, and how these link into the above thoughts.

## Categories of MisLeadership

In Chapters 2 to 5 we looked in some detail at the four types of MisLeadership and one step towards resolution for each. We emphasised that these four steps, summarised in Figure 6.3, will not completely resolve all aspects of MisLeadership but that they are four important steps on the journey.

| Category of MisLeadership | | Globally Fit Leadership Element |
|---|---|---|
| Missing | → | Effective Decision Making |
| Misguided | → | Global Perspective |
| Misinformed | → | New Paradigm |
| Machiavellian | → | Contemporary Mission |

**Figure 6.3     Elements of Globally Fit Leadership**
*Source*: The Authors.

Each of the four categories has so far been assumed to link smoothly to a specific element of GFL with the assumption that improving any element will help tackle the related category of MisLeadership and improve the overall fitness level. To close the gap between actual and globally fit leadership we need to identify and reduce the MisLeadership that is taking place. It is a continuum so every improvement we make to actual fitness will move up the continuum.

The way forward is of course more complex than we describe above. In reality there are likely to be many forms of MisLeadership and many elements to GFL. It is also fair to say that there is not an exact match or causality between specific categories and elements as depicted in Figure 6.3. We encourage you to reflect on our categories and elements – are they clear, unambiguous, separate and comprehensive? What others could be added? If you feel those offered are wrong or too simplistic we encourage you to develop more appropriate ones and share them with us. We hope the four categories and elements discussed are sufficient however to illustrate the points we wish to highlight and to spark your imagination.

It is also not as clear cut as we have shown when deciding where a particular act of leadership fits on our Leadership Fitness Continuum: is it effective leadership or actually MisLeadership? For example, some competition is recognised as being desirable but it is also possible to be excessively competitive:

at what level does competition become a negative influence? Leadership involves a lot of uncertainty and risk taking and an action that was initiated with the best possible intentions may go wrong. It is also not straightforward to identify which category a particular issue fits into. In practice issues may be large and complex, involve many different perspectives and there are likely to be several categories of MisLeadership involved in each. This last point is illustrated in Table 6.1 where we give our own idea as to how much of each category of MisLeadership is contained in three of the case studies from earlier chapters.

**Table 6.1     Categories of MisLeadership in cases discussed**

| Case | Authors' % weighting of relative importance of MisLeadership categories involved | | | |
| --- | --- | --- | --- | --- |
| | Missing | Misguided | Misinformed | Machiavellian |
| Resource depletion | 50 | 10 | 20 | 20 |
| Toxic childhood | 20 | 50 | 20 | 10 |
| A level grades | 20 | 70 | 0 | 10 |

You may care to reflect on the weightings you would give each case illustrated in Table 6.1 and consider possible reasons for any significant differences between those in the table and yours.

Given that a particular issue may contain several categories of MisLeadership and there is not a perfect match between specific categories and GFL elements, the search for a solution to a particular issue becomes quite involved. A further complexity is that the importance and effects of specific acts and decisions may be hard to predict and measure due to the number of facets involved including their scope, depth, breadth, consequences of error, longevity and possibility of retraction.

But nobody said it would be easy: complex issues are likely to require complex solutions. What is encouraging is the fact that the complex nature of specific issues does not detract from the value of our approach; in fact it strengthens it. When a number of cases are studied (as in earlier chapters and to come in Chapter 7), it becomes apparent that similar issues keep recurring and that they fall within the gambit of our models. Thus we argue that the

MisLeadership/GFL approach is an important step towards resolving many contemporary leadership issues and bringing about a general reduction in MisLeadership and improved global fitness of leaders, thereby making a substantial move toward Rutte's (2005) heaven on earth concept.

## DOES CATEGORISATION MATTER?

Despite the mismatch outlined above between particular issues, MisLeadership categories and GFL elements, we strongly believe that thinking about the suggested categories and elements helps raise awareness of the scope and extent of MisLeadership in the modern world and ways and means of improvement. This develops sensitivity to and awareness of the MisLeadership that we ourselves may be perpetrating as leaders, condoning as followers, or allowing to pass into future generations through the education and role modelling we give our children. Individual and Institutional MisLeadership is everywhere and, armed with this increased sensitivity and awareness, we hope you will recognise it and be able to think differently, challenge its existence and perform an effective leadership role. You will move toward being a Globally Fit Leader.

## What Has Been Covered So Far

We now summarise the main points that have been highlighted in Chapters 2 to 5.

In Chapter 2, the focus was on Missing Leadership, effective decision-making and the ASK SIR L model. Here we raised the point that if any of the stages in the model were completed badly then the effectiveness of the final decision would suffer. We highlighted that it is often the ASK phase that is not completed as fully as is often required. If we do not appreciate that a problem exists and specify the exact nature of the problem so as to understand its importance, we will make no attempt to solve it. The learning phase was also highlighted as crucial as this is the means by which we minimise repetition of mistakes and encourage adoption of successful approaches and ideas in the future.

Chapter 3 examined Misguided Leadership, the need for a global perspective and the Global Fitness Framework. Global leadership was shown as having two possible meanings. It can be seen as leadership across borders and nations as given by those in the corridors of global power: the White House, the Kremlin, Beijing, the UN, CEOs and boardrooms of multinational corporations. Equally important, it can be interpreted as 'all round', 'all encompassing' holistic leadership including physical, mental and spiritual elements. The spiritual elements include values – whether moral, ethical, societal, or utilitarian, and including spiritual values. For the first interpretation of global leadership to be truly effective the second interpretation also needs to be applied, both at the highest levels and more personally and local.

It included the crucial thought that spirituality could be positive, negative or non-existent. Negative spirituality reflects such concepts as deliberate exclusion of other philosophies and values; misconstruing other's beliefs or demonising their followers; being excessively competitive, exploitative, prejudiced, parochial; measuring success purely in terms of money; allowing continuation of inequalities of resource distribution; reluctance to acknowledge or correct past injustice; and adopting a 'might is right' or 'not in my back yard' attitude.

Chapter 4 considered Misinformed Leadership and the need for a new paradigm. We argued this new paradigm needed to include the requirements for leaders to act ethically, honestly and with integrity; be aware of global issues; recognise their role in shaping the future of humanity and the planet; work with the whole person and recognise that all aspects of their followers' lives are important, and need to be valued and nurtured, including the fact that all people are spiritual beings who need to understand the meaning of what they do and a sense that it matters.

Machiavellian Leadership was covered in Chapter 5 and shown to be wholly negative causing such reactions as loss of trust, insecurity, under-achievement of broader objectives, lost time and effort attempting to 'second-guess' what leaders' hidden objectives are, stress, burn out and retaliation and the danger that future leaders see it as the right way to lead.

This summary of Chapters 2 to 5 reveals many ways in which MisLeadership can flourish. It also provides a number of suggestions for logical incremental initial steps that can be taken to reduce the incidence of MisLeadership and increase the global fitness of leaders. A golden thread that runs throughout is the need for change brought about by challenging existing habits and values and re-educating ourselves for the global era.

## A Force-Field Analysis

Force-Field Analysis is a change tool developed by Kurt Lewin in the 1960s. It refers to consideration of the forces which exist for and against successful implementation of a plan, and the relative strengths of these forces. It derives from the basic law of physics that in a state of equilibrium forces acting on an object must be in balance and in order to move an object in a particular direction, the forces pushing that way must be greater than those pushing the other way. By combining the ideas in Figures 6.1 and 6.3 we arrived at the force-field analysis in Figure 6.4.

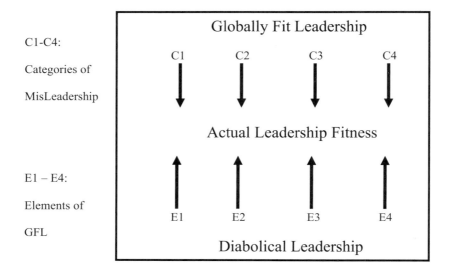

**Figure 6.4      Leadership Fitness Force Field**
*Source*: The Authors.

Figure 6.4 depicts the four categories of MisLeadership as pushing actual leadership fitness down toward diabolical leadership, and the four elements of GFL pushing up toward higher leadership fitness (actual achievement and well-being of humanity is not shown but is assumed to be linked to actual leadership fitness). This would mean that if we had perfect leadership we would also have no MisLeadership. As we can see from this analysis, according to this model, to improve actual leadership fitness we have to lessen the amount of MisLeadership or increase the effectiveness of the elements of GFL. We have tended to refer to these two aspects as opposites of the same coin, so for example as the force of effective decision-making grows, the force of Missing Leadership dwindles and overall fitness of leadership increases, leading to automatic improvement in well-being of humanity.

We believe this model in Figure 6.4 has a fascinating and crucial twist to it. As drawn it implies the result of the forces would be a particular leadership fitness level and result in all of humanity having a particular level of well-being. There are two points to consider: does all of humanity experience a similar level of well-being and are we in a state of equilibrium.

## Does All of Humanity Experience a Similar Level of Well-Being?

Chapter 1 included examples of the extent of suffering in the world:

- More than one billion people in the world living on less than US$1 a day

- 2.7 billion struggling to survive on less than US$2 per day

- More than 800 million people going to bed hungry every day, including 300 million children

- A person dying of starvation every 3.6 seconds, most of them being children under the age of 5

- 6,000 people every day who die from HIV/AIDS and another 8,200 who are infected with the deadly virus. (Source: Rural Poverty Portal.)

Other chapters included a large number of illustrations of the way in which certain individuals and societies receive more than their fair share, an example in Chapter 4 being that the typical 'Fortune 500' company pays their CEOs 350 times what their average worker earns.

These facts show that the level of inequity is extremely high. Those benefiting from existing leadership actions are likely to view their lives as relatively close to heaven on earth and thus current leadership as very fit, those suffering extreme poverty and ill-health feeling their lives are close to hell on earth and current leadership as diabolical. Because the level of inequity is so high, from a global perspective actual leadership fitness must be at a low level.

## Explanation Using the Leadership Fitness Force-Field

One way of relating this to Figure 6.4 would be if instead of the forces being spread evenly along opposite sides of the object, we have strong forces pushing up on the left (as drawn) but equally strong ones pushing down on the right. This is illustrated in Figure 6.5 as a see-saw.

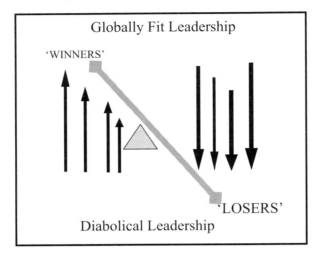

**Figure 6.5      Leadership Fitness See-Saw**
*Source*: The Authors.

This could happen if actions of leaders had opposite effects on different individuals, these effects being represented by different positions on the see-saw. This is a 'win-lose' outcome likely to result in some individuals gaining tremendously while very many others lose out. The more determined and able such a leader became, the more of a lop-sided effect their actions would have, with increased upward force for those benefiting but consequential downward force for those suffering. This links very well with the Drucker quote (2003:102) we gave in Chapter 3:

> *No century has seen more leaders with more charisma than our 20th century and never have political leaders done greater damage than the four great charismatic leaders of this century. Stalin, Mussolini, Hitler and Mao. What matters is not charisma. What matters is whether the leader leads in the right direction or misleads.*

What we urge is a search for an effective global approach which results in 'win-win' solutions.

## Are We in Equilibrium?

As stated above, we argue that humanity's current position on the force-field analysis is one where the see-saw is very significantly tilted such that different people have vastly different circumstances. If the see-saw was moving back towards the horizontal we could focus on raising actual leadership fitness. Our belief, however, is that the see-saw is tipping increasingly on its end such that we may all soon fall off. This could be thought of as looming system failure as shown by the growing number of UGIs illustrated in Table 1.1. Many of these are of recent origin and their number and importance is clear evidence that there are fundamental and growing flaws in how we are running the planet. In Diamond's terms (2005) we have reached the point of potential collapse and what we do in the next few years may decide whether we fail or survive as a species. Diamond's study looked at various societies and their failure or survival but what is particularly concerning now is that because of the extent of globalisation if our society collapses it could mean the end of humanity. A global society has to have global leadership to survive.

As we can see from this see-saw force-field one of the main reasons for the increasingly urgent position humanity finds itself in, with so little action taking place to rectify the crisis, may be that the people with the power to act tend to be those who believe they are riding high so have a vested interest in the status quo. These people may be reluctant to change unless they recognise and are concerned about the situation faced by those at the other end, the billions who are suffering from the current market driven economy and leadership approach who would see their environment as highly toxic and close to hell.

If you have a narrowly focused self-centred mission it is relatively easy to see which actions will help achieve it and to ignore or be blind to the circumstances of those on the far end of the see-saw, suffering the down-side of your actions. Trying to deal with global issues is hugely challenging and complex and we do not really know how to do this. We have never experienced this before and never been trained for it. It is hard, frightening and threatening and much, much easier simply not to think about it and just focus on the little things we can understand. To use an analogy related to the *Titanic* case study in Chapter 2, it feels like the variety of peoples' reactions immediately after the ship hit the iceberg.

There is a saying 'rearranging the deckchairs on the *Titanic*' but from the case we saw that quite quickly the leaders in fact realised the true situation and attempted to devise a solution. Many passengers continued to do whatever they had been doing for various reasons, some refused to accept that the ship could sink, others could not handle the information psychologically other than by ignoring it, others continued to carry out their duties in an attempt to maintain morale; a few tried to use the lifeboats, but many others refused to get on; some continued to enforce rules and approaches that were evidently not relevant to the new situation.

Perhaps our circumstances are not as dire as they proved to be for the *Titanic* and there may be solutions – possibly we have not hit the iceberg yet but will we heed the warnings:

### ICEBURG, DEAD AHEAD, ONE HUNDRED YARDS

At one level it may be argued that the powerful individuals who can have most effect on changing the current situation only have a moral obligation to commit to resolution of UGIs – the clear problem here being that any moral obligation they feel has not led to effective actions to date. There are, however, many other reasons why such individuals should act.

Leaders are only powerful as long as they are being followed, and followers are becoming increasingly aware of global and spiritual issues and questioning the attitudes and decisions taken by their leaders. Failure to solve global problems will place immense pressure on the validity of their claim to be globally fit leaders, that is, ones who are leading their followers to a positive future. Followers are becoming more questioning and able to communicate with each other very effectively through the internet as will be shown in the AVAAZ case in Chapter 7. If they become disillusioned with their leaders, they have the potential to remove them from power.

Ultimately, failure to solve certain UGIs will threaten the security, wealth and very survival of even the most powerful individuals and corporations. Thus, if the powerful, often multi-national business leaders fail to recognise the severity and inter-connectedness of global problems and take appropriate action, their power base will be threatened. The very high rate of attrition among major corporations during and since the recent global financial market disruptions is witness to the fact that unless they keep in tune with global events and environment change such leaders are highly vulnerable and even then, they are at risk since the effects of UGIs are extremely hard to predict in terms of incidence or magnitude. Thus, rather than protecting their position, by not acting these leaders are in fact exposing themselves and their organisations to the risk of ultimate and devastating failure.

In Chapter 1 we noted that one of the biggest difficulties with tackling MisLeadership is that it has been apparently tremendously successful, particularly when seen from its own viewpoint. The use of Machiavellian Leadership can result in large short-term financial and other gains for individuals but at the ultimate expense of others. Why would someone who is benefiting tremendously from this strategy want to change their approach and put their excess gains at risk? This brings us to a fundamental difficulty with the recent approach to capitalism which has been to place high levels of trust in the markets and assume that minimal government intervention will result in optimum outcomes for all. DeWoot (2009:40) argues of such a market ideology:

> *It ignores the fact that economic progress does not constitute the whole of human progress, even it if is a condition of it, and that it must be subject to the ethical and political imperatives that express the common good.*

Bill Gates in *Time* magazine (2008) said:

> *Capitalism has improved the lives of billions of people ... But it has left out billions more ... we need a more creative capitalism: an attempt to stretch the market forces so that more companies can benefit from doing work that makes more people better off.*

Those who believe they are doing well from the status quo will tend to be those who have high levels of power and influence as noted above, but also other significant rewards such as position, salary and bonus. It may be the people who tend to attain such positions are politically astute and skilled at working in the current system of Institutional MisLeadership. If political game playing and use of power achieves promotion, these people are likely to see that as confirmation that they are politically astute and able to manipulate others; it is this that has led to their success; and that this is the best way to behave. They are the least likely to see that such manipulation may be a strong negative force causing global issues and that they should change their ways. Power and political games are discussed in more detail later in this chapter.

Those leaders who attempt to take a global approach may find the correct actions more difficult to determine since there are many additional factors to consider and the scale is increased. This problem is exacerbated by the fact that many other leaders will be acting in a Machiavellian way to deliberately confuse and mislead, thereby retaining their high seat on the see-saw.

This was demonstrated in the Financial Markets case study in Chapter 4. Nick Leeson initially focused on making high profits for his organisation so he would gain promotion, high bonuses and a reputation for being top dog. When it started to go wrong, he took massive risks with vast amounts of other people's money to try to regain his personal position. This attitude was repeated by individuals in the banks when they adopted increasingly risky gearing levels and lent money to increasingly risky customers in an attempt to justify their status and earnings. In both circumstances the perpetrators seemed oblivious of the down side of their actions while senior managers were unaware of the situation, the risks faced and their global consequences.

It also applies when we consider international corporations as in the asbestos and cigarette industries and baby milk powder cases where they are shown to be willing to exploit their manoeuvrability by outflanking nations so as to avoid paying tax, exploit workers in developing countries and sell harmful products to unsuspecting and desperate people.

This brings us to consider what may be the most dangerous interpretations of our see-saw analogy. A Machiavellian leader may see it as confirming that:

- it is the vast numbers of deprived people who are dragging down that side of the see-saw – if we could get rid of them, the rest of us could have an even higher standard of living

- to maintain their high seat, they have to keep the disadvantaged down: any move toward equality will move the see-saw back toward the horizontal, clearly lessening their advantageous position.

## In Defence of Modern Managers

Given the above scenario it is evident that from a global perspective the overall fitness for purpose of modern leaders has been extremely low since they have led us into this global crisis situation.

From this it might be tempting to assume all modern leaders are unfit in our terms. We certainly are not suggesting this. Although the combined effects of modern leadership fitness levels may have led us to this crisis, it does not follow that every leader is unfit. We quoted Drucker's views above (2003:102) on Stalin, Mussolini, Hitler and Mao but it must be recognised that at the same time as these diabolical leaders were in power there were people like Churchill and Eisenhower fighting against them, possibly displaying equally high levels of GFL but in their case positive.

The root cause of our parlous state may not in fact be the fitness of leadership per se but that the leadership role is becoming harder to perform. Many of the urgent global issues listed in Table 1.1 above were of no concern to managers gone by, not because they were necessarily Machiavellian but because the scale of human activity was completely different. Many of the issues identified in Table 1.1 share root causes such as high and growing global population, increased expectations, increased capability to exploit resources and situations, and increased resource consumption per capita.

With globalisation and related developments such as Information Technology, the complexity, speed and expectations placed on the leadership role have multiplied to such an extent that it may now be becoming almost impossible for humans to perform a leadership role. Ridderstrale (2009), author of 'Funky Business' and 'Re-energising the Corporation' argues that the knowledge growth of individuals is linear, whereas for humanity as a whole it is exponential, thus individuals are becoming relatively stupid.

Leadership education and development has improved but at the same relatively slow pace, hence the rapidly widening gap which reflects the leadership crisis referred to in Chapter 1 and repeatedly throughout the book.

Our view is that the vast majority of leaders are doing their best in an unworkable system, with Institutional MisLeadership at its core. In many instances leaders are working so hard they are burning themselves out as evidenced by the high incidence of stress we touched on in Chapter 2. Many leaders complain of stress due to work overload, as illustrated in a 2008 Management Today survey (Clements 2008) which showed that stress at work is an incredibly damaging force, people are over-worked, stressed, burned-out or physically ill and they lack the necessary competence to cope.

The complexities faced by modern managers are demonstrated in an article by Age Concern, an extract from which is in Figure 6.6. The article accepts the fact that the population in the UK is ageing but feels that the problem could be tackled by keeping more of them at work. This is, however, only a valid solution if there is a shortage of overall manpower; otherwise, keeping more older people employed has the knock-on effect of reducing job opportunities for younger people.

---

**Myth of demographic 'time bomb' exploded**

Over 50s currently create a quarter of the UK's economic wealth[1] and have the potential to produce even more if given the opportunity. A ground-breaking, independent report published today by Age Concern reveals that up to 1 million more older people who are not currently in paid work could be, adding up to £30 billion to the annual economic output now.[2]

'The Economic Contribution of Older People' demonstrates how a rise of just a third of a percent per year in workers from 50 to 69 will be more than enough to meet the economic challenge of the ageing population. This increase would add a massive, additional £63 billion to economic output by 2021 than if employment rates remain static.[3]

The report challenges the view of an ageing population as a burden. Its findings clearly quantify for the first time how this alarmist vision obscures how much older people do and could add to the economy. The current contribution of older people from paid work has an annual value of £201 billion. In addition, unpaid work by older people including grand-parenting, caring for partners and volunteering is valued at £24 billion a year (see ref1).

Despite their enormous input, under-employment of the over 50s rather than the ageing demographic itself poses a serious threat to the future of the UK economy. By 2021, 40% of the population will be over 50 [4] yet many older people cannot get jobs. A small increase in those working could make a big improvement to the nation's wealth.

Author of the report, leading economist Pamela Meadows said:
"A debate that characterises older people as dependent on others in society is misleading. Existing contributions to national well-being, whether through paid employment or through unpaid work, are significant. But the economic contribution by older people could be greater still."

---

**Figure 6.6     Myth of demographic 'time bomb' exploded article**
*Source*: Age Concern 2004.

What we are looking for is a way to break free from all the things that prevent effective action by modern managers. Things like embedded values, ethical fading, Institutional MisLeadership, comfort zone of familiar approaches, backsliding due to fear and anxiety, and lack of motivation. We argue that one of the most significant ways to address many of these is through effective leadership education. This is often carried out in business schools across the world but to develop leaders capable of working with the hugely complex and rapidly changing environment will require a paradigm shift in the way leadership education is researched, designed and delivered. We consider the issues involved in creating this shift in the next section.

## The Role of Business Schools

According to Hawawini (2005:771), one of the most pressing issues facing business schools is the effect of globalisation on business education. Whilst there is debate on how to respond to this phenomenon, we agree with Lorange (2002:18 and 204) who suggests that business schools' response has to be proactive and they have to lead change – 'drive the market' as he terms it. Business schools have to lead the development and promulgation of new ideas, developing leaders fit to lead in the new environment, rather than relying on existing philosophies and striving to meet demands from the marketplace. If they do not perform this much needed role they will soon be overtaken by other organisations able and willing to do so, including private educational providers and the internal business academies that many major global organisations have established.

The key question here is 'Are business schools fit for this role?' Pfeffer and Fong (2002) indicate that the jury is still out when they argue that despite being identified as one of the major success stories in higher education over the last 30 years, business schools are now at a crossroads in their development. From Mintzberg's (2004) extensive research into the effectiveness of MBAs, it seems that programmes are too often focused on developing the mental strength and stamina of individuals. Thomas (2007) argues that business schools are *'failing to build ethical, global, and team orientated thinking into their curriculum.'* Capra (1997, cited in Kriger and Seng 2005:773) criticises the current position adopted by many business schools, and his argument below (as quoted in Chapter 3) also supports the holistic, interconnected emphasis within the GFF:

> *The more we study the major problems of our time, the more we come to realize that they cannot be understood in isolation. They are systemic problems, which means they are interconnected and interdependent ... There are solutions to the major problems of our time, some of them even simple. But they require a radical shift in our perceptions, our thinking, our values ... [However] the recognition that a profound change of perception and thinking is needed, if we are to survive, has not yet reached most of our corporate leaders, either, or the administrators and professors of our large universities.*

As Hawawini (2005:774) and Mitroff and Denton (1999:17) identify, typical business school courses have a large emphasis on quantitative management skills and techniques, with, for example, programmes like the MBA including modules on finance and accounting, marketing, human resources and strategic management. They fail to develop leaders 'fit to lead' in the new environment, and rarely include modules specifically relating to elements of what Hawawini (2005:774) terms 'societal skills', which cover the types of concerns addressed in this book, including the need for new paradigms of business thought and ways to tackle the UGIs identified in Table 1.1.

This situation exists despite increasing calls for business schools to change their approach and programme content. As an example of these calls, Cornuel (2007:90) from the European Foundation for Management Development says:

> The top business schools of the future will train their students to meet the increasingly complex worldwide demands by challenging management education; they will implement substantial changes in the way they prepare the next generation of leaders.

Another example of these calls comes from the Bangkok Manifesto on Global Responsibility (2002, as cited in Lorange 2003:127):

> Global actors of today are developing in a still over-regulated nationally and under-regulated globally environment; hence the importance of focusing our attention and our education on global governance and globally responsible leaders and decision makers.

This same manifesto also recommends the objective of developing new capabilities in schools and companies to deal with these global responsibility issues.

From the above and our recent research (Rayment and Smith, 2009), we conclude that many business schools are not currently fit to lead future thinking in organisations. As a first step to remedying this situation, business schools need to fully acknowledge their leading role in developing and promulgating business philosophies, approaches, tools and knowledge that are fit for contemporary circumstances. This must include facilitating business' understanding and solution of UGIs such as those identified in Table 1.1 above.

There may, however, be a more significant underlying issue. Business schools need to consider whether they are also operating from the same outmoded paradigm as the businesses they are there to help. They also need to consider whether they have done what Ghoshal suggests (2005) and actually created inappropriate management practices through the scientific model of teaching they have adopted. Ghoshal argues (2005:76) that by necessity this model of teaching has had to deny any moral or ethical considerations – considerations which are now so fundamental if leaders are to embrace the need for businesses to play their part in resolving the UGIs. We argue that if business schools are to play a leading role in the crucial future strategies outlined in this book they have to appreciate that they are part of the problem, not the solution.

As will be shown in Chapter 8 many organisations are already adopting these new paradigms and increasing numbers are likely to follow. If business schools embrace these changes then as Cornuel (2007:91) identifies:

> *Putting globally responsible leadership and corporate responsibility at the heart of business school curricula will present business schools with a rich opportunity to expand and enrich their academic offering …*

Of course there are significant challenges if business schools are to do this. As Tom Peters puts it (cited in Covey 1999b:179):

> *It's nothing less than 180-degree shift in the way we think about managing and leading.*

And if business schools do not change, what then? Well, business leaders will continue to be taught that the current business paradigm, with all the weaknesses and issues identified above, is still viable. They will continue to take decisions based on that paradigm and UGIs will not be tackled, thus becoming ever more urgent and wide-spread. Diamond, as quoted earlier in this book, has predicted the extent of the ultimate disaster.

## The Psychology of MisLeadership: Why Ideas are Not Implemented

In this chapter we have summarised the proposals made throughout the book. While some, such as the need for a new paradigm, have been proposed by others, the specifics provided and combination of elements that work with and support each other is what makes our proposals new, exciting and significant steps forward.

Although some of the elements have been proposed by others previously, it should be recognised that these have often not been implemented to any great extent. For example, the need for a new paradigm is increasingly talked about but the vast majority of people and organisations continue to work from the old paradigm. This section will explore some of the underlying reasons why proposed new strategies are often not implemented, helping ensure such factors are considered when we seek to implement our proposals.

As we saw in Chapter 1, one of the main reasons MisLeadership is prevalent, difficult to identify and challenge is that it is so pervasive throughout our upbringing, socialisation and education. From birth we face a continual barrage of Institutional MisLeadership which as our Embedded Values Cycle (Figure 1.1) shows, informs our thinking and influences our behaviour, habits, values and attitudes. We reinforce these and pass them on to our children through our own Misguided Leadership until it becomes accepted as the right way to lead. As it has become so embedded and accepted, few will recognise that MisLeadership is taking place. As shown in Chapter 2, the first step in solving a problem is to appreciate its existence, which is the principal aim in this book. While we explore their scope and scale, causes and potential solutions, our immediate aim is to build awareness of the fundamental flaws in contemporary society.

Johnson's (2009:201) discussion of ethical fading in relation to ethical leadership is significant here, as he suggests that the moral aspects of a decision fade into the background if we use euphemisms to disguise unethical behaviour or numb our conscience through repeated MisLeadership acts, as we do with repeated exposure to Institutional MisLeadership. We argue that the more a person sees and experiences MisLeadership the more de-sensitised they become to it and the ethical challenges it presents, until they ultimately work with it and start to demonstrate it themselves without realising they are doing so. It becomes the informed, expected and accepted way to lead so there is nothing to challenge or overcome.

Continuing to do things in old familiar ways is also likely to be quicker and easier initially than finding new ways so people may be reluctant to search for, test and implement new approaches. This is particularly so if they feel overloaded or are faced with challenging situations, as we are experiencing now with the crisis in leadership, global financial crises and urgent global issues. As noted in Chapter 2, leaders may feel locked into a system and fearful about challenging the status quo, the education they receive or their peers. Fear may also be seen in followers who are reluctant to challenge or question their leader or suggest alternative actions. All this may ultimately come back to fears about being wrong and the consequences of error including being made to look foolish, being bullied or ostracised by a group or peers, or of losing their jobs, income, livelihood or the respect of people. Fear is a huge issue for a great many of us. Interestingly a lot of the underpinning fears can be developed from childhood experiences and MisLeadership that occurred at that time.

In such circumstances we tend to fall back to what we know and are comfortable with. This is known as backsliding and as Senge et al. (2008:10) point out:

> Our actions are most likely to revert to what is habitual when we are in a state of fear or anxiety. Collective actions are no different. Even as conditions in the world change dramatically most businesses, governments, schools and other large organisations driven by 'fear' continue to take the same kinds of institutional actions that they always have.

So we set out with the best of intentions for improving a situation but then slip back into the habitual ways of working we know.

Solutions to MisLeadership may not be implemented because of a lack of motivation. This could be a lack of motivation to question, challenge, find information, enquire or try new things. Vroom's (1964) Expectancy Theory of Motivation tells us that a person's lack of motivation could be because the outcomes of their efforts are not sufficiently clear or do not matter enough to that individual. For our MisLeadership exploration this could mean that the negative outcomes of MisLeadership are not clear or are not sufficiently motivating for the individual to do anything to change the situation.

An example to illustrate this point is whether this lack of motivation is the underlying issue behind the extent of use of the car today? Everyone knows that carbon emissions from petrol and diesel engines are to some extent contributing to global warming, but the vast majority who are lucky enough to have a car still use it without much thought even for the shortest journey. Is it a lack of motivation to walk or cycle, to find an alternative, or do something different? Is this lack of motivation really because the consequences are unclear, unreal or too remote? As an example, do you know how much a five-mile journey to the shops in your car increases the earth's temperature, and how much this increase in temperature affects sea levels, plant and animal life?

Carnall (2007:210) proposes a formula related to motivation to change:

$$EC = A \times B \times D$$

where:
    EC  =  The Energy for change
    A   =  Felt dissatisfaction with the present situation
    B   =  Level of knowledge of practical steps forward
    D   =  Shared vision

He also argues that for change to occur EC has to be greater than the perceived cost of making the change.

With our car example it is easy to see the energy for change, level of knowledge of the steps forward and shared vision all being low, and the perceived cost of change being high, which may be why little happens.

## POWER

We now turn to what we see as one of the main underpinning reasons why strategies to address MisLeadership are not implemented: power. Power is a seductive phenomenon in the world of leadership as it can make the leaders feel very good about themselves and their achievements. As Lord Acton said *'Power tends to corrupt, and absolute power corrupts absolutely.'* According to Yukl (2006), power is the capacity to influence the attitudes and behaviour of people in a desired direction. French and Raven (1959) identify seven different types of power, which are useful in helping us to understand the many different aspects of power that can encourage MisLeadership:

- Legitimate Power – Being put in a leadership position the agent then has power to make requests, and this is seen as a legitimate use of authority by followers.

- Reward Power – A person holding this type of power is seen as being in a position to offer rewards and people comply with their requests or activities in order to obtain rewards.

- Coercive Power – Person complies in order to avoid punishment.

- Information Power – An agent holding this form of power has access to or control over information.

- Ecological Power – Agent controls the physical environment, technology and organisation of work.

- Referent Power – Person admires the agent and wants to gain approval.

- Expert Power – Person complies as they believe the agent has specialist knowledge or expertise.

Any of these forms of power has the capacity to influence the attitudes and behaviour of people in a desired direction. As we have discussed in Chapter 1, this direction can be for the common good but so often is not.

Holding these forms of power can be very seductive for a leader because it gives them the capacity to influence the behaviour and direction of people to do the things the leader wants done. It is easy to understand that a person holding a little of one form of power can desire to hold more of this and other forms, which provides them with even more control over the attitudes and behaviours of people. Where this power is not gained legitimately or where there is a danger of a person losing the very gratifying power they hold, it is easy to see the use of more underhand tactics coming into play to hold or gain power as we saw in Chapter 3 with the actions of King Henry V.

This can result in political games being played. Ferris (1989, as cited by Hargie 2004) defines politics within organisations as the behaviour strategically designed to maximise the self interests of individuals – classic Machiavellian Leadership. Mintzberg (1998) identifies 13 different political games that can be played by leaders to gain or build power.

- Insurgency Game – played by lower level employees to resist authority

- Counterinsurgency Game – played by those in authority to fight back using political means

- Sponsorship Game – to build power base by attaching oneself to individuals with more status professing loyalty for power

- Alliance Building Game – played by managers to negotiate support with other managers to build power base for organisational advancement

- Empire Building Game – played by managers to build power with subordinates

- Budgeting Game – similar to Empire Building but the prize is greater resource/finance

- Expertise Game – using expertise to build power, exploiting technical skills and keeping knowledge to oneself

- Lording Game – 'lording' legitimate power over those with less of it

- Line vs. Staff Game – played to defeat rival groups, exploiting legitimate power illegitimately

- Rival Camps Game – played to defeat a rival between two people, groups or competing visions

- Strategic Candidates Game – played to effect change, individuals promoting their own strategic change through political means

- Whistle-Blowing Game – played to effect change, highlighting to a third party questionable or illegal behaviour by an organisation or individual

- Young Turks Game – played by a group close to the centre of an organisation seeking to change something, replace culture or rid current leaders.

Note the use of the word 'game' to describe these various behaviours. This is Misguided Leadership in that it encourages the reader to believe these 'games' are not to be taken seriously, don't really matter and are a fun and legitimate way to act. The reader can become misinformed and start to act in a similar fashion in the mistaken belief that it is the right thing to do – the Embedded Value Cycle again.

Holding power has a double aspect; it can be gratifying in itself but leaders may also think it is better to hold power themselves than let other people have power over them. Thus fear of being dominated may drive the leaders to seek and hold onto power.

*Power in education*     We will now turn our attention to this issue of power within the process of education that a leader may receive. In this analysis we will draw on the work of Pierre Bourdieu (n.d) who introduced the concept of habitus, and the focus of our analysis are the leaders or future leaders that are being educated in business schools. Habitus is a system of dispositions which are lasting, acquired schemes of perception, thought and action. These are developed by individuals in response to objective conditions they encounter (in part, business school teaching, but can also be applied to general upbringing and teaching in schools and at work). This ultimately leads to creation of doxa – fundamental, deeply held, but unquestioned beliefs which become internally accepted as self-evident, universal 'truths' that inform the individual's actions.

'Symbolic capital' (prestige, honour, expectation on the right to be listened to) and 'cultural capital' (accepted qualifications, the right experience or background) are viewed by Bourdieu as critical sources of power. If those who hold this power (lecturers) use it against an individual who holds less (the student), seeking thereby to alter their beliefs and actions, they exercise what Bourdieu calls symbolic violence. This imposes categories of thought and perception on dominated individuals who unquestioningly take this view as correct and just. Symbolic violence ensures that the arbitrariness of the established social order is ignored, or misrecognised as natural, thus continuing the apparent legitimacy of 'traditional' social structures – Institutional MisLeadership.

## FOLLOWERS AS MISLEADERS

We have explored some of the reasons why actions to address MisLeadership, while often straightforward, have not been addressed. We return now to the important issue that was raised in Chapter 1 concerning followers, and look at how followers can encourage MisLeadership, or restrict the improvement in leadership. Leaders can only lead if they have people who will follow so understanding the actions of followers is key to understanding MisLeadership.

We now look at two short cases to illustrate where followers have had an influence on the actions of leaders, the first being the swine flu epidemic that threatened the UK in 2009.

## Swine Flu and Tamiflu

---

**TAMIFLU SWINE FLU POLICY 'SHOULD BE REVIEWED URGENTLY'**

Prescribing experts have called for an urgent review of the NHS's use of Tamiflu in tackling the swine flu pandemic – amid concerns that the public have been misled about the drug's effectiveness.

*Source*: Duffin 2009.

---

The H1N1 Swine Flu virus was a new strain that had been creating havoc across the world with large numbers of people becoming ill and some dying. As with any new strain of a virus, there was limited knowledge available and medical teams were attempting to establish its symptoms, scale and scope and how best to treat it. In particular little was known of the long-term effects on humans, plants or animals of the main antiviral medication being used (Generic name – oseltamivir; brand name – Tamiflu).

An editorial in the BMJ's Drug and Therapeutics Bulletin (2009) argued that the drug had failed to prevent widespread transmission of swine flu and that the side effects and costs linked to it were not made widely known in advance, including:

> *The limited evidence base and the low mortality rates so far in the pandemic underlie the scepticism about widespread use of oseltamivir. It is regrettable that obvious potential problems from the widespread use of oseltamivir were not presented openly from the outset.'*

Despite the limited evidence base and WHO advice to the contrary (Godlee 2009), the government and doctors in the UK opted for relatively indiscriminate use of antivirals after self-diagnosis, doctors prescribed Tamiflu and gave indications to patients that they knew how to treat this strain of flu. While at first sight this appears to be an example of Misinformed Leadership by the doctors, we believe they were justified in using this approach as it helped avoid panic and kept the public reassured.

In situations like this, the majority of patients want someone to take control, take their concerns and pain away, and give them answers as to how best to treat their ailment. Some are not emotionally mature enough to cope with the truth: that the doctors have limited knowledge of efficacy and side effects of the treatment and that there are risks involved. According to news reports, UK Government ministers took this to the extreme by claiming it would be:

> ...*publicly unacceptable to withhold antiviral drugs, even after it became clear that swine flu was generally a mild illness.*

The BMJ's Drug and Therapeutics Bulletin (2009) adopted the opposite view:

> *The risk benefit analysis of the policy on oseltamivir deserved more open and balanced public discussion. On this measure, at least, the policy has failed and should be reviewed urgently.*

Of course open and balanced public discussion is important but one also has to deal with public perceptions, norms and expectations, and what people have learned and been socialised into with regard to MisLeadership. One can easily imagine public hysteria and frenzied media activity if doctors admitted the true position as summarised above.

This case illustrates the complex and embedded nature of MisLeadership in the psyche of both leaders and followers, and also shows how followers' expectations and behaviour can encourage leaders into acts of MisLeadership.

## The Police

Our second example is rather similar regarding followers' expectations and MisLeadership and relates to the police. It draws on Smith's (2005) research with the UK police. Smith identified the huge expectations that are placed on police officers from the public and police organisation itself.

Imagine a major road traffic accident where there are many people killed, injured and dying. Those involved in the accident together with bystanders and loved ones of the injured are desperately seeking people to help them, take their pain away and take control of the situation. People want and expect a police officer to get to that scene quickly and to do this. Just imagine though if the police officer who arrived on the scene exhibited perhaps some of the more natural human reactions of shock, fear and upset. Imagine if they broke down into floods of tears and walked away from the horrific scene. It would be a natural reaction and they would avoid having to see and deal with the horrendous sights, smells and sounds they are likely to encounter but there would be public uproar.

The public expect a police officer not to react in this natural manner but to take and then be in control, know what to do, and act quickly and 'professionally' at all times. As a result there are huge expectations placed on police officers by the public, the police service and the officers themselves to act as if they are in control. To enable the officers to do this they have to put on a performance as Goffman (1987:26) describes, detach themselves from their feelings and emotions and don a metaphorical suit of armour.

These performances are clearly aimed at misguiding the public and possibly the police officers themselves, but are they MisLeadership? As we said in Chapter 1 we see MisLeadership as being any leadership action which results in less than optimum achievement of an entity's overall objectives. The police are very good at considering humanity's overall objectives and they do a great deal to protect and serve the public. However, what we see in this example is the potential for less than optimum functioning of the police organisation itself over the long-term.

The weakness here, and the Misguided Leadership that occurs in this instance relates to the care and development of police officers. There can be a large impact on police officers themselves from being required to misguide the public on a regular basis, which Smith and Charles (2009) argue can be seen in terms of reduced life expectancy, high suicide, divorce rates, alcohol and drug abuse, ill health and medical retirements. This is not good for police officers, for the police organisation or society as a whole, but in some ways is forced on the police service because of the MisLeadership expectations of the general public.

## Other Reasons Followers May Condone MisLeadership

Having considered the complexities of follower and leader relationships between doctors and patients and the police and public, we now consider two further reasons why followers may condone MisLeadership in an organisational setting. One is they may feel they have little choice – put up with the MisLeadership that is occurring and conform, or leave. This situation reflects the power balance and its effects and is a clear case of Machiavellian Leadership.

Our other reason followers may not challenge MisLeadership relates to Groupthink (Janis 1972). Groupthink can result in groups making extremely poor decisions, which some of the individuals involved should definitely have known were wrong. The reasons for this type of behaviour include:

- lack of individual responsibility

- unwillingness to break group norms or appear disloyal

- placing consequences on themselves above the overall consequences of the decision (for example, fear of being disciplined for 'breaking ranks'), and

- automatically following a standard approach.

This scenario tends to occur with most dramatic effect when a group is faced with a slowly worsening situation and no one wants to be the first to point it out. An extremely well-known example was the Battle of the Somme, with individual officers perfectly aware that continual assaults on enemy lines were basically futile and extremely costly in terms of casualties, but not prepared to force through a change of tactic. Another example is the actions of the Kennedy Cabinet during the Bay of Pigs Invasion (n.d.).

Any long-standing group could suffer from this phenomenon, with the House of Commons a very clear example: everyone knows their rules, regulations and processes are terribly out of date, with repeated promises being made as to improved provision of facilities for female MPs, and much earlier start and finish times for parliamentary sessions, but little progress is made. The failure to tackle known problems may have been a root cause of the recent MPs' expenses scandal where a large number were found to have broken the spirit and many the letter of the law. Initial attempts to claim they were only following the rules and House practice gained short shrift and in many respects made their position worse as they lost respect and trust when people saw through and reacted against such blatant Machiavellian Leadership.

Another example is NASA's Challenger space mission (see Griffin n.d:235) which exploded shortly after take-off. It is claimed that, despite strong warnings from the engineers involved in the project that the craft was not safe, the NASA committee responsible for the launch decided to go ahead. Several individuals on the committee were interviewed and admitted that they had extreme misgivings about the launch, one even stating that he had gone home to his wife and told her that disaster was inevitable. None had been prepared to be the one to call a halt.

'The Emperor's New Clothes', a well-known tale by Hans Christian Andersen, is an excellent illustration of this kind of situation/behaviour. Everyone knew that the emperor was naked, but no one was prepared to say so. Of course, there may have been any number of reasons why they kept quiet – some people might enjoy the sight of the emperor revealed in all his glory and looking extremely foolish. As with most tales of this nature, it can be read in many different ways and at different levels. Another interpretation is to do with 'power': very often people in powerful positions try to push through their desires based on false/invalid arguments – in other words, they have 'no clothes'. This interpretation fits extremely well here in that one reason for Groupthink is the reluctance of subordinates to openly contradict the viewpoint of their superiors even if they know them to be wrong.

The end of the story illustrates how the problem can often be dealt with. A young boy, blissfully unaware of the niceties of the situation, stated what everyone knew: the emperor has got no clothes! Insiders who attempt to play this role often attempt to justify their actions by use of such phrases as 'playing devil's advocate' but the very fact that they feel the need to do so highlights the quandary they are faced with. In the Middle Ages the monarch was surrounded by her/his court, and one of the important members was the court jester, whose main function was to carry out the role under discussion. Given the instability of court life and constant fear of rebellion or treason it would have been very dangerous for a high ranking and powerful individual to criticise the monarch's plans but someone had to do it. Hence the idea of a Fool who could speak the unspeakable, be openly mocked but on occasion ensure that important aspects were in fact considered.

## Summary

This chapter began by summarising the exploration that has taken place in Chapters 1 to 5 where four categories of MisLeadership are identified and one key action to help address each proposed. In this chapter we have termed the combination of these four key elements Globally Fit Leadership but drawn attention to this being a simplification in that MisLeadership and its resolution is a far more complex problem than the model implies.

The model of a Leadership Fitness Continuum introduced in Chapter 1 was expanded to include non-leadership factors and the concepts of heaven on earth and hell on earth.

Similar issues and solutions keep recurring in specific examples of leadership practice and they are well covered by indicators in our models. Thus we argue that the MisLeadership/GFL approach is an important step towards resolving many contemporary leadership issues. Thinking about different categories of MisLeadership and elements of GFL helps raise awareness of the scope and extent of MisLeadership in the modern world and ways and means of improvement.

A model of the Leadership Fitness Force-Field was presented and discussed, a particularly important aspect being the potential effect of leaders with high GFL but negative spirituality and self-centred missions: diabolical leadership. It is possible and highly important to recognise our current situation, which to us is lop-sided forces resulting in those few who benefit from the current global environment and leadership believing we are close to heaven so not inclined to act while billions are suffering from the leadership such that their environment is toxic and they are close to hell. Worse still, we believe we are currently moving in the wrong direction – the see-saw is tipping increasingly on its end such that we may all soon fall off – or put in more academic language, total system failure. This is evidenced by the growing number of urgent global issues illustrated in Table 1.1.

The root cause of our parlous state may in fact not be the fitness of leadership per se but that the leadership role is becoming harder to perform. Our view is that the vast majority of leaders are doing their best in an unworkable system. In many instances they are working so hard that they are burning themselves out.

Our overarching solution is to consider the categories of MisLeadership and how to minimise them, and elements of GFL and ways to increase them.

In the next chapter we examine four cases that illustrate how complex many situations are and that the leaders involved are often doing their best to cope with tools designed for a bygone age. We also illustrate examples of good practice currently being adopted. This sets the scene for Chapter 8 which summarises the whole book, draws our proposed approaches together and ends with an action summary.

---

**POINTS FOR REFLECTION**

1. What prevents you as a follower from challenging the MisLeadership that is occurring?

2. If you were having a conversation with Henry VIII, what would you like to ask him in relation to the issues we have discussed so far in this book?

3. What would you like to ask your parents in relation to the issues we have discussed so far in this book?

4. We invite you to consider the current and likely future situation in the conflict between Israel and Palestine from the following viewpoints:

   a. A Palestinian whose house, where he and his ancestors have lived for hundreds of years, has been bulldozed by the 'other side' who claim their god promised the land to them thousands of years ago;

   b. An Israeli settler who is certain his claim is legitimate and feels threatened by reprisals and suicide bombers;

   c. A Christian who believes God may have promised the land to the Israelis, but surely there must be a better way;

   d. A Chinese atheist who sees the whole thing as yet another illustration of 'might is right' and just as big a war crime as those carried out by Nazi Germany on the Jews only 70 years ago.

5. What if, instead of using force and superior weapons, the Israelis had *bought* the land at a generous price? Say this had cost one-quarter of their defence spending? What might the situation be now and looking ahead?

---

## References

Age Concern. (2004). [Online]. Available at: http://www.ageconcern.org.uk/Age Concern/BC9A9A793C104423BC4D70AC64154754.asp [accessed: 19/10/09].

*Bay of Pigs Invasion*. (n.d.). [Online]. Available at: http://faculty.css.edu/dswenson/web/TWAssoc/groupthink.html) [accessed: 28/9/09].

Bourdieu, P. (n.d.). *Bourdieu's theory of power and practice*. [Online]. Available at: http://en.wikipedia.org/wiki/Bourdieu#Bourdieu.27s_theory of power and practice [accessed: 17/9/09].

Carnall, C. (2007). *Managing Change in Organizations*. 5th Edition. Harlow: Prentice-Hall.

Clements, A. (2008). Workplace: Stress Survey 2008 – get a grip on your stressed-out staff workers workplace. (online) Available at: http://www.managementtoday.co.uk/search/arlice/796383/workplace.htm     [accessed: 30/07/09].

Cornuel, E. (2007). Challenges facing business schools in the future. *Journal of Management Development*, vol. 26, no.1, 87–92.

Covey, S.R. (1999b). *Principle-Centred Leadership*. London: Simon and Schuster UK Ltd.

Daly, J., Speedy, S. and Jackson, D. (2007). *Nursing Leadership*. New South Wales: Elsevier.

De Woot, P. (2009). *Should Prometheus be Bound?* Basingstoke: Palgrave Macmillan.

Diamond, J. (2005). *Collapse: How Societies Choose to Fail or Survive*. London: Penguin Books.

Drucker, P.F. (2003). *The New Realities* New Jersey: Transaction Publishers.

Drug and Therapeutics Bulletin. (2009). *British Medical Journal*, 20 August, BMJ 2009, 339:b3394.

Duffin, C. (2009). *Tamiflu swine flu policy 'should be reviewed urgently'*. [Online, 10 September]. Available at: http://www.pulsetoday.co.uk/story.asp?sectioncode=23andstorycode=4123609andc=1 [accessed: 16/9/09].

French, J. and Raven, B.H. (1959). The basis of social power. In Cartwright, D. (ed.). *Studies of Social Power*. Institute of Social Research.

Gates, B. (2008). *Time* magazine. August.

Ghoshal, S. (2005). Bad Management Theories Are Destroying Good Management Practices. *Academy of Management Learning and Education*, vol. 4(1), 75–91.

Godlee, F. (ed.). (2009). Editor's Choice Pandemic flu: Will there be a second wave? *British Medical Journal*, 2009, 339:b3394.

Goffman, E. (1987). *The Presentation of Self in Everyday Life*. Middlesex: Penguin.

Gooding, L, (2005). Stress poses dire threat to NHS. *Nursing Standard*, vol. 19, no. 24.

Griffin, E. (n.d). *Group Think by Erving Janis: A First Look at Communication Theory*. [Online]. Available at: http://www.afirstlook.com/docs/groupthink.pdf [accessed 28/9/09].

Hargie, O. (2004). *The Handbook of Communication Skills*. Hove: Routledge.

Hawawini, G. (2005). The future of business schools. *Journal of Management Development*, vol. 24, no. 9, 770–82.

Janis, I. (1972). *Victims of Groupthink*. New York: Houghton Mifflin.

Johnson, E. (2009). *Meeting the Ethical Challenges of Leadership Casting Light or Shadow*. 3rd Edition. California: SAGE Publications, Inc.

Kriger, M. and Seng, Y. (2005). Leadership with inner meaning: A contingency theory of leadership based on the worldviews of five religions. *The Leadership Quarterly*, 16, 771–806.

Lorange, P. (2002). *New Visions of Management Education: Leadership Challenges*. Oxford: Elsevier.

Lorange, P. (2003). Global responsibility – business education and business schools – roles in promoting a global perspective. *Corporate Governance*, vol. 3, no. 3, 126–35.

Mintzberg, H. (1998). *Strategy Safari – A Guided Tour Through The Wilds of Strategic Management*. New York: The Free Press.

Mintzberg, H. (2004). *Managers not MBAs: A Hard Look at the Soft Practice of Managing and Management Development*. London: Financial Times Prentice Hall.

Mitroff, I. and Denton, E. (1999). *A Spiritual Audit of Corporate America: A Hard Look at Spirituality, Religion and Values in the Workplace*. San Francisco: Jossey – Bass Inc.

Pfeffer, J. and Fong, C. (2002). The end of business schools? Less success than meets the eye. *Academy of Management Learning and Education*, 1(1), 78–95.

Ridderstrale, J. (2009). Speech given at the Employee Engagement conference of Impact at Windermere, UK, 16–18 June 2009.

Rutte, M. (2006). The Work of Humanity: Project Heaven on Earth. In *Seeking the Sacred: Leading a Spiritual Life in a Secular World*. Ontarion: ECW Press.

Smith, J.A. (2005). *Training for the Whole Person: An Exploration of Possibilities for Enhancing the Spiritual Dimension of Police Training*. PhD Diss., University of Hull.

Smith, J.A. and Charles, G. (2009). The Relevance of Spirituality in Policing: A Meta-Analysis. Paper submitted to the *International Journal of Police Science and Management*. October, 2009.

Thomas, H. (2007). An analysis of the environment and competitive dynamics of management education. *Journal of Management Development*, vol. 26, no.1, 9–21.

Senge, P., Scharmer, C.O., Jaworskil, J. and Flowers, B.S. (2008). *Presence: Exploring Profound Change in People, Organizations and Society*. London: Nicholas Brealey Publishing.

Vroom, V.H. (1964). *Work and Motivation*. Oxford: Wiley.

Yukl, G. (2006). *Leadership in Organisations*. 6th Edition. New Jersey: Prentice Hall.

# 7

# Case Studies

A wide range of situations and applications have been used so far in the book to illustrate specific categories of MisLeadership and elements of GFL. Following the discussion in Chapter 6, we now examine four cases that illustrate how complex many situations are, the extent of any MisLeadership, that many of the leaders involved are doing their best, they are struggling with tools designed for a bygone age, and that improvements are available through Globally Fit Leadership. These are followed by examples of organisations that have taken initial steps toward tackling MisLeadership.

## Forced Marriage

Forced marriage is a complex, contentious topic which contains a number of MisLeadership categories and requires several elements of GFL to work towards a solution. There is a definite gap between the results of forced marriages and what Globally Fit Leadership would lead to.

According to Her Majesty's Government (2009) a forced marriage is a marriage in which one or both spouses do not consent to the marriage and duress is involved. Duress can include physical, psychological, financial, sexual and emotional pressure. A forced marriage is not the same as an arranged marriage when those getting married have a choice as to whether to accept the arrangement or not. Although the issue of forced marriages is not restricted to a particular racial, ethnic or religious group, according to Samad and Eade (n.d.:2) it does seem to be more common where the practice of arranged marriage is the norm. Her Majesty's Government (2009) point out, however, that the tradition of arranged marriages has operated successfully within many communities and countries for a very long time.

**Figure 7.1     The Forced Marriage Unit**

The topic of marriage is a difficult and thorny subject itself before we even get into the issues of consent and duress. Marriage does not seem to be a particularly successful idea with nearly 45 per cent of marriages in countries like America and the UK ending in divorce (The Free Library 2009), and many others continue due to the desire not to upset other parties including children or other pressures similar to those mentioned above for forced marriages. Samad and Eade (n.d.:26) also identify that in the UK the number of marriages taking place is at the lowest level since 1917 and the divorce rate is the highest in the European Union.

Getting married can be a significant milestone in people's lives and demonstrates a major commitment to the other person in the marriage. It also has significant implications for the long-term happiness and well being not only of the people getting married but also their parents and grandparents, children and grandchildren, communities, religious groups and society. There is a mix of complex emotions involved – love, sex, fear, safety and security, food and shelter, desire to have children and meet family and social expectations – which all impact on the decision as to who and whether to marry. It is a decision that will affect those involved for the rest of their lives, and is often made when the people are relatively young and immature.

Poverty is also a critical factor and a common reason why parents may encourage a child to marry. Where poverty is acute, a girl may be regarded as an economic burden and her marriage to a much older – sometimes even elderly – man believed to benefit the child and her family both financially and socially. In communities where child marriage is practised marriage is regarded as a transaction, often representing a significant economic activity for a family. A daughter may be the only commodity a family has left to be traded and sometimes girls can be used as currency or to settle debts. A girl's marriage may also take place as a perceived means of creating stability. In uncertain times, poor harvest conditions or war, a family may believe it is necessary to ensure the economical 'safety' of their daughter and family through marriage.

> Victims of forced marriages could total 4,000 says study.
>
> *Source:* Taylor 2008.

When studying forced marriage the already complex situation related to marriage is added to the issues of racism, sexism, homophobia and religious discrimination. Because marriage is such a significant milestone it can bring to a head all these issues as well as any intergenerational debates and conflicts that may have existed in a family or community for many years, even generations.

Getting into a situation, though, where one person is forcing another to marry against their will is probably something that few people actually want. It is more likely to be the unfortunate outcome of poverty or the above conflicts that have been running for many years and which have come to a head at this crucial juncture in life. At this time there is likely to be a stand-off usually between parents and child as to what is going to take place, and this ends up in the child either being forced to marry against their will or running away and leaving their home, family and friends behind. The victims can face emotional and physical abuse where there can be kidnap, child abuse, sexual assaults, beatings and even murder taking place according to Taylor (2008). It is apparent that, whether the marriage takes place or not, the above duress is clear evidence of MisLeadership.

The conflict leading to the forcing of a marriage often seems to be about differences in values and beliefs between generations. Sometimes this seems to reflect the conflict between Eastern and Western worldviews. One perspective might emphasise the importance of the group, argue life is about duty, respecting parent's and elder's wishes, preserving the clan, and people protecting their families both financially and socially. As Samad and Eade (n.d.:109) point out, in this situation family honour can motivate men and women to regulate the behaviour of their children, in particular girls, and if these children flagrantly disregard the parents' social norms it can trigger processes that culminate in forced marriages. Another perspective might argue that life is much more about the individual, about rights and individual happiness.

The idea of forcing anyone to marry is a difficult one for many to understand, but in reality it might actually occur in very many instances of marriage. Perhaps not as overtly as the ones Her Majesty's Government (2009) are focused on but parents, families and communities all over the world can and often do exert considerable psychological pressure and utilise many different forms of power over their child to marry a particular person they approve of. As Samad and Eade (n.d.:2) point out, marriage practices among white people still often tend to see partners coming from the same nationality, ethnic and racial group, socio-economic background and religion. Those who do not conform to these norms may suffer sanctions ranging from disapproval to ostracism from parents, family, friends, work colleagues or communities. We argue this same observation applies to all racial and ethnic groups.

So while forced marriage is likely to demonstrate MisLeadership at some point it is difficult to say which form of MisLeadership as that depends on the particular circumstances. It may be a result of Missing Leadership and be linked to a toxic childhood, as explored in Chapter 2. It may be that some of the parties involved are misinformed perhaps about the role of, and acceptable approaches to, parenthood, or the requirements and expectations of community groups or family members. It may be misguided as parents try to maintain cultural traditions and norms that *may* have been valid in earlier times but do not fit with modern views of freedom and choice. It may also be Machiavellian as those parents seek to reap personal benefit from particular unions, as may be the case in some of the situations described by Buchanan (2009). This may include a gain in finance or power, access to living in a particular country, or an increased standing in the community or country.

## APPLICATION OF GLOBALLY FIT LEADERSHIP

The following comments are made from our perspective as academics from the UK. We have tried hard to be unbiased and consider all perspectives but the Embedded Values Cycle, Institutionalised MisLeadership, and experiences we have had throughout our lives will have influenced our thoughts and may mean that the perspective we give is more biased towards individual rights and happiness than duty, respecting parent's and elder's wishes and preserving the clan. The need to recognise this reinforces the complexities in the case.

As stated above we believe that fundamentally few people actually want to force their children into a marriage which that child does not want to enter into. Parents are more likely to be doing their best, and feel that the marriage is the best alternative available given the circumstances. It is likely that the issue coming to a head in forced marriage is really a conflict between different values and beliefs.

It may be useful for all parties to consider the embedded values cycle and potential effects of MisLeadership and reflect on all the teachings and experiences they will have been exposed to over the course of their lives. These will have come from many sources including parents, peers, religious teachings, school teachers, friends, the media, television, and visitors from other lands. This process will enable the influences on each individual's values and attitudes to be moved into the conscious mind so they can be considered more objectively from the individual's current position, and the current global situation.

The problem-solving model we discussed in Chapter 2 can then be used to try to reach a decision that all parties are happy with. As we said there, the ASK phase of the model is often done badly if at all. By exploring the embedded values cycle and considering the various influences objectively a greater appreciation of the issues will be involved. They can then specify the exact nature of the conflict, see more clearly where they originate and be in a clearer position to start moving through the remaining stages of ASK SIR L.

This whole process is complicated by poverty and also by the influence of emotions and embedded values. It is a challenging and difficult process to work through and is likely to require skilled assistance from a third party. A suitable third party may not always be available and we believe a fundamental role of education should be to work through these processes with students so they are more able to apply it themselves in the future.

This is not just a mental process between two sets of people. It involves physical, mental and spiritual aspects of individuals, groups and societies and requires high levels of fitness from those involved if a solution is to be found – hence our emphasis on the importance of holistic approaches as demonstrated in our Global Fitness Framework.

Here we have explored the issue of forced marriage but shown that the route to tackling this issue effectively can be applied in many situations in a leader's development and practice. This will include those applicable to the business world.

## Religion

In this case we look at religion as a generic form, seeking to adopt a detached, objective position as a way of raising issues and questions related to the MisLeadership elements identified in this book. The difficulty of doing this was clear in the previous case where we had to adopt and state a particular stance. As religion is often largely based on some form of faith it is perhaps particularly susceptible to issues of MisLeadership.

People who believe the world is around 5,000 years old tend to also believe God created a man and a woman shortly after that and the whole of humanity has descended from them, through tribes and nations who spread throughout the world. That is their religion based on what their parents and other important adults often including a religious teacher told them, passed down through the generations and forming part of their embedded values as described in Chapter 1.

Those who believe in evolution may believe that as humanity developed each tribe would have slowly created its own set of beliefs as to such fundamental questions as where the wind and rain come from, the movements of the sun and moon and what happens to a person's life force when they die. These beliefs would have been passed from parents to children and again become part of the tribe's embedded values.

Contact with other tribes may have led to exchange of ideas and adoption, with modifications, of each other's beliefs if they had appeal. Over time, a particular individual would have emerged who seemed to have a good understanding of such concepts and became the tribe's authority on such matters. This would have been an important role to them so they would have attempted to ensure it passed on to either their own offspring or some other trusted person who had similar understanding.

As tribes grew into nations it was likely that spiritual leaders would experience some problems in maintaining control. One way of overcoming this would be to formalise the faith by establishing rituals, specific beliefs, a hierarchy of control (as discussed in Chapter 5) and a system of rewards (heaven?) and punishments (hell?). Such steps are perhaps what differentiates religion from a broader spirituality and may cause some people to resist if they feel the formal teachings do not meet their own beliefs. Often the power of the religious leaders has been such that few would have dared to openly disagree with their teaching.

Such measures may have enabled the religious leaders to retain and pass on their power unless and until a major event caused the demise of their belief system. At some point the event would be the leader's own death but even then as stated above the religious leader would want the belief system to continue so would have prepared for the event by grooming a successor.

Other potential events threatening the continuity of a religion include conquest by another nation, a natural disaster undermining the claimed relationship between the religious leaders and their god(s), revelation of a truth that their belief system could not embrace or the establishment of a different religion. To resist the last of these religious leaders have been known to attack and punish anyone preaching different beliefs and/or challenging the current dominant view. At the same time, they were keen to spread their sphere of influence by encouraging followers to convert non-believers to their religion. Lessening the threat through conquest could be achieved by spreading the religion into neighbouring countries, evangelising being an important element of most religions.

To support the validity of their claim to be representatives of god on earth, some religious leaders first attempted to prove the existence of their god(s) including suggesting the working of miracles or some other form of divine intervention. Second, they attempted to prove their special relationship with that god by such means as creating a lineage, establishing rituals and rites, support from royal families, display of physical power (domineering and awe-inspiring buildings, gold and treasures, rich and expansive garments, military might), special prayers and incantations, and use of magic and potions including relics of saints. The word of god, written in a book which is held in special reverence, also supports their position. Some of these may be seen as attempts to mislead existing and potential followers.

To the extent that different religious beliefs conflict with each other, one belief may have all the right interpretations, they each may have a partial truth, or all may be wrong. In areas where the different beliefs do not conflict they are effectively the same religion. All this seems logical and yet we rarely see this fact being presented by the leaders of different religions. More often we see each claiming strongly that they have all the right interpretations, the one true faith and the followers of other religions are at best misguided and at worst evil. It may be that their beliefs are the same in the vast majority of important aspects, yet leaders and followers tend to focus on their differences. Time spent in this manner does little to solve UGIs or approach Heaven on Earth. They have often ridiculed each other's beliefs, while holding onto beliefs that can look equally ridiculous to objective outsiders. This approach has often resulted in conflicts and wars. Whichever particular perspective you have, some element of the above scenario must be MisLeadership aimed at maintaining or increasing identity, power, wealth or dominance.

Many religions want to be seen as constant and unchanging, claiming their beliefs are based literally on the word of god(s) and thus eternal, which as shown above may be a fundamental element of their claim to power. This causes difficulty when scientific discoveries or new social norms appear to conflict with the written word. Figure 7.2 looks at a specific case which relates to the conflict between scientific discoveries and beliefs, and how this conflict was handled. It relates to the Catholic Church but similar examples can be seen in many different beliefs. It concerns Galileo, his use of a telescope to discover that planets are globes spinning round the sun, and his deduction that the earth did the same. This deduction was, however, in direct conflict with the teachings of the church at that time; teachings that said the earth was in the middle with heaven above and hell below.

Figure 7.3 on page 178 contains Galileo's confession.

## APPLICATION OF GLOBALLY FIT LEADERSHIP

This is a fascinating case particularly as we know Galileo's deductions ultimately proved to be accurate. Although times and social norms have changed and we look at things through a different lens now there is still a lot we can learn from this case about MisLeadership and how to overcome it.

On 15 January 1633, Galileo wrote to his friend Ella Diodati setting out his views on why the Bible should not be treated as literally true. At this time he was in deep trouble over his claims that the earth moved and was facing a trial which took place a few months later. The translation of Galileo's comments said:

"When I ask: whose work is the Sun, the Moon, the Earth, the Stars, their motions and dispositions, I shall probably be told that they are God's work. When I continue to ask whose work is Holy Scripture, I shall certainly be told that it is the work of the Holy Ghost, i.e., God's work also. If now I ask if the Holy Ghost uses words which are manifest contradictions of the truth so as to satisfy the understanding of the generally uneducated - masses, I am convinced that I shall be told, with many citations from all the sanctified writers, that this is indeed the custom of Holy Scripture, containing as it does hundreds of passages that taken literally would be nothing but heresy and blasphemy, for in them God appears as a Being full of hatred, guilt and forgetfulness. If now I ask whether God, so as to be understood by the masses, had ever altered His works, or else if Nature, unchangeable and inaccessible as it is to human desires, has always retained the same kinds of motion, forms and divisions of the Universe... To condense all this into one phrase: Nobody will maintain that Nature has ever changed in order to make its works palatable to men. If this be the case, then I ask why it is that, in order to arrive at an understanding of the different parts of the world, we must begin with the investigation of the Words of God, rather than of His Works. Is then the Work less venerable than the Word? If someone had held it to be heresy to say that the Earth moves, and if later verification and experiments were to show us that it does indeed do so, what difficulties would the church not encounter! If, on the contrary, whenever the works and the Word cannot be made to agree, we consider Holy Scripture as secondary, no harm will befall it, for it has often been modified to suit the masses and has frequently attributed false qualities to God. Therefore I must ask why it is that we insist that whenever it speaks of the Sun or of the Earth, Holy Scripture be considered as quite infallible?"

**Figure 7.2    The Galileo case**

*Source*: St Andrews University 2009.

Is this case an example of MisLeadership by the then cardinals of the church? Could these cardinals have been feeling that there was insufficient evidence to challenge their teachings as it had only come from one person? Is this an example of attempts by those high in the church to purposely mislead followers in order to maintain the perceived correctness of their teachings? Is it an example of a broader MisLeadership by the Catholic or Christian church? If any of these are the case, what might the purpose of this MisLeadership have been – greater good of humanity; maintaining power, wealth and influence; maintaining the perceived correctness of their teachings; or fear of the unknown? As we highlighted in Chapter 6 Machiavellian Leadership can

*On 22 June 1633 Galileo, having been found guilty at his trial, was forced to make a 'confession' to the Cardinals of the Holy Office of the Church. He read from the text of which a translation is given below:*

*"I, Galileo Galilei, son of the late Vincenzio Galilei of Florence, aged seventy years, being brought personally to judgment, and kneeling before you, Most Eminent and Most Reverend Lords Cardinals, General Inquisitors of the Universal Christian Commonwealth against heretical depravity, having before my eyes the Holy Gospels which I touch with my own hands, swear that I have always believed, and, with the help of God, will in future believe, every article which the Holy Catholic and Apostolic Church of Rome holds, teaches, and preaches. But because I have been enjoined, by this Holy Office, altogether to abandon the false opinion which maintains that the Sun is the centre and immovable, and forbidden to hold, defend, or teach, the said false doctrine in any manner ... I am willing to remove from the minds of your Eminences, and of every Catholic Christian, this vehement suspicion rightly entertained towards me, therefore, with a sincere heart and unfeigned faith, I abjure, curse, and detest the said errors and heresies, and generally every other error and sect contrary to the said Holy Church; and I swear that I will never more in future say, or assert anything, verbally or in writing, which may give rise to a similar suspicion of me; but that if I shall know any heretic, or any one suspected of heresy, I will denounce him to this Holy Office, or to the Inquisitor and Ordinary of the place in which I may be. I swear, moreover, and promise that I will fulfil and observe fully all the penances which have been or shall be laid on me by this Holy Office. But if it shall happen that I violate any of my said promises, oaths, and protestations (which God avert!), I subject myself to all the pains and punishments which have been decreed and promulgated by the sacred canons and other general and particular constitutions against delinquents of this description. So, may God help me, and His Holy Gospels, which I touch with my own hands, I, the above named Galileo Galilei, have abjured, sworn, promised, and bound myself as above; and, in witness thereof, with my own hand have subscribed this present writing of my abjuration, which I have recited word for word."*

**Figure 7.3     Galileo's confession**

*Source*: St Andrews University 2009.

only be successful if followers are unaware of the MisLeadership taking place or are willing to condone it. Some of the church leaders would have been aware of Galileo's deductions and possibly accepted his conclusion. How did they feel about and react to the MisLeadership that occurred and why did they react in that manner?

This new scientific discovery by Galileo called into question some of the underpinning teachings of the church and had the potential to undermine its credibility. Dealing with this new information effectively would require high levels of physical, mental and spiritual strength, stamina and particularly suppleness as identified in the Global Fitness Framework in Chapter 3.

Or could this case have been an example of those leaders in the church actually misleading themselves as they desperately tried to hold onto what they believed and had committed their lives too? Perhaps fear prevented them from fully considering the evidence. Drawing again on the Global Fitness Framework in Chapter 3, this is an example of the need for mental and spiritual suppleness. Instead of being supple and fully considering all the evidence through engaging in a critically constructive dialogue with Galileo, which would have demonstrated the type of effective problem-solving approach outlined in Chapter 2, we see that the church leaders used their huge power base to crush Galileo and force a confession from him on the errors of his thinking.

Galileo's case may indicate Machiavellian and Misguided Leadership if the reason the leaders acted as they did was to cling to power and refuse to consider the possibility that they might be wrong despite the evidence. It also reflects the fact that these leaders had themselves been misinformed by previous leaders. At some point someone must have invented the 'heaven above, hell below' myth and it had been passed down through subsequent generations without challenge by anyone powerful enough to achieve change. Perhaps this is one of the greatest examples of groupthink.

As we have shown, Globally Fit Leadership requires a global outlook and effective problem-solving processes, particularly the ASK elements of the model discussed in Chapter 2, and all aspects in the Global Fitness Framework in Chapter 3. Perhaps more willingness to consider and investigate Galileo's deductions and a more open, honest and transparent stance would have assisted people to uncover and deal effectively with the actual situation of the Earth rotating round the Sun. Fear of one form or another seems to be a key reason influencing the actions of the church leaders but their actions actually display a lack of faith in their god which in the long-term may have undermined credibility of both them and their religion.

Or perhaps the church leaders were indeed showing effective problem-solving skills. By crushing Galileo and making an example of him, they literally put the fear of God into him and his followers to ensure they kept silent for enough time for the leaders to carefully consider how to react. It is also true to say that this was a tremendous test of faith for them and their followers.

Perhaps the best way to cope with such a change was to initially deny it but then gradually change the church's teaching to encompass it which would also give them a chance to accept and internalise it and try to work out its ramifications. That is in fact what happened and is the approach adopted by many ancient, venerable organisations faced with changes beyond their comfort zones. The Catholic Church has existed for some 1600 years so must be doing something right.

Whatever the real reasons, and even taking into account the changing times and historical context, it is a clear and rather shocking example of MisLeadership. This all took place in 1633, nearly 400 years ago, but has similarities to the type of issue religious communities are still struggling with today. In 1948, over 300 years after Galileo and just 60 years ago, Mahatma Gandhi said (according to Williams 2009):

> *In the name of God we have indulged in lies and in massacres of*
> *people without caring whether they were innocent or guilty, men or*
> *women, children or infants. We have indulged in abductions, forcible*
> *conversions – and we have done this shamelessly. I am not aware if*
> *anyone has done these things in the name of Truth.*

It is relevant to recall the abuse of children in institutions run by religious congregations in Ireland as discussed in Chapter 2 in the Toxic Childhood case.

Just 10 years ago, the Geneva Spiritual Appeal (1999) called on all religious communities, and indeed the whole world, to adhere to three basic principles: a refusal to invoke a religious or spiritual power to justify violence of any kind; a refusal to invoke a religious or spiritual source to justify discrimination or exclusion; a refusal to exploit or dominate others by means of strength, intellectual capacity of spiritual persuasion, wealth or social status. Some of this sounds much like what happened to Galileo nearly 400 years earlier.

Today the Anglican Church is in crisis according to Burrell (2008), Rural Dean in the Diocese of Coventry and formerly Archdeacon of Pretoria East. Burrell argues that as far as the Christian church is concerned, the crisis manifests itself in the increasing secularisation of the world, the dechristianisation of the West, a growing gap between rich and poor and younger churches becoming more autonomous. One of the speakers at the 14th Lambeth Conference in 2008, Dr Brian McLaren (as cited in Burell 2008:1), said:

*The old model of the church was a bridge that stood strong and firm in the desert; the river now flowed elsewhere. It has been built for modernity, but the world was postmodern ... We are deep into a paradigm shift ... We have to be ready for a season of unlearning and new learning.*

Recent research by Richmond, Chaplain at Coventry Cathedral and Spencer, Research Director at the London Institute for Contemporary Christianity (Richmond and Spencer 2005:160) also highlights a great deal of criticism of the church being made by respondents. They saw it as: 'dull, narrow, bigoted, hypocritical, embarrassing, unreal, prescriptive, unspiritual, judgemental, patriarchal, credulous, inflexible, corrupt, a waste of time and unable to handle doubt'. Again much of what we saw occurring in the Galileo case.

Richmond and Spenser (2005:12) consider for the UK whether:

*A Christian skeleton – which has long held and structured people's spiritual lives – has decayed and left in its place a slowly unravelling and increasingly amorphous body of often powerfully-held spiritual beliefs, many of which are shaped by ghosts of Christian doctrine.*

Respondents in their research indicated they had strong spiritual beliefs or big spiritual questions, supporting the importance of the spiritual domain in the Global Fitness Framework. The main challenge for the Christian church today seems to be how to respond to the need for assistance with these big questions and the finding of a new paradigm, and how to embrace a 'season of new learning'. We would argue these are common challenges, not just for the church and it is something we return to in Chapter 8.

This case study commenced with a brief outline of the basic ideas of creationism and evolution. Interestingly, many monotheists are somewhere in the middle having been told the former story when they were very young and still attracted to the appeal of a loving god and eternal life, but gradually been pulled toward the other as they studied or heard about various aspects of science such as geology, palaeontology and evolution. DNA is proving to be a particularly challenging discovery for those who believe the world is only a few thousand years old. Perhaps the process from Galileo through Darwin and to the present day is one of religions gradually reacting to scientific revelations that rock their foundations.

The Galileo case also seems to have striking similarities to the approach being taken today by many of the leaders of large multinational corporations and nations of the world to the evidence on global warming and other urgent global issues illustrated in Table 1.1. Denial, fear, claims of insufficient evidence, and overriding focus on the maintenance of power and wealth for example are common.

## The Tour de France

One of the greatest global sporting events that has taken place nearly every year since 1903 and one of the greatest tests of human endurance is the Tour de France cycling race. It covers 3,500 kilometres around France and bordering countries in three weeks including ascending some of the highest and severest climbs imaginable. But even this great sporting event has not escaped the clutches of MisLeadership.

Many examples are documented in the race's earlier years of competitors trying to mislead race organisers, other competitors and the general public by taking short cuts and hitching rides on cars, trucks and trains in an attempt to cheat their way to victory. Sadly the sport is best known though for its MisLeadership over the use of drugs by participating riders. This is well documented in many publications including Sports Scientist (2007), where much of the information on this case was obtained.

The Tour de France has suffered from doping since the early 1900s when riders were drinking wine laced with strychnine to 'dull the pain'. With World War II came the introduction of amphetamines which had been created to assist soldiers in battle to remain alert and focused but were soon used by professional cyclists, among them Tom Simpson, who famously died near the summit of the Mont Ventoux in the 1960s. In the book *Put me back on my bike* by Fotheringham, Simpson is credited with the following quote:

> *I know from the way they ride the next day that they are taking dope. I don't want to have to take it – I have too much respect for my body – but if I don't win a big event soon, I shall have to start taking it.*

Also at this time, one of the men to have won the Tour five times, Jacques Anquetil, reportedly perfected the use of 'the Anquetil cocktail' comprising a painkiller, morphine or palfium, injected directly into painful muscles even whilst cycling; an amphetamine to offset the somnolent effect of morphine;

and a sleeping tablet, Gardenal, to allow sleep when the stimulatory effects of the amphetamines were still active. Anquetil's recorded comment is that:

> *You would have to be an imbecile or a crook to imagine that a professional cyclist who races for 235 days a year can hold the pace without stimulants.*

Anquetil also reportedly stated:

> *For 50 years bike racers have been taking stimulants. Obviously we can do without them in a race, but then we will pedal 15 miles an hour (instead of 25). Since we are constantly asked to go faster and to make even greater efforts, we are obliged to take stimulants.*

(All above quotations are cited in Sports Scientist 2007.)

There are numerous stories about how cyclists have tried many ingenious methods to mislead doping controllers. One example given in Moore (2008:61) is of the 1978 Tour de France race leader, Michel Pollentier, trying to mislead doping controls by using a bulb and tube, operated from the armpits and passing down through the shorts, to dispense old, 'clean' urine into the doping controllers test tube. In the Festina affair in 1998 (BBC 2000) customs officials found the Festina team masseur was carrying 400 bottles and capsules of doping products three days before the Tour was due to start in Dublin. During police questioning the team doctor admitted the whole Festina team used doping under medical supervision and the team was banned. During that year's race, one leg was delayed and another abandoned due to other riders protesting about investigations into other teams. The biggest doping scandal ever to befall cycling according to Moore (2008:263) was in the aftermath of the 2006 Tour de France when Tour favourites Jan Ullrich and Ivan Basso and six other riders were excluded from the race after being implicated in blood doping; and the winner Floyd Landis tested positive for testosterone.

One example of the debate over drugs and the validity of tests performed relates to the use of EPO. Asplund (2003) stated:

> *Although no direct links have been made between EPO and cycling deaths, anecdotal evidence is abundant. Too much r-EPO can increase hematocrit to the point that overall blood viscosity is increased making the blood like sludge. This thickened blood could cause the heart to work excessively hard, which may lead to a heart attack. Increasing*

*hematocrit also increases the risk in the cyclist for clotting events, raises blood pressure, and resultant iron overload can ultimately lead to organ failure. Evidence has shown that long-term EPO use may also possibly contribute to blood borne cancers.*

*Despite the potentially fatal risks, it is apparent that many professional cyclists may be using EPO to improve performance. Because EPO potentially gives an unfair advantage in competition, it has been banned by the Union Cycliste Internationale (UCI). As EPO is a natural body substance it is very hard to detect by conventional (direct) testing methods. Levels of synthetic EPO can be detected, but the half-life is so short, that r-EPO is out of the system within 6–12 hours. Other detection methods have been focused on abnormally high hematocrit levels. In Geneva in 1997, the UCI implemented an upper level of normal for hematocrit of 50 per cent, and 2.4 for the reticulocyte count. Those cyclists testing higher than these levels are then subjected to the more accurate French urine test, which is an indirect test that looks for specific biomechanical properties of synthetic EPO using sophisticated laboratory techniques (gel electrophoresis).*

According to Millar (as cited in Moore 2008:340) less than 5 per cent of the population get anywhere near the 50 per cent hematocrit level and those blood values go down with training and racing. And yet the professional cyclists all have near the 50 per cent limit – how can their levels be so high? According to Obree (as cited in Moore 2008:286) it is because 99 per cent of elite riders are taking EPO or a similar drug, and control their use of the drug so they stay just below the 50 per cent maximum level permitted.

Nobody who follows or is involved in the sport can be oblivious to the suspicion that, at the top level, the use of performance enhancing products is prevalent. But Moore (2008:254) suggests drugs in cycling is viewed like speeding on the motorway – *'driving fast is not the problem, getting caught is.'* Could this be because the socialisation of MisLeadership that has occurred throughout the racers' careers has as we outlined in Chapter 1 de-sensitised people to their and other people's acts of MisLeadership?

Bellocq argued (in Moore 2008:259):

*It's not physiologically possible to compete for four consecutive days at over 200 km including three or four cols at over 1,500 metres in*

*altitude. At this level, cycling is no longer a pleasurable pastime but a*
*very dangerous sport as far as health is concerned.*

This is another clear example of Misguided Leadership as competitors attempt to mislead themselves, other competitors, doping controllers and the general public as to the physical, mental and spiritual strength and stamina of the professional cyclists. They try to make us believe they have superhuman abilities to be able to cycle much further, faster, higher and longer than mere mortals. We argue that it is not just the competitors, however, who are trying to mislead. Drug use in the sport is so rife that everyone knows about it – doctors, managers, sponsors, race organisers, drugs testers, controlling bodies and the fans. They all allow it to go on, turning a blind eye, deliberately attempting to misinform the public in the misguided belief that this causes the greatness of the spectacle and feats of human endurance to be marvelled at by spectators when it is clear that those spectators have seen the true situation and are actually turning away from the sport. Thus they are not only putting riders' lives and health at risk but are also ruining the sport. As Robert Millar, one of the most famous British cyclists of all time puts it (cited in Moore 2008:341):

> *It's not as simple as blaming just the riders because everyone involved,*
> *from the team management all the way up to the ruling bodies have*
> *some responsibility.*

Bellocq (cited in Moore 2008:257) considered the subject of doping in professional cycling to be *'riddled with inconsistencies, falsehoods and hypocrisy'* – all classic signs and symptoms of Machiavellian MisLeadership in action.

There is strong evidence that the approach taken to drugs within professional cycling has radically harmed the sport. Particularly since the Festina affair in 1998, public confidence and belief in the feats of cyclists have waned. As Fiedler (2009) put it after Landis tested positive after an improbable 80-mile solo attack during stage 17 of the 2006 tour though the Alps:

> *For many, it was like having their hearts ripped out and stomped on*
> *with bike shoes.*

Fiedler (2009) suggests some believe:

> *'Cycling's image is tarnished beyond repair', and 'it'll be painful to*
> *finally clean up the mess' (of drug taking) once and for all, but these are*

*necessary steps for professional cycling to take if there is to be any hope*
*of one day luring back the sponsors and fans who have vanished as a*
*result of these dark episodes.*

## APPLICATION OF GLOBALLY FIT LEADERSHIP

It is clear that drug-taking in professional cycling is an embedded systemic
problem affecting all elements of the profession. It may not be possible to solve
it quickly or easily and there are likely to be many significant implications,
repercussions and emotions involved. Even so, the decision to be made is clear
and simple and due to its systemic nature must involve all stakeholders but
driven from the top, in this case cycling's ruling bodies.

These bodies need to be strong and bold, take responsibility for the issue
and show clear and effective leadership. They need to be transparent and
honest about what they do and do not know about drugs and drug testing in
the sport, and what is accepted in relation to doping and what is not. They need
to set rules that can be enforced, then carry out such enforcement fairly but
ruthlessly. A very important facet will be obtaining the support of other parties
involved, including the riders, sponsors and team bosses.

It is very likely that there will be difficulties to be overcome in taking action
against those who break the rules that have been set, but these have to be faced.
Some racers and teams may attempt to sue but the vast majority of people in
the sport are likely to respond favourably to attempts to make the issues more
clear and transparent. Most riders presumably only take the inherent risks
because of peer pressure and knowing they will not be able to compete against
those who take illegal drugs.

Open discussion will help them persuade these stakeholders of the benefits
to be gained from cleaning up the sport and making it more transparent. These
include health and safety of riders, genuine sporting prowess being appreciated
and rewarded, genuine performance records being established, more accurate
and valid comparisons over time and regaining the trust and respect of
the spectators, thereby increasing sponsorship and their own feelings of
achievement. The negative aspects of having cheats winning events should also
be recognised including its effects on spiritual fitness such as that it discourages
honesty and openness of all kinds, is bad for motivation and morale, shows
low morals and undermines the whole ethos of sport. It clearly sets a very bad
example to people thinking of taking up the sport, basically telling anyone who
is not prepared to cheat and risk their health that they cannot win.

The ruling bodies seem to assume that the general public would react negatively to such an approach but the opposite may well be true, the leaders being misguided in their belief due to allowing their own misinformed assumptions to dominate their thinking despite evidence to the contrary. They seem to be frightened to take action due to this fear, but should instead show spiritual and mental fitness by taking what they know in their hearts is the right decision and facing the consequences. If their fears are well founded, at least they will have acted courageously but if their fears prove false, they will have saved the sport they love and given support and leadership to all other people who feel they cannot act. In short they must be globally fit leaders.

## The Asbestos Industry

Information for this analysis was drawn from the extensive study by Janet Moran (2009) of 'The Ethics and Morality of Asbestos Sales' undertaken as part of her MBA dissertation at Anglia Ruskin University. Thanks and recognition go to her for this extensive and valuable piece of work.

The asbestos debate offers a fascinating and powerful global case study which demonstrates mankind's intrinsic capability to mislead and knowingly inflict fatal consequences upon countless vulnerable victims. It is a *'synoptic account of Man's inhumanity to Man in the context of asbestos'* according to Greenberg (2006:87).

At the same time, however, asbestos has some extraordinary qualities which would make it an ideal material for many building applications were it not for its fatal flaw that it causes incurable and fatal cancers. It is virtually fire proof, retains a significant resistance to all chemicals, has the tensile strength of steel and is extreme versatile. By 1958 asbestos could be found in over 3,000 products and was hailed for its life saving qualities.

Tweedale (2003) provides a compelling insight into one of the largest UK asbestos manufacturers Turner and Newell and exposes many instances of systemic and embedded MisLeadership by that organisation's management, the UK government, factory inspectors and medical professionals. Bowker (2003) did a study based on an asbestos mining town in Montana, USA, owned by one of the largest asbestos manufacturers in the world throughout the 1990s, Johns-Manville Corporation and revealed a similar tale of greed, cruel deceit, unfortunate circumstance and powerful human tragedy.

Campbell and Kitson (2008:47) suggest that industrialists such as Turner and Newell were driven by a sole focus on profit for the sake of shareholders regardless of the cost to life, and yet were considered to be dignified and devoted members of the Methodist Church who bestowed local communities with an array of charitable donations. Greenberg (2006: 87) also highlights how far Turner and Newell were prepared to go to disguise the growing death rate, through a persistent onslaught of deception to government inspectors, employees, the local community and customers. He says:

> The Turners followed the behaviour of fellow tycoons in combining brutal and even illegal industrial and commercial practice with public charity.

Bowker (2003: 57) highlights a similar situation in the Johns-Manville Corporation. A disturbing acknowledgement of missed opportunities and Missing Leadership, particularly as it dates back as far as 1932 and refers to the preceding 25 years, was observed by Thomas Legge a former Medical Inspector of Factories at the Commission on Compensatable Diseases (1906–1913) (as cited by Harrington 1999:2):

> The story of asbestos is a long one ... I was impressed as to the injurious nature of the dust by that evidence (1906). At various times during the next 20 years, the injurious character of the industry was investigated, but no detailed medical examination of the work people ... was ever made. Looking back in the light of present knowledge, it is impossible not to feel that opportunities and prevention were badly missed (pp. 190–1).

This type of MisLeadership was not exclusive to the UK and appears to have been global.

Today, the Health and Safety Executive (n.d.) considers asbestos to be the *'greatest single cause of work related deaths in the UK.'* A similar situation can be found within all countries that were producing and consuming asbestos throughout the 1900s. The World Health Organization (WHO 2006) estimates a staggering 90,000 global deaths per annum are associated to exposure to asbestos, and as a result more than 40 countries, including all member states of the European Union (EU), have now prohibited its production, supply and use.

Asbestosis, lung cancer and mesothelioma are the three fatal diseases associated to asbestos that besieged the workers of the mines, factories and mills and continue to threaten the lives of current and future generations. The HSE confirm a UK annual death rate of 4,000, expected to continue to rise, and that one in 17 British carpenters born in the 1940s will die of mesothelioma. For plumbers, electricians and decorators born in the same decade the risk is one in 50 and for other construction workers one in 125. Mesothelioma has been reported in some individuals who had no known exposure to asbestos, including Leigh Carlisle who died in 2008, aged just 28, believed to have been the youngest UK victim of an asbestos related disease with no known exposure (MailOnline 2008).

Between 1988 and 1992 Lloyds lost almost £8bn (as reported by the BBC 2006), some £4bn relating to asbestos claims from the US. The growing death rate brings with it a mounting weight of claims which currently grow at an estimated rate of 50,000 every year. By 2000, insurance companies had paid out approximately US$21.6 billion  in addition to the US$31 billion that had been settled by individual organisations prosecuted within the USA (Hure 2004:7–8). Within Europe, WHO anticipate an estimated cost of over US$500 billion in settlement of insurance and compensation claims in respect to the anticipated 400,000 people that will die from an asbestos related disease over the next few decades (Neira 2008:1).

Despite the 'magical mineral' of the industrial revolution becoming such a significant health hazard and economic burden in the developed world it remains in global production and use. According to the United States Geological Society (USGS 2007:86) the global asbestos market in 2007 was estimated to be 2.2 million tonnes. This is being produced by Russia, China, Kazakhstan, Brazil, Canada, and Zimbabwe to meet growing demand from countries such as Ukraine, Uzbekistan, India, Thailand, Indonesia, Vietnam and the Republic of Korea – a combination of nations that are either sustaining economic growth or besieged with poverty (USGS 2006).

Asbestos is used to provide much needed shelter and water supply to millions of impoverished individuals. Its durability and low production cost make it the obvious choice for such people.

Producers argue that the risk is insignificant, and substitute materials are uneconomical. Russia, the largest producer of asbestos since 1975, claims that up to 500,000 workers in the country could lose their jobs if there was a global ban on production (AFP 2007). Walker (2009) states that the town of Asbest in the Ural area has 76,000 residents dependent on the continued production of asbestos with more than 70 per cent of the families having at least one member who works within the mines and factories.

An estimated 170,000 workers in India's and China's asbestos mining and manufacturing industries and many hundreds of thousands more in other producing and consuming nations could lose a secured income. Many of these have a low level of education and lack awareness of occupational health and safety issues (World Asbestos Report 2007a and b).

## COMPLEXITY

We can therefore see two competing pressures in this case. On the one hand we have clear evidence of the health risks, growing death rate and rising health and insurance costs associated with asbestos production and use. On the other, we see a multi-billion pound industry, providing jobs for hundreds of thousands of people, producing an inexpensive and durable product that requires simple technology to make, does not require large capital investments and provides shelter for hundreds of millions of the poorest people in the world.

These tensions raise major ethical, moral and financial issues and reflect the complex nature of many problems facing modern leaders. To further cloud the issue there is debate over the risks associated with the one remaining type of asbestos in production – chrysotile (white). The fibre structure in this form of asbestos differs from all other forms and many of the current producers and consumers argue that the risk in respect to chrysotile is insignificant. LaDou (2004:6), however, identifies many who show that on a per-fibre basis, the highest risks of lung cancer have been shown for chrysotile. The IPCS (1998:144) conclude *'exposure to chrysotile asbestos poses increased risks for asbestosis, lung cancer and mesothelioma.'* The World Health Organization, World Trade Organization, International Labour Organization, International Social Security Association and the European Union have all recognised a need for a global ban on worldwide production.

Machiavellian Leadership was evident within the asbestos industry world wide during much of the twentieth century and may be continuing in the present day. Johnson (2009:20) suggests leaders in the industry are using *'dysfunctional impression management to send deceptive messages, undermine relationships, and distort information, which leads to poor conclusions and decisions'* in the debate concerning the risks from using chrysotile asbestos. This would mean Machiavellian Leadership was still being practised.

We wonder:

- Does the relationship between the developed and developing world, and the power concerned, have any bearing on this?

- How much the continued supply is influenced by MisLeadership practices?

## THE TOBACCO INDUSTRY

The tobacco industry provides a very similar case to that of asbestos and before moving to look at how the asbestos industry could move ahead, we briefly outline the tobacco industry case. Tobacco is the second major cause of death in the world. According to the World Health Organization (WHO 2008) it has killed 100 million people in the twentieth century and is currently killing 5.4 million every year. WHO suggest that unless urgent action is taken, by 2030 there will be 8 million deaths every year and 80 per cent of these deaths will be in developing countries and they estimate there will be one billion deaths during the twenty-first century.

Given these rather startling figures one has to ask why smoking has not been completely banned. Drawing extensively on McDaniel, Intinarelli and Malone (2008) we argue that part of the reasons has been the MisLeadership occurring within the various tobacco industries.

According to Brandt (2007:452) during the last half of the twentieth century increased knowledge of the risks of tobacco use led to increased regulation and declining consumption in Western nations. Given this information related to the increased risk of tobacco use, the tobacco industry would obviously be presented with somewhat of a moral dilemma. On the one hand a cessation of all production would be the best strategy for overall public good, but on the other this would be catastrophic for their own industry, resulting profits and the livelihoods of people employed in the industry.

It is clearly a moral dilemma, which may be most effectively addressed by adopting a Globally Fit Leadership strategy as will be outlined below. With the weight of public opinion in developed countries this strategy might have been difficult and instead the tobacco industry response (according to Brandt 2007:452–3) was to adopt a Machiavellian MisLeadership strategy in order to defend their industry at home while expanding their international operations.

They supported trade liberalisation policies and brought sophisticated and aggressive marketing techniques to countries with few smoking restrictions and limited knowledge of the health consequences of smoking. McDaniel et al. (2008:2) also argue that the tobacco manufacturers established a series of cross-company 'issues management' organisations and national manufacturers' associations to develop common strategies to thwart tobacco control effects at national and regional levels and to maintain tobacco-friendly environments, particularly in developing countries.

McDaniel et al. highlight a large number of research studies that have revealed how the industry has:

> Deceived the public and policy makers about the harms of tobacco, manipulated science, used third parties to promote its agenda, targeted vulnerable populations, and interfered with regulatory and public policy processes.

This strategy did not pay off in the long-term. In 1997 the US Attorney-General, Janet Reno (1997 as cited by De Woot 2009:86), said:

> [They] deceived the public about the risks of cancer caused by tobacco, conducted their business without regard for the truth, the law, the health of the American people, campaigning to preserve their enormous profits whatever the cost in human lives, in suffering and in medical expenditure, organizing a public relations campaign to create false debate on these points, lying about the dependency of the smoker with regard to tobacco, recruiting new smokers among children in order to replace those who had died.

On the 22 May 2009 CBC News (2009) reported:

> A U.S. Federal Appeal Court on Friday largely agreed with a landmark ruling that found cigarette makers deceived the public for decades about the health hazards of smoking.

McDaniel et al. (2008:2) point out:

> These behaviours are not unique to the tobacco industry; research on internal asbestos and chemical industry documents has uncovered similar actions.

## APPLICATION OF GLOBALLY FIT LEADERSHIP

The tobacco and asbestos industries are good examples of the worst aspects of MisLeadership in action: individuals, companies and countries have acted selfishly in their own interest and have been willing to ignore externalities such as other people's health. Some would argue that they are still continuing to do this today. Spiritual and societal aspects have been given little consideration; cheap natural resources have been exploited to increase business growth, their adverse effects being kept hidden for as long as possible by the manufacturers; companies have been forced to implement high standards of health care in the developed world but such standards have not been applied in the undeveloped world; attempts have been made to continue use of risky products by muddying the argument through circulation of misleading information to government inspectors, employees, the local community and customers; a confrontational approach has been adopted by the parties to the debate:

> *Moving the risks elsewhere does not fit in with the aim of fair globalization that offers opportunities for everyone. It is a big but important challenge to expand the asbestos ban to all countries in the world. To that end, the international community must provide knowledge and assistance to help them cope with the necessary restructuring measures, create alternative jobs and promote the use of asbestos substitutes around the world. (Source: Jukka Takala, Director of the European Agency for Safety and Health at Work (as cited in Mines and Communities (MAC 2006).)*

Some of these MisLeadership actions may have stemmed from ethical fading as discussed in Chapter 6. It often seems to be the case that people who are in an industry that turns out to have adverse health consequences become desensitised to the issue as it develops and thus continue to make products that they may have shunned if coming into the industry at a later stage. Such embedded, institutionalised and systematic MisLeadership can be a major reason for it continuing over many years.

The tobacco industry is, to our mind, clearly based on MisLeadership. If those involved in the asbestos industry, however, adopted the kind of approaches suggested throughout this book we believe an informed debate could take place as to the societal risks and benefits of asbestos use. Such an honest, transparent and open debate would help ensure all those affected would be able to make informed decisions.

The economic and societal circumstances in the developing world are markedly different to those in the developed world and it is unrealistic to apply the same health and safety standards to both. The benefits from using asbestos are substantial so if there are little dangers from chrysotile asbestos such open, honest and transparent debate might lead to the safe use of asbestos and enable all countries to benefit from its extraordinary qualities. This transparent exploration would also switch the debate from wasted time and resources on defence and maintaining one's position to genuine exploration and learning. This could seek ways of using asbestos safely, and help explore what other alternatives may be developed.

## Positive Initial Steps

Having discussed four cases illustrating MisLeadership and its complexities, we now give a few examples of individuals and organisations that have taken initial steps toward tackling these issues.

| |
|---|
| **Globally Responsible Leadership Initiative** |
| **Avaaz** |
| **State Of The World Forum** |
| **Al Gore** |
| **Center For Spirituality And The Workplace** |
| **CIMA's Business Trust: A Critical Time Initiative** |
| **Aspen Institute's Corporate Values Strategy Group** |
| **The Gates Foundation** |

We have tried to draw on examples from a variety of situations which highlight that MisLeadership is not just limited to one profession, culture or society and nor is the call and scope for action. They set the scene for our final chapter where we summarise the learning points and suggest ways in which we as individuals, groups and societies can begin to make the changes required in the new age.

## Globally Responsible Leadership Initiative

The GRLI is a global initiative with 63 partners from business and business schools from around the world. It has 10 Strategic Levers for Change:

1.  The Principles for Responsible Management Education (PRME) Initiative which requires business schools to commit to six

principles of responsible education in carrying out their role (more information at www.prme.org)

2.     Advocacy through being a resource centre

3.     Research and publications on twenty-first century corporations, the purpose of business schools and management education, and the process for cultural change in organisations

4.     The diffusion of good practices

5.     New approaches to learning and education with a focus on whole-person learning

6.     GRLI Ambassadors are students who debate concepts and their integration into the curricula and business practices of their employers. These ambassadors will form the emerging community of responsible young leaders

7.     Award and recognition programme for examples of good practice within businesses and business schools

8.     CEOs and Deans international forum

9.     Developing accreditation criteria for business school activities to ensure they include the development of globally responsible leaders

10.    Communities of Responsible Action focuses on global awareness activities in local areas.

More information is available at: www.grli.org.

## Avaaz

Avaaz.org is an independent, not-for-profit global campaigning organisation that works to ensure that the views and values of the world's people inform global decision-making. (Avaaz means 'voice' in many languages.) They operate through the internet, making use of Facebook, Myspace, Bebo and Twitter and specialise in raising awareness of issues via obtaining electronic signatures to petitions, then delivering them to key personnel at key meetings. The results of one of their recent campaigns are shown below:

**G8 Summit** – 130,000 Avaaz members signed a petition in 48 hours calling for the G8 industrial countries to limit global warming to 2 degrees celsius – focusing on shaming 3 countries who were blocking progress. The petition was delivered at the summit to UK Prime Minister Gordon Brown along with giant personalized postcards.

*Source:* https://secure.avaaz.org/en/report_back_2/

More details available at: http://www.avaaz.org/en/contact.

## State of the World Forum

As will be seen from the 2020 Climate Leader Manifesto in Figure 7.4, this forum is very clearly working at the global, spiritual and societal level. It is also proactive and seeking strong commitment from participants who are expected to take responsibility.

To become a climate leader and join the global 2020 Climate Leadership Campaign movement, please visit www.2020Brasil.com.br August 2, 2009.

## Al Gore

Former Vice President of America, Al Gore is well known for his DVD 'An Inconvenient Truth' (Gore 2006a) and views on global warming. In a speech at the New York University School of Law (Gore 2006b) he revealed his concern for the way many aspects of MisLeadership have applied to the search for solutions. It was slow to start partly because some leaders still find it more convenient to deny the reality of the crisis (Misinformed Leadership) but also because the maximum change that seems politically feasible still falls far short of the minimum that would be effective in solving the crisis:

> *If we acknowledge candidly that what we need to do is beyond the limits of our current political capacities, that really is just another way of saying that we have to urgently expand the limits of what is politically possible. (Gore 2006b)*

1. One planet, one humanity
I have one home that gives life to me and my human family. We will not get a second chance to keep our home healthy and my life will reflect this fact.
2. I will lead so my children don't lose
 Our children are facing a world wracked by unsustainable economic, ecological and energy systems. I will not allow this trend to continue. They will not lose because I refused to lead.
3. Climate leadership will earn my vote
I am a climate leader and a climate citizen: I will vote for leaders and policies that demonstrate a commitment to a 2020 action framework.
4. Climate leadership will earn my money
I am a climate leader and a climate consumer: I will buy products and services from companies that demonstrate a commitment to a 2020 action-framework
5. I am powerful
My life and my world will be what I make it. There is great power in a clear decision, and I have decided to be a 2020 Climate Leader.
6. Human civilization has a deeper purpose
My family and I are part of an amazing, awe-inspiring and rich story of human growth, progress and evolution. Human civilization has a deeper purpose to represent the highest reaches of love, beauty, stewardship, and progress in the unfolding story of the Earth. My life is a reflection of this deeper purpose.
7. I will act today
My actions today create my reality tomorrow. I will act today and will not wait for others to create my future.
8. I have a sense of belonging
As a climate leader I reaffirm my commitment to the health and wellbeing of my community, my country and my planet.
9. I am present
I will breathe deeply into the challenges, opportunities, fears and hopes of the emerging future that I am helping to create today.
10. Climate leadership is a decision. I'm in!
My power and my commitment comes from the simple force of my decision to be a climate leader.

**Figure 7.4    The 2020 Climate Leader Manifesto**
*Source*: State of the World Forum, 2009.

Gore believes that to conquer our fear we have to insist on a higher level of honesty in political dialogue and that when big mistakes are made it is usually because the people have not been given an honest accounting of the choices before them (Machiavellian Leadership). It also is often because too many members of both parties who knew better did not have the courage to do better (Missing Leadership).

*Our children have a right to hold us to a higher standard when their future*
*– indeed the future of all human civilization – is hanging in the balance'*

(Globally Fit Leadership). *'They deserve better than the spectacle of censorship of the best scientific evidence about the truth of our situation and harassment of honest scientists who are trying to warn us about the looming catastrophe'* (Machiavellian Leadership). *'They deserve better than politicians who sit on their hands and do nothing to confront the greatest challenge that humankind has ever faced – even as the danger bears down on us'* (Missing Leadership). *(Gore 2006b)*

This is not a political issue. This is a moral issue. It affects the survival of human civilisation. It is not a question of left vs. right; it is a question of right vs. wrong. Put simply, it is wrong to destroy the habitability of our planet and ruin the prospects of every generation that follows ours.

This is an opportunity for bipartisanship and transcendence, an opportunity to find our better selves and in rising to meet this challenge, create a better brighter future – a future worthy of the generations who come after us and who have a right to be able to depend on us.

## Center for Spirituality and the Workplace

The centre is based in St Mary's University, Halifax, Nova Scotia, Canada. Their mission is:

> *Positively and strategically influencing the conversations and accomplishments about spirituality and the workplace globally.*

Their focus is on workplace spirituality, which they define in very similar fashion to our general definition of spirituality, but they have an academic flavour to their approach and output which includes texts, doctoral theses and published articles. This is an interesting combination which they pull off very successfully.

### WHAT THEY MEAN BY SPIRITUALITY IN THE WORKPLACE

When they say spirituality in the workplace, they mean a process of inquiry:

> *We all hunger for a connection to something larger than ourselves. For many people that hunger is fed at home, at a place of worship, or through a personal spiritual practice. At the same time, many people wonder whether it's also possible to feed that hunger while they're at work.*

Looking forward, the Center is being asked to go deeper and broader in its work – to increase its impact – to help change the way people and organisations work. They intend to devote their entrepreneurial energy, academic discipline, and global reach to four areas of activity:

- Building and Nurturing Community

- Deepening and Sharing our Understanding of Spirituality and Work

- Introducing Students and Leaders to Spirituality and Work

- Contributing Energy to an International Network.

More information at www.spiritualityandtheworkplace.ca.

## CIMA's Responsible Business Initiative

The Chartered Institute of Management Accountants is one of the largest professional accounting bodies in the world. It focuses on accounting needs of managers and has recognised the crisis facing their profession and the wider community. With this in mind they held a roundtable to develop recommendations for future business ethics as shown in Figure 7.5.

CIMA emphasise that they cannot achieve their vision of an ethical future alone. Strengthening business ethics will require action by government, regulators, business leaders, educators and individuals.

More information is available: http://www.cimaglobal.com.

## Aspen Institute's Corporate Values Strategy Group

Twenty-eight leaders representing business, investment, government, academia, and labour joined the Aspen Institute Business and Society Program's Corporate Values Strategy Group to endorse a bold call to end the focus on value-destroying short-termism in our financial markets and create public policies that reward long-term value creation for investors and the public good. This is summarised in Figure 7.6.

---

**Regulation**

Business needs regulation that ensures high ethical standards. Regulation must be appropriate, specifically targeting high risk areas. It should be based on principles rather than rules and – crucially– must be enforced, with regulators being given the correct powers. However, regulation alone is not sufficient to deliver an economically and ecologically sustainable future.

**Education**

CIMA has a vital role to play in educating the business leaders of tomorrow, giving them the awareness, skills and capabilities to apply ethical values in business. Teaching ethical values should start even earlier than this, though, in schools and colleges. Concern for social and environmental justice appears to be increasing, especially amongst young people, but only time will tell whether this is just a temporary reaction to turbulent economic times.

**Leadership**

An ethical 'tone at the top' is critical to embedding ethical standards in business. Leaders must do more than simply toe the corporate line - they need the skills and capabilities to challenge colleagues constructively and must show courage when putting these skills into action.

**Collaboration**

Business leaders have a responsibility to take a lead, but only targeting the behaviour of senior individuals will not deliver the improvements needed. A collaborative approach is required, with action at many levels.

**Systemic change**

Feedback loops that encourage business to focus on long-term rather than short-term performance need to be established and reinforced. The shareholders who own companies could influence a shift towards this, but the system must allow their voices to be heard. Remuneration, in particular, is a powerful incentive and must be used to reinforce ethical values. However, it is also possible that we need to think more deeply about our economic system and whether it can be economically, socially and ecologically sustainable in its current form.

---

**Figure 7.5    CIMA's Business Trust Recommendations**
*Source*: CIMA, 2009.

Among the signers are John Bogle, Warren Buffett, Barbara Hackman Franklin, Jack Ehnes, Louis Gerstner, Martin Lipton, Ira Millstein, John Olson, Peter Peterson, Felix Rohatyn, Charles Rossotti, Richard Trumka, John Whitehead, and James Wolfensohn.

## The Gates Foundation

In 2000, Bill and Melinda Gates set up a foundation to help all people, regardless of birthplace or heritage, to get the opportunity to live a healthy, productive life. Endowment assets available for charitable activities totalled $29.5 billion at the end of 2008, all to be spent within 50 years of the Gates' deaths.

The statement, "Overcoming Short-termism: A Call for a More Responsible Approach to Investment and Business Management," identifies three leverage points for encouraging a renewed focus on long-term value creation and for addressing one part of market short-termism, shareholder short-termism:

1. Market incentives: encourage more patient capital through tax policy
2. Alignment: better align the interests of financial intermediaries and their ultimate investors
3. Transparency: strengthen investor disclosures

Ira Millstein commented that he joined this diverse group to help move discussion about reform beyond "pious wishful thinking, to the core issue in our market economy - how to incentivize capital to go long term." He adds, "The current system cannot achieve that result. The proposals presented in our statement are intended to place this issue front and center and to engender serious, realistic debate."

The statement highlights the need to focus on the system and not just the corporation, recognizing that a complex dance involving corporate managers, boards, investment advisers, providers of capital, and government drives the results we have now. This distinguished and diverse group is unified in calling for a comprehensive examination of market short-termism in our economy. The signatories hope that policy makers in Congress, the Executive branch, and relevant regulatory agencies will heed this call.

**Figure 7.6      Aspen Institute's Call**
*Source*: Aspen Institute 2009.

A letter on their website (Gates 2009) explains how their motivation sprang from an article about the millions of children who die every year from preventable diseases. They believe every human life has equal worth, whether they be:

> *An impoverished child in a developing country ... (or) a middle-class kid in a developed one ... (If) scientific and technological advances ... are focused on the problems of the people with the most urgent needs and the fewest champions, then within this century billions of people will grow up healthier, get a better education, and gain the power to lift themselves out of poverty.*

## Summary

This chapter has considered four case studies. These have shown how many leaders are extremely dedicated and are attempting to tackle extremely complex issues with out-dated tools, unsuitable for the new environment. They also considered the extent of MisLeadership displayed and ways in which a Globally Fit Leadership approach could help. In the space available it was not possible to present all the arguments relevant to each case but we hope to have given the reader a good feel for the issues involved and possible first steps in resolving these complex issues.

It has also introduced the steps taken by several organisations toward tackling these issues. Many others exist which gives us a source of hope. The final chapter pulls together the suggestions made throughout the book as to ways in which you too can start to change our world.

---

**POINTS FOR REFLECTION**

1.   Which of the cases presented in this chapter has helped you the most?
2.   Which was most disturbing, and why?
3.   What examples from your own experience demonstrate the complexities of contemporary leadership practice?
4.   How would the concept and models of Globally Fit Leadership help address your examples?

---

## Further Reading

The Geneva Spiritual Appeal at:
   www.geneve.ch/appelgeneve/welcome.html
Leadership Lessons for hard times at:
   www.mckinseyquarterly.com/leadership_lessons_for_hard_times
The Fair Trade Foundation at:
   www.fairtrade.org.uk

## References

AFP. (2007). *Russia protests as global forum urges asbestos ban*. [On-line]. Available at: http://afp.google.com/article/ALeqM5iu5bHcrS05_7drMa4dcNQWX7zULA [accessed: 13/10/09].
Aspen Institute. (2009). [Online]. Available at: http://www.aspeninstitute.org/ sites/default/files/content/docs/business per cent20and per cent20society per cent20program/overcome_short_state0909.pdf [accessed: 16/10/09].
Asplund, C. (2003). *EPO and Bicycling*. [Online]. Available at: http://www.road cycling.com/cgi-bin/artman/exec/view.cgi/3/251/printer [accessed: 19/10/09].
BBC. (2000). *'Festina Affair': A time line*. [Online]. Available at: http://newsbbc. co.uk/sport1/hi/other_sports/988530.stm [accessed: 13/10/09].
BBC. (2006). *Lloyd's offloads asbestos claims*. [Online]. Available at: http://news. bbc.co.uk/1/hi/business/6070634.stm [accessed: 3/5/09].
Bowker, M. (2003). *Fatal Deception. The Untold Story of Asbestos: Why It is Still Legal and Still Killing Us*. USA: Rodale, Inc.

Brandt, A.M. (2007). *The Cigarette Century: The Rise, Fall, and Deadly persistence of the Product that defined America*. New York: Basic Books.

Buchanan, E. (2009). *Tough choice between freedom and honour*. [Online]. Available at: http://news.bbc.co.uk/1/hi/uk/7754280.stm [accessed: 16/9/09].

Burrell, J. (2008). *Reflections on the Anglican Communion*. [Online, 4 August]. Available at: http://www.iofc.org/node/32762 [accessed: 16/9/09].

Campbell, R. and Kitson, A. (2008). *The Ethical Organisation*. London: Palgrave.

CBC News. (2009). [Online]. Available at: http://www.cbc.ca/consumer/story/2009/05/22/tobacco-lawsuit.html?ref=rss [accessed: 19/10/09].

CIMA (Chartered Institute of Management Accountants). (2009). *Business Trust: A Critical Time Perspective*. [Online]. Available at: www.cimaglobal.com/responsiblebusiness [accessed: 13/10/09].

De Woot, P. (2009). *Should Prometheus be Bound?* Basingstoke: Palgrave Macmillan.

Fiedler, D. (2009). *Drugs and Doping in Professional Cycling*. [Online]. Available at: http://bicycling.about.com/od/professionalcycling/a/cheating.htm [accessed: 17/9/09].

Gates. (2009). *Letter from Bill and Melinda Gates*. [Online]. Available at: http://www.gatesfoundation.org/about/Pages/bill-melinda-gates-letter.aspx [accessed: 20/10/09].

Geneva Spiritual Appeal. (1999). [Online]. Available at: http://www.geneve.ch/appelgeneve/welcome.html [accessed: 16/9/09].

Gore, A. (2006a). An Inconvenient Truth: A Global Warning. Paramount Classics, Paramount Pictures DVD. [Online]. Available at: http://www.climatecrisis.net/ [accessed: 1/10/09].

Gore, A. (2006b). Speech at the New York University School of Law on Monday 18 September 2006. 'Global Warming Is an Immediate Crisis.'

Greenberg, C. (2006). Asbestos Medical and Legal Aspects. *International Journal on Environmental Health*, 12(1).

Harrington, J. (1999). Legge's Legacy to Modern Occupational Health. *Annual Occupational Hygiene*, 43(1), 1–6.

Health and Safety Executive (HSE). (n.d). [Online]. Available at: hse.gov.uk/asbestos/index [accessed: 29/9/09].

Her Majesty's Government. (2009). *Multi-agency practice guidelines: Handling cases of Forced Marriage*. [Online]. Available at: http://www.fco.gov.uk/resources/en/pdf/3849543/forced-marriage-guidelines09.pdf [accessed: 16/9/09].

Hure, P. (2004). *Respiratory diseases linked to exposure to products such as asbestos: Are preventive measures sufficient?* Technical report 20, ISSA. [Online]. Available at: http://www.issa.int/aiss/content/download/55879/1022558/file/TR-20–2.pdf [accessed: 12/2/09].

IPCS (International Programme on Chemical Safety). (1998). *Environmental Health Criteria 203 Chrysotile Asbestos*. Finland: Vammala.

Johnson, E. (2009). *Meeting the Ethical Challenges of Leadership Casting Light or Shadow*. 3rd Edition. California: SAGE Publications, Inc.

LaDou, J. (2004). *The Asbestos Cancer Epidemic*. [Online]. Available at: http://www.mesdscape.com/viewarticle/471144_print [accessed: 17/2/09].

MAC: Mines and Communities. (2006). *ILO to promote global asbestos ban*. [Online]. Available at: http://www.minesandcommunities.org//article. php?a=1977 [accessed: 13/10/09].

Mail On Line. (2008). *Britain's youngest Asbestos victim dies at 28: Did she contract it at school?* [Online]. Available at: http://www.dailymail.co.uk/news/article-1050955/Britains-youngest-Asbestos-victim-dies-28-Did-contract-school. html [accessed: 13/10/09].

McDaniel, P.A., Intinarelli, G. and Malone, R.E. (2008). Tobacco Industry issues management organisations: Creating a global corporate network to undermine public health. *Globalization and Health*, vol. 4, no. 2.

Moore, R. (2008). *In Search of Robert Millar*. London: Harper Sport.

Moran, J. (2009). The Efficacy and Value of the Global Leadership and Global Fitness Frameworks Offered by Rayment and Smith. MBA Dissertation. Anglia Ruskin University.

Neira, M. (2008). *Sound chemicals management: relieving the burden on public health*. (Statement) World Health Organisation: Rotterdam. [Online]. Available at: http://www.who.int/ipcs/capacity_building/cop4_statement.pdf [accessed: 13/10/09].

Richmond, Y. and Spencer, N. (2005). *Beyond the Fringe: Researching a Spiritual Age*. Derbyshire: Cliff College Publishing.

Samad,Y. and Eade, J. (n.d.). *Community Perceptions of Forced Marriage*. Community Liaison Unit. University of Bradford and University of Surrey Roehampton. [Online]. Available at: http://www.fco.gov.uk/resources/en/pdf/pdf1/fco_forcedmarriagereport121102 [accessed: 17/9/09].

Sports Scientist. (2007). [Online]. Available at: http://www.sportsscientists.com/2007/06/culture-of-doping-in-cycling-anything.html [accessed: 17/9/09].

St Andrews University. (2009). *Galileo's 'Confession'*. [Online]. Available at: http://www-history.mcs.st-andrews.ac.uk/Extras/Galileo_confession.html [accessed: 19/10/09].

State of the World Forum. (2009). *The 2020 Climate Leader Manifesto*. [Online]. Available at: http://www.worldforum.org/index.htm [accessed: 20/10/09].

Taylor, M. (2008). Victims of forced marriages could total 4,000, says study. *Guardian*, Tuesday 11 March.

The Free Library. (2009). *World Divorce Rates*. [Online]. Available at: http://www. thefreelibrary.com/ [accessed: 25/9/09].

Tweedale, G. (2003). *Magic Mineral To Killer Dust Turner and Newall And The Asbestos Hazard*. New York: Oxford Press Inc.

USGS. (2006). *Worldwide Asbestos Supply and Consumption Trends from 1900 through 2003*. Circular 1298. [Online]. Available at: http://pubs.usgs.gov/circ/2006/1298/c1298.pdf [accessed: 2/4/09].

USGS. (2007). *Worldwide Asbestos Supply and Consumption Trends*. [Online]. Available at: http://minerals.usgs.gov/minerals/pubs/commodity/asbestos/mcs-2009-asbes.pdf [accessed: 2/4/09].

Walker, S. (2009). *A Town Called Asbestos*. [Online]. Available at: http://www.slate.com/id/2217220/ [accessed: 8/5/09].

Williams, P. (2009). *Initiatives of Change*. [Online]. Available at: http://www.hopeinthecities.org/node/41952 [accessed: 16/9/09].

World Asbestos Report. (2007a). *Asbestos Experiences of Asian Countries: China*. [Online]. Available at: http://worldasbestosreport.org/asbestosasia/China_experience.html [accessed: 26/4/09].

World Asbestos Report. (2007b). *Asbestos Experiences of Asian Countries: India*. [Online]. Available at: http://worldasbestosreport.org/asbestosasia/India_experience.html [accessed: 26/4/09].

World Health Organization. (2006). *Elimination of asbestos-related diseases*. WHO/SDE/OEH/06.03. [Online]. Available at: http://whqlibdoc.who.int/hq/2006/WHO_SDE_OEH_06.03_eng.pdf [accessed: 2/5/09].

World Health Organization. (WHO, 2008). *WHO Report on the Global Tobacco Epidemic*. [Online]. Available at: http://www.who.int/tobacco/mpower/mpower_report_full_2008.pdf [accessed: 16/9/09].

# Implementation Strategies

*Your task is simple: Eliminate the difference between how things should be and how they really are.*

*William Faulkner*

*In the battle of life it is not the critic who counts. Not the man (sic) who points out how the strong man stumbled or where the doer of deeds could have done better. The credit belongs to the man who is actually in the arena; whose face is marred by dust and sweat and blood; who strives valiantly; who errs and comes short again and again; who knows the great enthusiasms, the great devotions and spends himself in a worthy cause. Who, at the best, knows in the end the triumph of high achievement; and who, at the worst, if he fails, at least fails while daring greatly, so that his place shall never be with those cold and timid souls who know neither victory nor defeat.*

*Theodore Roosevelt*

And so we come to our final chapter. In this chapter we focus on illustrating actions individuals at all levels can take to implement the ideas we have discussed. We focus on eight key actions and at the end of the chapter provide a checklist of these action points. These are only a start, and our ideas. No doubt as you have been reading through the book and reflecting on the controversial and challenging issues we have raised you have identified your own set of action points also. That is great news.

If you have read through this book and thought *'fantastic, great points, insightful, thought provoking and challenging'* then put it down and carried on with what you are doing, then we will have failed. We are at a critical point in our history where talk is not enough, we all – you – have to move to action so that we shall *'never be with those cold and timid souls who know neither victory nor defeat'* as Roosevelt puts it above.

Our key actions are split into two parts. The first four cover action that we believe will assist to address all the dimensions of MisLeadership we have identified. The remaining four actions focus on specific categories of MisLeadership and are the initial steps we identified in Chapters 2 to 5.

## 1. Wake Up!

As we said in Chapter 1, part of the purpose of this book is to raise awareness of the real situation regarding leadership. How vital it is to our collective and long-term survival on this planet, and how often what we see, know about, and practice in leadership is not in fact leadership but *MisLeadership*. It is embedded and prevalent in our psyche because this is how we have been brought up and educated to see leadership, how we have seen others lead and how we are pressurised to lead. It is Institutional MisLeadership on a global scale.

In Chapter 6 we also argued that it was important to recognise our current situation. We suggested this is one represented in Figure 6.5 as a see-saw with lop-sided forces resulting in those few who benefit from the current global environment and current MisLeadership believing we are close to heaven so not inclined to act while billions are suffering from the leadership such that their environment is highly toxic and they are close to hell. Worse still, we believe we are currently moving in the wrong direction – the see-saw is tipping increasingly on its end such that we may all soon fall off. This is evidenced by the growing number of urgent global issues illustrated in Table 1.1.

If you have a narrow self-centred focus it is easier to see which actions will help achieve your goal and it is also easier to ignore or be blind to the circumstances of those on the far end of the see-saw, suffering the down-side of your actions. Those who are the most successful and powerful may also have the largest challenge. They are the ones most able to achieve a desired change but are also the ones who perceive they may have the most to lose.

In Chapter 6, we showed that two of the reasons why solutions to tackle MisLeadership are not implemented are because MisLeadership practices are so embedded and socialised that we are often unaware and de-sensitised to them. Returning to the analogy of a see-saw, a see-saw is something we have grown up with, learned to use and learned to play on – much like a system or paradigm. But a see-saw is designed in such a way that as one side goes up, the other side must come down. When this is just being used for fun and there is no long-term adverse effect, this is fine. In any case, part of the fun is that we take turns at being at the top, the person at the bottom having the power to push their end up so they have a turn on top.

With the Leadership Fitness See-saw, there are long-term winners and losers. The system, paradigm, see-saw is designed that way – this is the Institutionalised MisLeadership we have grown up with, learnt to play with and had embedded into our values. It underpins the current capitalist, market economy.

One fundamental problem is that it is the winners who have the power so are able to keep themselves at the top. A major theme running through Diamond's book 'Collapse: How Societies Choose to Fail or Survive' (Diamond 2006) is that the only way to survival for humanity is to solve our problems here and now, but is it realistic to expect people who are overwhelming winners under the existing system to change it and voluntarily relinquish their power?

In reality, the only way that we are going to change things is to leave the see-saw behind. We need to find a new paradigm and system that is solid and gives everyone an equal chance – perhaps a climbing frame?

But having got to this point in the book you can no longer be unaware of this situation and hopefully as we have progressed through you have identified many other examples from your own experiences of MisLeadership. Having this awareness is half the challenge complete already. All you have to do now is start doing something about it and our other seven ideas below may assist you in this task.

## 2. Take Responsibility

A lot of the MisLeadership that is occurring, particularly missing leadership is related to this issue of taking responsibility. Often people can see what is going wrong, what is needed but walk away or simply criticise other people's actions. In Chapter 6 we talked about the danger of group think where poor decisions are made because individuals do not take responsibility for the processes that are occurring. We need to change this approach to one of every individual taking responsibility for doing something. Individual small actions can collectively result in a major improvement.

A golden thread that runs throughout the book is the Embedded Values Cycle introduced in Figure 1.1 and the need to challenge existing habits and values and re-educating ourselves for the global era.

Fear can often hold us back and prevent us from taking the responsibility. As we showed in Chapter 6 sometimes this fear can be an irrational one that comes from childhood experiences and may no longer be relevant. Even if the fear is still valid, the challenge must be faced and overcome.

## 3. Have Transparency in All That You Do

One of the main factors that underpins and fuels MisLeadership, particularly the Institutional MisLeadership we have identified throughout this book, is a lack of transparency. Transparency here means being open with your thoughts and ideas and what is taking place. By being transparent you get away from having to mislead people and instead can work to build their capabilities to deal with the real situation. Transparency has close links with honesty and trust, which we discuss below.

Talbott (2009:227), in his exploration of the financial sector, suggests we need greater transparency. Carey et al. (2009) undertook a series of interviews with 14 CEOs and chairmen of major companies which sheds light on the foundations of effective corporate leadership. They identify six key points and two of these relate to transparency – transparency with employees and investors. Carey et al. (2009:6) argue:

> *Being open about what is happening in a company is partly a question of integrity: employees deserve honesty. Openness also builds respect, trust, and solidarity, all of which in turn help employees stay focused on the task of running the business at a time when financial rewards might be limited and the future uncertain. Openness helps build morale as well. A CEO cannot mislead people and certainly shouldn't panic them, but explaining problems and the actions being taken to deal with them builds confidence in the quality of the CEO's leadership.*

### HONESTY IS THE BEST POLICY

A lot of the fundamental points to MisLeadership come back to a lack of honesty. We highlighted Talbott's (2009:221) view on this in Chapter 1:

*There is much lying and cheating going on in the system, both on Wall Street and in Washington, but very little progress will be made until the root causes of this crisis are uncovered and corrected.*

We argue, however, that the lying and cheating is not just peculiar to one location, but in all leadership across the globe. Lying and cheating is a strategy that will only work in the short-term as the truth will out and when it does the leader's position is undermined significantly. By being honest you build the next of our important factors.

## BUILD AND HONOUR TRUST

Trust is a fragile and precious thing as with it you do not have to work on your own, but are able to realise the benefits of true collaborative working. Real trust takes a great deal of time to build, though, and can be destroyed in an instant. The elements of MisLeadership we have discussed in this book are effective ways to destroy trust in families, communities and workplaces.

## 4. Prepare a Force-Field Analysis

The power and flexibility of force-field analysis was shown in Chapter 6 and we encourage you to carry out such an analysis to understand the potential influence of MisLeadership on any situation you would like to influence and your own leadership. It would also be of potential benefit in assessing the forces for and against any action you would like to implement. For you to achieve a desired change, the driving forces (Figure 8.1) in favour of the change have to be sufficient to overcome the resisting forces.

Our next four suggested actions are important initial steps we have identified to help address specific aspects of MisLeadership. These have been discussed in Chapters 2 to 5.

## 5. Adopt Effective Problem Solving Approaches

Problem solving in individual, group and societal levels needs to be in the context of today's global realities. We all live in the global village and the age of information has shrunk time and distance.

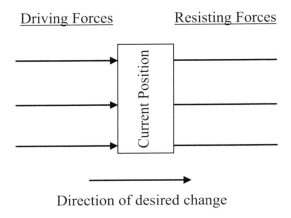

**Figure 8.1    Force-Field Analysis**

In Chapter 2 the focus was on effective problem-solving and the ASK SIR L model. We argued here that there can sometimes, particularly in the West, be a desire to jump to the SIR solution phases of the model. We emphasised the importance of the ASK phase. If we do not fully appreciate that a problem exists, specify the exact nature of that problem so as to understand its importance, or understand the root causes we will either make no attempt to solve the problem, or if we do we will not be as successful as we need to be. The learning phase was also highlighted as the means by which we minimise repetition of mistakes and encourage adoption of successful approaches and ideas in the future.

To fully appreciate all the issues involved in each situation, so that the incidences of MisLeadership can be addressed will require an ongoing critical but constructive dialogue between the many different stakeholders involved in the process. Depending on the situation this might include the political world, business leaders, customers, members of the public and various experts in the field. It will also require rethinking the way these various leaders are educated and trained. This will require a fundamental shift at all levels of education but business schools have a prime role in this and must re-think their approach.

As was highlighted in Chapter 2, however, the complexity, amount of information available and issues raised from critical constructive dialogue can mean there is a danger of long circuitous debates and analysis paralysis, where nothing actually gets done. We emphasised that it is important to keep a bias in favour of action and, where a path forward is not clear, take small iterative steps to test new ideas and changes whilst keeping site of the long-term goal.

## 6. Take a Global Perspective

With globalisation, the explosion of information technology and the ease of travel, no longer can we think simply of our own specific entity. The number of Urgent Global Issues is testament to the need to include consideration of the bigger picture and how our actions today will affect those around the world tomorrow.

Global leadership was shown as having two important aspects. Firstly they need to recognise that all individuals, groups and societies in the world are interconnected and interdependent, so leaders must now think beyond traditional organisational, sectoral and national boundaries. Individuals working alone simply cannot keep pace with the speed of change and have to hook into the collective and all the permutations of possible inter-connections. So tap into the internet, start emailing, set up networks and arrange meetings in your local area. If we are to improve our world we need everyone to get involved and do something. Participate, collaborate and act.

One of the difficulties to implementing solutions to MisLeadership that was identified in Chapter 6 was that of backsliding; slipping back into our comfort zones and habits when things become challenging and tough, or when you are busy. Tapping into the collective and seeking support from others can be helpful in guarding against this, because those who are supporting you can give you a gentle nudge when you start to backslide.

Your support network can be extremely helpful as well in addressing the fear issues which often prevent action. *'A problem shared is a problem halved'* and the fears that are holding you back from taking responsibility and action may not seem as formidable when you have the support and understanding of others. The benefits of support also apply to you giving support to others.

The second part to our taking a global perspective is that thinking globally also means thinking holistically and the Global Fitness Framework outlined in Chapter 3 is offered as a way of guiding you in all the areas you now need to consider in this holistic approach.

## 7. Work Towards a New Paradigm of Thought

In Chapter 4 we discussed the weaknesses with the current economic and social paradigm and highlighted the need for a new paradigm. This included the need for leaders to act ethically, honestly and with integrity; be aware of global issues; recognise their role in shaping the future of humanity and the planet; work with the whole person and recognise that all aspects of their followers' lives are important.

It is much easier to say these things than actually do them though and it may be useful to work through the Embedded Values Cycle shown in Figure 1.1 to understand how you have developed your current paradigm of thought. It will also be important to have a thorough grasp of Chapter 4 to appreciate why this current paradigm is no longer sustainable as a long-term approach.

## 8. Develop a Contemporary Mission

The significant challenges we face on the planet are big, global issues that cannot be solved with quick fixes, easy solutions and short-term focus. Indeed, a lot of the difficulties we are now experiencing are because of the short-term focus that a lot of our corporations and leaders have adopted for many years. Short-term issues need to be dealt with but have to be approached from a perspective that balances short and long-term needs. This balance is a fundamental element of a Contemporary Mission, whether that mission is for an individual, group, society or humanity as a whole.

We suggest that an overarching mission for organisations today – a new definition of the purpose of business – might include:

> *Developing a sustainable, just and fulfilling human presence on the planet.*

## Action Points

These eight steps have been summarised in the check list of action points shown below. As you will see there are another five spaces at the bottom of this table where we hope you will add your own ideas.

| Point | Action | Your activity |
|---|---|---|
| 1 | Wake up! | |
| 2 | Take responsibility | |
| 3 | Transparency in all that you do | |
| 4 | Force-field analysis | |
| 5 | Effective problem-solving | |
| 6 | Global perspective | |
| 7 | New paradigm | |
| 8 | Contemporary mission | |
| 9 | | |
| 10 | | |
| 11 | | |
| 12 | | |
| 13 | | |

## Summary

And so we come to the end of this book. Hopefully a challenging and thought-provoking read but we hope only the start of the journey. There is much to be done and the need has never been greater to move from thoughts and well meaning words, statements and books into action.

> *All people dream, but not equally.*
> *Those who dream by night in the dusty recesses of their mind,*
> *wake in the morning to find that it was vanity.*
> *But the dreamers of the day are dangerous people,*
> *for they dream their dreams with open eyes,*
> *and make them come true.*

*T.E. Lawrence*

# References

Carey, D., Patsalos-Fox, M. and Useem, M. (2009). Leadership lessons for hard times. *McKinsey Quarterly* [Online]. Available at: http://www.mckinsey quarterly.com/Leadership_lessons_for_hard_times [accessed: 9/9/09].

Diamond, J. (2006). *Collapse: How Societies Choose to Fail or Survive*. London: Penguin Books.

Talbott, J.R. (2009). *The 86 Biggest Lies on Wall Street*. London: Constable and Robinson.

# Index

# If you have found this book useful you may be interested in other titles from Gower Applied Research

**The Rise and Fall of Management: A Brief History of Practice, Theory and Context**
Gordon Pearson
978-0-566-08976-3

**Transformation Management: Towards the Integral Enterprise**
Ronnie Lessem and Alexander Schieffer
978-0-566-08896-4

**Globalization's Limits: Conflicting National Interests in Trade and Finance**
Dimitris N. Chorafas
978-0-566-08885-8

**Wealth, Welfare and the Global Free Market: A Social Audit of Capitalist Economics**
Ibrahim Ozer Ertuna
978-0-566-08905-3

**Risky Business: Psychological, Physical and Financial Costs of High Risk Behavior in Organizations**
Professor Ronald J. Burke and Professor Cary L. Cooper
978-0-566-08915-2

**Complex Adaptive Leadership: Embracing Paradox and Uncertainty**
Nick Obolensky
978-0-566-08932-9

**Integral Research and Innovation: Transforming Enterprise and Society**
Ronnie Lessem and Alexander Schieffer
978-0-566-08918-3

# GOWER